Starting FORTH

Starting FORTH

An Introduction to the FORTH Language and Operating System for Beginners and Professionals

Leo Brodie,

FORTH, Inc.

With a foreword by
Charles H. Moore

Prentice-Hall, Inc., Englewood Cliffs, NJ 07632

Library of Congress Cataloging in Publication Data

BRODIE, LEO.

Starting FORTH.

1. FORTH (Computer program language) I. Title.

QA76.73.F24B76 001.64'24 81-11837

ISBN 0-13-842930-8 AACR2

ISBN 0-13-842922-7 (pbk.)

Publisher's credits:
Editorial/production supervision: Kathryn Gollin Marshak
Manufacturing buyer: Gordon Osbourne
Paper cover design: FORTH, Inc. and Alon Jaediker
Case cover design: Edsal Enterprises

The pages of this book were reproduced
from camera ready copy
designed and prepared by FORTH, Inc.

Printed in the United States of America

10 9 8 7 6 5

Prentice-Hall International, Inc., *London*
Prentice-Hall of Australia Pty. Limited, *Sydney*
Prentice-Hall of Canada, Ltd., *Toronto*
Prentice-Hall of India Private Limited, *New Delhi*
Prentice-Hall of Japan, Inc., *Tokyo*
Prentice-Hall of Southeast Asia Pte. Ltd., *Singapore*
Whitehall Books Limited, *Wellington, New Zealand*

ABOUT THE AUTHOR

Leo Brodie's inability to express even the most complex technical concepts without adding a twist of humor comes from an early love of comedy. He specialized in playwriting at UCLA and has had several comedies produced there and in local theater. He has also written freelance magazine articles and has worked as a copywriter for an ad agency. When a company he was working for installed a computer, he became inspired to try designing a microprocessor-based toy. Although he never got the toy running, he learned a lot about computers and programming. He now works at FORTH, Inc. as a technical and marketing writer, where he can play on the computers as the muse determines without having to be a fanatical computer jockey, and is allowed to write books such as this.

Leo's other interests include singing, driving classic Volvos, and dancing to 50's music.

FOREWORD

The FORTH community can celebrate a significant event with the publication of Starting FORTH. A greater effort, talent, and commitment have gone into this book than into any previous introductory manual. I, particularly, am pleased at this evidence of the growing popularity of FORTH, the language.

I developed FORTH over a period of some years as an interface between me and the computers I programmed. The traditional languages were not providing the power, ease, or flexibility that I wanted. I disregarded much conventional wisdom in order to include exactly the capabilities needed by a productive programmer. The most important of these is the ability to add whatever capabilities later become necessary.

The first time I combined the ideas I had been developing into a single entity, I was working on an IBM 1130, a "third-generation" computer. The result seemed so powerful that I considered it a "fourth-generation computer language." I would have called it FOURTH, except that the 1130 permitted only five-character identifiers. So FOURTH became FORTH, a nicer play on words anyway.

One principle that guided the evolution of FORTH, and continues to guide its application, is bluntly: Keep It Simple. A simple solution has elegance. It is the result of exacting effort to understand the real problem and is recognized by its compelling sense of rightness. I stress this point because it contradicts the conventional view that power increases with complexity. Simplicity provides confidence, reliability, compactness, and speed.

Starting FORTH was written and illustrated by Leo Brodie, a remarkably capable person whose insight and imagination will become apparent. This book is an original and detailed prescription for learning. It deftly guides the novice over the thresholds of understanding that all FORTH programmers must cross.

Although I am the only person who has never had to learn FORTH, I do know that its study is a formidable one. As with a human language, the usage of many words must be memorized. For beginners, Leo's droll comments and superbly cast characters appear to make this study easy and enjoyable. For those like myself who already know FORTH, a quick reading provides a delightful trip and fresh views of familiar terrain. But I hope this book is not so easy and enjoyable that it seems trivial. Be warned that there is heavy content here and that you can learn much about computers and compilers as well as about programming.

FORTH provides a natural means of communication between man and the smart machines he is surrounding himself with. This requires that it share characteristics of human languages, including compactness, versatility, and extensibility. I cannot imagine a better language for writing programs, expressing algorithms, or understanding computers. As you read this book, I hope that you may come to agree.

Charles H. Moore
Inventor of FORTH

ABOUT THIS BOOK

Welcome to Starting FORTH, your introduction to an exciting and powerful computer language called FORTH.

If you're a beginner who wants to learn more about computers, FORTH is a great way to learn. FORTH is more fun to write programs with than any language that I know of. (See the "Introduction for Beginners.")

If you are a seasoned professional who wants to learn FORTH, this book is just what you need. FORTH is a very different approach to computers, so different that everyone, from newcomers to old hands, learns FORTH best from the ground up. If you're adept at other computer languages, put them out of your mind, and remember only what you know about computers. (See the "Introduction for Professionals.")

Since many people with different backgrounds are interested in FORTH, I've arranged this book so that you'll only have to read what you need to know, with footnotes addressed to different kinds of readers. The first half of Chap. 7 provides a background in computer arithmetic for beginners only.

This book explains how to write simple applications in FORTH. It includes all standard FORTH words that you need to write a high-level, single-task application. This word set is an extremely powerful one, including everything from simple math operators to compiler-controlling words. (See Appendix 3, "FORTH-79 Standard.")

Excluded from this book are all commands that are related to the assembler, multiprogrammer, printing and disking utilities, and target compiler. These commands are available on some versions of FORTH such as polyFORTH. (See Appendix 2, "Further Features of polyFORTH.")

I've chosen examples that will actually work at a FORTH system with a terminal and disk. Don't infer from this that FORTH is limited to batch or string-handling tasks, since there is really no limit to FORTH's usefulness.

Here are some features of this book that will make it easy to use:

All commands are listed twice: first, in the section in which the word is introduced, and second, in the summary at the end of that chapter. Appendix 4 provides an index to the tables.

Each chapter also has a review of terms and a set of exercise problems. Appendix 1 lists the answers.

Several "Handy Hints" have been included to reveal procedural tips or optional routines that are useful for learners but that don't merit an explanation as to how or why they work.

A personal note: FORTH is a very unusual language. It violates many cardinal rules of programming. My first reaction to FORTH was extremely skeptical, but as I tried to develop complicated applications I began to see its beauty and power. You owe it to yourslf to keep an open mind while reading about some of its peculiarities. I'll warn you now: few programmers who learn FORTH ever go back to other languages.

Good luck, and enjoy learning!

Leo Brodie
FORTH, Inc.

ACKNOWLEDGEMENTS

I'd like to thank the following people who helped to make this book possible:

For consultation on FORTH technique and style: Dean Sanderson, Michael LaManna, James Dewey, Edward K. Conklin, and Elizabeth D. Rather, all of FORTH, Inc.; for providing insights into the art of teaching FORTH and for writing several of the problems in this book: Kim Harris of the FORTH Interest Group; for proofreading, editorial suggestions, and enormous amounts of work formatting the pages: Carolyn A. Rosenberg; for help with typing and other necessities: Sue Linstrot, Carolyn Lubisich, Kevin Weaver, Kris Cramer, and Stephanie Brown Brodie; for help with the graphics: Carolyn Lubisich, Jim Roberts, Janine Ritscher, Dana Rather, Winnie Shows, Natasha Elbert, Barbara Roberts, and John Dotson of Sunrise Printery (Redondo Beach, CA); for technical assistance, Bill Patterson and Gary Friedlander; for constructive criticism, much patience and love: Stephanie Brown Brodie; and for inventing FORTH, Charles H. Moore.

TABLE OF CONTENTS

TABLE OF HANDY HINTS

Starting FORTH

INTRODUCTIONS

Introduction for Beginners: What Is a Computer Language?

At first, when beginners hear the term "computer language," they wonder, "What kind of language could a computer possibly speak? It must be awfully hard for people to understand. It probably looks like:

976#!@NX714&+

if it looks like anything at all."

Actually, a computer language should not be difficult to understand. Its purpose is simply to serve as a convenient compromise for communication between person and computer.

Consider the marionette. You can make a marionette "walk" simply by working the wooden control, without even touching the strings. You could say that rocking the control means "walking" in the language of the marionette. The puppeteer guides the marionette in a way that the marionette can understand and that the puppeteer can easily master.

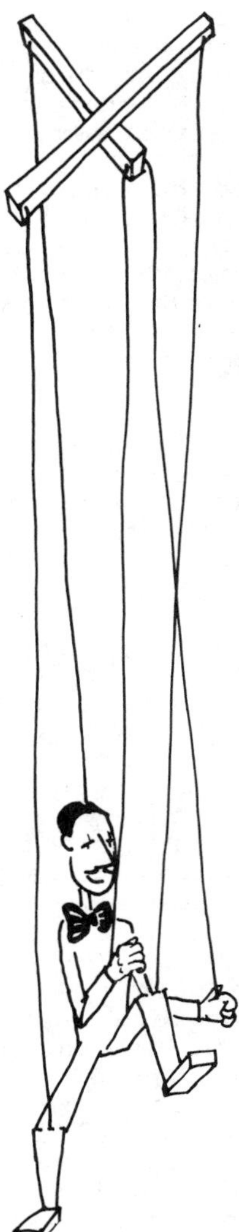

Computers are machines just like the marionette. They must be told exactly what to do, in specific language. And so we need a language which possesses two seemingly opposite traits:

On the one hand, it must be precise in its meaning to the computer, conveying all the information that the computer needs to know to perform the operation. On the other hand, it must be simple and easy-to-use by the programmer.

Many languages have been developed since the birth of computers: FORTRAN is the elder statesman of the field; COBOL is the standard language for business data processing; BASIC was designed as a beginner's language along the road toward languages like FORTRAN and COBOL. This book is about a very different kind of language: FORTH. FORTH's popularity has been gaining steadily over the past several years, and its popularity is shared among programmers in all fields.

All the languages mentioned above, including FORTH, are called "high-level" languages. It's important for beginners to recognize the difference between a high-level language and the computer it runs on. A high-level language looks the same to a programmer regardless of which make or model of computer it's running on. But each make or model has its own internal language, or "machine language." To explain what a machine language is, let's return to the marionette.

Imagine that there is no wooden control and that the puppeteer has to deal directly with the strings. Each string corresponds to exactly one part of the marionette's body. The harmonious combinations of movements of the individual strings could be called the marionette's "machine language."

Now tie the strings to a control. The control is like a high-level language. With a simple turn of the wrist, the puppeteer can move many strings simultaneously.

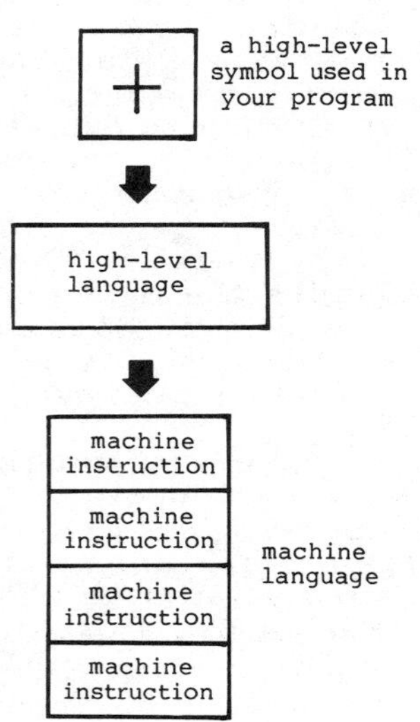

So it is with a high-level computer language, where the simple and familiar symbol "+" causes many internal functions to be performed in the process of addition.

Here's a very clever thing about a computer: it can be programmed to translate high-level symbols (such as "+") into the computer's own machine language. Then it can proceed to carry out the machine instructions. A high-level language is a computer program that translates humanly understandable words and symbols into the machine language of the particular make and model of computer.

What's the difference between FORTH and other high-level languages? To put it very briefly: it has to do with the compromise between man and computer. A language should be designed for the convenience of its human users, but at the same time for compatibility with the operation of the computer.

FORTH is unique among languages because its solution to this problem is unique. This book will explain how.

Introduction for Professionals: FORTH in the Real World

FORTH has enjoyed a rising tide of popularity in recent years, perhaps most visibly among enthusiasts and hobbyists. But this development is only a new wrinkle in the history of FORTH. FORTH has been in use for over ten years in critical scientific and industrial applications. In fact, if you use a mini- or microcomputer professionally, chances are that FORTH can run your application--more efficiently than the language you're presently using.

Now you'll probably ask rhetorically, "If FORTH is so efficient, how come I'm not using it?" The answer is that you, like most people, don't know what FORTH is.

To really get an understanding of FORTH, you should read this book and, if possible, find a FORTH system and try it for yourself. For those of you who are still at the bookstore browsing, however, this section will answer two questions: "What is FORTH?" and "What is it *good* for?"

FORTH is many things:

--a high-level language
--an assembly language
--an operating system
--a set of development tools
--a software design philosophy

As a language, FORTH begins with a powerful set of standard commands, then provides the mechanism by which you can define your own commands. The structured process of building definitions upon previous definitions is FORTH's equivalent of high-level coding. Alternatively, words may be defined directly in assembler mnemonics, using FORTH's assembler. All commands are interpreted by the same interpreter and compiled by the same compiler, giving the language tremendous flexibility.

The highest level of your code will resemble an English-language description of your application. FORTH has been called a "meta-application language"--a language that you can use to create problem-oriented languages.

As an operating system, FORTH does everything that traditional operating systems do, including interpretation, compilation, assembling, virtual memory handling, I/O, text editing, etc.

But because the FORTH operating system is much simpler than its traditional counterparts due to FORTH's design, it runs much more quickly, much more conveniently, and in far less memory.

What is FORTH good for? FORTH offers a simple means to maximize a processor's efficiency. For example:

FORTH is fast. _High-level_ FORTH executes faster than other high-level languages and between 20 and 75% slower than equivalent assembly-language programs, while time-critical code may be written in assembler to run at full processor speed. Without a traditional operating system, FORTH eliminates redundancy and needless run-time error checking.

FORTH compiled code is compact. FORTH applications require less memory than their equivalent _assembly-language_ programs! Written in FORTH, the entire operating system and its standard word set reside in less than 8K bytes. Support for a target application may require less than 1K bytes.

FORTH is transportable. It has been implemented on just about every mini- and microcomputer known to the industry.

FORTH has been known to cut program development time by a factor of ten for equivalent assembly-language programming and by a factor of two for equivalent high-level programming. Productivity increases because FORTH epitomizes "structured programming" and because it is interactive and modular.

Here are a few samples of FORTH in the real world:

> _Process Control_--FORTH is being used to steer the robot motion-picture cameras to create the special effects used in the film "Battle Beyond the Stars." FORTH was chosen because of its speed and its flexibility in providing an interface by which the operator can describe the camera motion. Other process-control applications range from a baggage handler for a major U.S. airline to a peach sorter for a California cannery.

> _Portable Intelligent Devices_--The variety of applications which run FORTH internally include a heart monitor for outpatients, an automotive ignition analyzer, a hand-held instrument to measure relative moisture in different types of grain, and the Craig Language Translator.

<u>Medical</u>--On a single PDP-11 at a major hospital, FORTH simultaneously maintains a large patient database; manages thirty-two terminals and an optical reader; performs statistical analysis on the database to correlate physical types, diseases, treatments, and results; and analyzes blood samples and monitors heartbeats in real time.

<u>Data Acquisition and Analysis</u>--A single PDP-11/34 running under FORTH controls an entire observatory, including an extraordinarily accurate telescope, the dome, several CRTs, a clock, a line printer, and a floppy disk drive--and still has time for taking data on infrared emissions from space, analyzing the data, and displaying the results on a graphics monitor. Applications of this type often make use of Fast Fourier and Walsh Transforms, numerical integration, and other math routines written in FORTH.

There's a catch, we must admit. It is that FORTH makes <u>you</u> responsible for your computer's efficiency. To draw an analogy: a manual transmission is tougher to master than an automatic, yet for many drivers it offers improved control over the vehicle.

Similarly, FORTH is tougher to master than traditional high-level languages, which essentially resemble one another (i.e., after learning one, it is not difficult to learn another). Once mastered, however, FORTH gives <u>you</u> the capability to minimize CPU time and memory space, as well as an organizing philosophy by which you can dramatically reduce project development time.

And remember, all of FORTH's elements enjoy the same protocol, including operating system, compiler, interpreters, text editor, virtual memory, assembler, and multiprogrammer. The learning curve for FORTH is much shorter than that for all these separate elements added together.

If any of this sounds exciting to you, turn the page and start FORTH.

1 FUNDAMENTAL FORTH

In this chapter we'll acquaint you with some of the unique properties of the FORTH language. After a few introductory pages we'll have you sitting at a FORTH terminal. If you don't have a FORTH terminal, don't worry. We'll show you the result of each step along the way.

A Living Language

Imagine that you're an office manager and you've just hired a new, eager assistant. On the first day, you teach the assistant the proper format for typing correspondence. (The assistant already knows how to type.) By the end of the day, all you have to say is "Please type this."

On the second day, you explain the filing system. It takes all morning to explain where everything goes, but by the afternoon all you have to say is "Please file this."

By the end of the week, you can communicate in a kind of shorthand, where "Please send this letter" means "Type it, get me to sign it, photocopy it, file the copy, and mail the original." Both you and your assistant are free to carry out your business more pleasantly and efficiently.

Good organization and effective communication require that you

1. define useful tasks and give each task a name, then

2. group related tasks together into larger tasks and give each of these a name, and so on.

FORTH lets you organize your own procedures and communicate them to a computer in just this way (except you don't have to say "Please").

As an example, imagine a microprocessor-controlled washing machine programmed in FORTH. The ultimate command in your example is named WASHER. Here is the definition of WASHER, as written in FORTH:

```
: WASHER   WASH SPIN RINSE SPIN ;
```

In FORTH, the colon indicates the beginning of a new definition. The first word after the colon, WASHER, is the name of the new procedure. The remaining words, WASH, SPIN, RINSE, and SPIN, comprise the "definition" of the new procedure. Finally, the semicolon indicates the end of the definition.

Each of the words comprising the definition of WASHER has already been defined in our washing-machine application. For example, let's look at our definition of RINSE:

```
: RINSE   FILL AGITATE DRAIN ;
```

As you can see, the definition of RINSE consists of a group of words: FILL, AGITATE, and DRAIN. Once again, each of these words has been already defined elsewhere in our washing-machine application. The definition of FILL might be

```
: FILL   FAUCETS OPEN  TILL-FULL  FAUCETS CLOSE ;
```

In this definition we are referring to <u>things</u> (faucets) as well as to <u>actions</u> (open and close). The word TILL-FULL has been defined to create a "delay loop" which does nothing but mark time until the water-level switch has been activated, indicating that the tub is full.

If we were to trace these definitions back, we would eventually find that they are all defined in terms of a group of very useful commands that form the basis of all FORTH systems. For example, polyFORTH includes about 300 such commands. Many of these commands are themselves "colon definitions" just like our example words; others are defined directly in the machine language of the particular computer. In FORTH, a defined command is called a "word."†

---

†For Old Hands

This meaning of "word" is not to be associated with a 16-bit value, which in the FORTH community is referred to as a "cell."

The ability to define a word in terms of other words is called "extensibility." Extensibility leads to a style of programming that is extremely simple, naturally well-organized, and as powerful as you want it to be.

Whether your application runs an assembly line, acquires data for a scientific environment, maintains a business application, or plays a game, you can create your own "living language" of words that relate to your particular need.

In this book we'll cover the most useful of the standard FORTH commands.

All This and ... Interactive!

One of FORTH's many unique features is that it lets you "execute"† a word by simply naming the word. If you're working at a terminal keyboard, this can be as simple as typing in the word and pressing the RETURN key.

Of course, you can also use the same word in the definition of any other word, simply by putting its name in the definition.

FORTH is called an "interactive" language because it carries out your commands the instant you enter them.

We're going to give an example that you can try yourself, showing the process of combining simple commands into more powerful commands. We'll use some simple FORTH words that control your terminal screen or printer. But first, let's get acquainted with the mechanics of "talking" to FORTH through your terminal's keyboard.

Take a seat at your real or imaginary FORTH terminal. We'll assume that someone has been kind enough to set everything up for you, or that you have followed all the instructions given for loading your particular computer.

---

† For Beginners

To "execute" a word is to order the computer to carry out a command.

Now press the key labeled:

RETURN†

The computer will respond by saying

ok

The RETURN key is your way of telling FORTH to acknowledge your request. The ok is FORTH's way of saying that it's done everything you asked it to do without any hangups. In this case, you didn't ask it to do anything, so FORTH obediently did nothing and said ok. (The ok may be either in upper case or in lower case, depending on your terminal.)

Now enter this:

15 SPACES

If you make a typing mistake, you can correct it by hitting the "backspace" key. Back up to the mistake, enter the correct letter, then continue. When you have typed the line correctly, press the RETURN key. (Once you press RETURN, it's too late to correct the line.)

In this book, we use the symbol RETURN to mark the point where you must press the RETURN key. We also underline the computer's output (even though the computer does not) to indicate who is typing what.

Here's what has happened:

15 SPACES RETURN   ok

As soon as you pressed the return key, FORTH printed fifteen blank spaces and then, having processed your request, it responded ok (at the end of the fifteen spaces).

Now enter this:

42 EMIT RETURN *ok

The phrase "42 EMIT" tells FORTH to print an asterisk (we'll

---

†For People at Terminals

RETURN may have a different name on your terminal. Other possible names are NEW LINE and ENTER.

Backspace may also have a different name on your terminal, such as DEL or RUBOUT.

discuss this command later on in the book.) Here FORTH printed the asterisk, then responded ok.

We can put more than one command on the same line. For example:

```
15 SPACES  42 EMIT  42 EMIT RETURN                **ok
```

This time FORTH printed fifteen spaces and two asterisks. A note about entering words and/or numbers: we can separate them from one another by as many spaces as we want for clarity. But they must be separated by at least one space for FORTH to be able to recognize them as words and/or numbers.

Instead of entering the phrase

```
42 EMIT
```

over and over, let's define it as a word called "STAR."

Enter this

```
: STAR   42 EMIT ; RETURN ok
```

Here "STAR" is the name; "42 EMIT" is the definition. Notice that we set off the colon and semicolon from adjacent words with a space. Also, to make FORTH definitions easy for human beings to read, we conventionally separate the name of a definition from its contents with three spaces.

After you have entered the above definition and pressed RETURN, FORTH responds ok, signifying that it has recognized your definition and will remember it. Now enter

```
STAR RETURN *ok
```

Voila! FORTH executes your definition of "STAR" and prints an asterisk.

There is no difference between a word such as STAR that you define yourself and a word such as EMIT that is already defined. In this book, however, we will put boxes around those words that are already defined, so that you can more easily tell the difference.

Another system-defined word is CR, which performs a carriage return and line feed at your terminal.† For example, enter this:

---

†For Beginners

Be sure to distinguish between the key labeled RETURN and the FORTH word CR.

```
CR RETURN
ok
```

As you can see, FORTH executed a carriage return, then printed an ok (on the next line).

Now try this:

```
CR STAR CR STAR CR STAR RETURN
*
*
*ok
```

Let's put a CR in a definition, like this:

```
: MARGIN   CR  30 SPACES ; RETURN ok
```

Now we can enter

```
MARGIN STAR MARGIN STAR MARGIN STAR RETURN
```

and get three stars lined up vertically, thirty spaces in from the left.

Our MARGIN STAR combination will be useful for what we intend to do, so let's define

```
: BLIP   MARGIN STAR ; RETURN ok
```

We will also need to print a horizontal row of stars. So let's enter the following definition (we'll explain how it works in a later chapter):

```
: STARS   0 DO STAR LOOP ; RETURN ok
```

Now we can say

```
5 STARS RETURN *****ok
```

or

```
35 STARS RETURN ***********************************ok
```

or any number of stars imaginable!

We will need a word which performs MARGIN, then prints five stars. Let's define it like this:

```
: BAR   MARGIN  5 STARS ; RETURN ok
```

Now we can enter

```
BAR BLIP BAR BLIP BLIP  CR
```

and get a letter "F" (for FORTH) made up of stars. It should look like this:

```
*****
*
*****
*
*
```

The final step is to make this new procedure a word. Let's call the word "F":

```
: F   BAR BLIP BAR BLIP BLIP  CR ; RETURN ok
```

You've just seen an example of the way simple FORTH commands can become the foundation for more complex commands. A FORTH application, when listed,† consists of a series of increasingly powerful definitions rather than a sequence of instructions to be executed in order.

To give you a sample of what a FORTH application really looks like, here's a listing of our experimental application:

```
( LARGE LETTER-F)
: STAR   42 EMIT ;
: STARS   0 DO STAR LOOP ;
: MARGIN   CR 30 SPACES ;
: BLIP   MARGIN STAR ;
: BAR   MARGIN 5 STARS ;
: F   BAR BLIP BAR BLIP BLIP  CR ;
```

---

†For Beginners

We'll explain more about listing, as it applies to FORTH, in Chapter 3.

The Dictionary

Each word and its definition are entered into FORTH's "dictionary." The dictionary already contained many words when you started, but your own words are now in the dictionary as well.

When you define a new word, FORTH translates your definition into dictionary form and writes the entry in the dictionary. This process is called "compiling."†

For example, when you enter the line

: STAR   42 EMIT ;RETURN

the compiler compiles the new definition into the dictionary. The compiler does not print the asterisk.

Once a word is in the dictionary, how is it executed? Let's say you enter the following line directly at your terminal (not inside a definition):

STAR 30 SPACESRETURN

This will activate a word called INTERPRET, also known as the "text interpreter."

---

†For Beginners

Compilation is a general computer term which normally means the translation of a high-level program into machine code that the computer can understand. In FORTH it means the same thing, but specifically it means writing in the dictionary.

The text interpreter scans the input stream, looking for strings of characters separated by spaces.

When he finds such a string, he looks it up in the dictionary.

If he finds the word in the dictionary, he points out the definition to a word called EXECUTE--

--who then executes the definition (in this case, he prints an asterisk). The interpreter says everything's "ok."

If the interpreter cannot find the string in the dictionary, he calls the numbers-runner (called NUMBER).

NUMBER knows a number when he sees one. If NUMBER finds a number, he runs it off to a temporary storage location for numbers.

What happens when you try to execute a word that is not in the dictionary? Enter this and see what happens:

XLERB RETURN <u>XLERB ?</u>

When the text interpreter cannot find XLERB in the dictionary, it tries to pass it off on NUMBER. NUMBER shines it on. Then the interpreter returns the string to you with a question mark.

In some versions of FORTH, including polyFORTH, the compiler does <u>not</u> copy the entire name of the definition into the dictionary--only the first three characters and the number of characters. For example, in polyFORTH, the text interpreter cannot distinguish between STAR and STAG because both words are four characters in length and both begin S-T-A.†

While many professional programmers prefer the three-character rule because it saves memory, certain programmers and many hobbyists enjoy the freedom to choose <u>any</u> name. The FORTH-79 Standard allows up to thirty-one characters of a name to be stored in the dictionary.

To summarize: when you type a pre-defined word at the terminal, it gets interpreted and then executed.

Now remember we said that : is a word? When you type the word :, as in

```
: STAR   42 EMIT ; RETURN
```

---

† For polyFORTH Users

The trick to avoiding conflicts is to

a) be conscious of your name choices, and
b) when naming a series of similar words, put the distinguishing character up front, like this:

```
1LINE  2LINE  3LINE  etc.
```

the following occurs:

The text interpreter finds the colon in the input stream,

and points it out to EXECUTE.

EXECUTE says, "Please start compiling."

The compiler translates the definition into dictionary form and writes it in the dictionary.

When the compiler gets to the semicolon, he stops,

and execution returns to the text interpreter, who gives the message ok.

Say What?

In FORTH, a word is a character or group of characters that have a definition. Almost any characters can be used in naming a word. The only characters that cannot be used are:

return	because the computer thinks you've finished entering,†
backspace	because the computer thinks you're trying to correct a typing error,
space	because the computer thinks it's the end of the word, and
caret (↑ or ^)	because the editor (if you're using it) thinks you mean something else. We'll discuss the editor in Chap. 3.

Here is a FORTH word whose name consists of two punctuation marks. The word is ." and is pronounced dot-quote. You can use ." inside a definition‡ to type a "string" of text at your terminal. Here's an example:

```
: GREET   ." HELLO, I SPEAK FORTH " ;RETURN ok
```

We've just defined a word called GREET. Its definition consists of just one FORTH word, .", followed by the text we want typed. The quotation mark at the *end* of the text will not be typed; it marks the end of the text. It's called a "delimiter."

---

†For Philosophers

No, the computer doesn't "think." Unfortunately, there's no better word for what it really does. We say "think" on the grounds that it's all right to say, "the lamp needs a new light bulb." Whether the lamp really *needs* a bulb depends on whether it *needs* to provide light (that is, incandescence is its karma). So let's just say the computer thinks.

‡FORTH-79 Standard

In systems that conform to the Standard, ." will execute outside of a colon definition as well.

When entering the definition of GREET, don't forget the closing [;] to end the definition.

Let's execute GREET:

GREET RETURN HELLO, I SPEAK FORTH ok

The Stack: FORTH's Worksite for Arithmetic

A computer would not be much good if it couldn't do arithmetic. If you've never studied computers before, it may seem pretty amazing that a computer (or even a pocket calculator) can do arithmetic at all. We can't cite all the mechanics in this book, but believe us, it's not a miracle.

In general, computers perform their operations by breaking everything they do into ridiculously tiny pieces of information and ridiculously easy things to do. To you and me, "3 + 4" is just "7," without even thinking. To a computer, "3 + 4" is actually a very long list of things to do and remember.

Without getting too specific, let's say you have a pocket calculator which expects its buttons to be pushed in this order:

in order to perform the addition and display the result. Here's a generalized picture of what might occur:

When you press

--the number 3 goes into one place (called Box A).

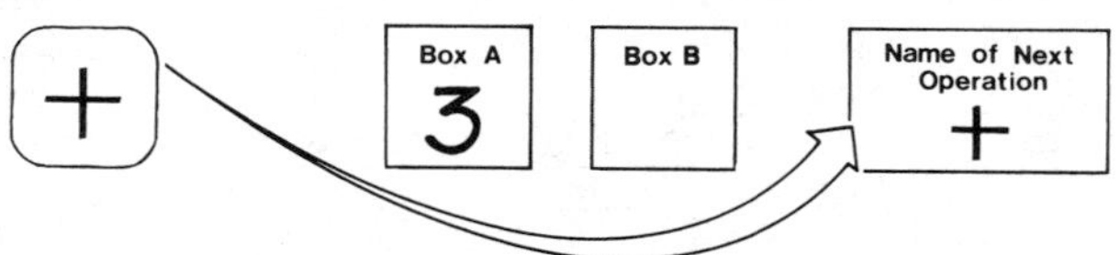

--the intended operation (addition) is remembered somehow.

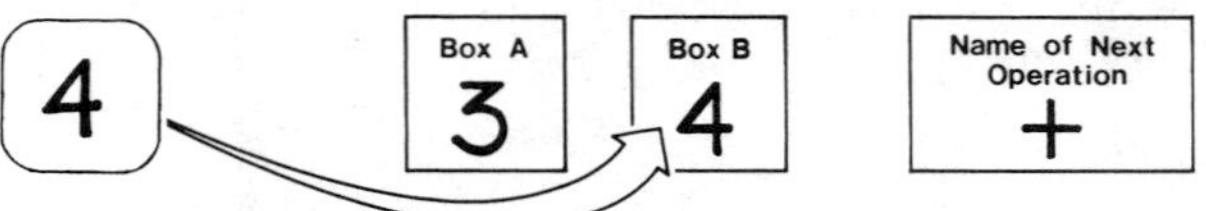

--the number 4 is stored into a second place (called Box B).

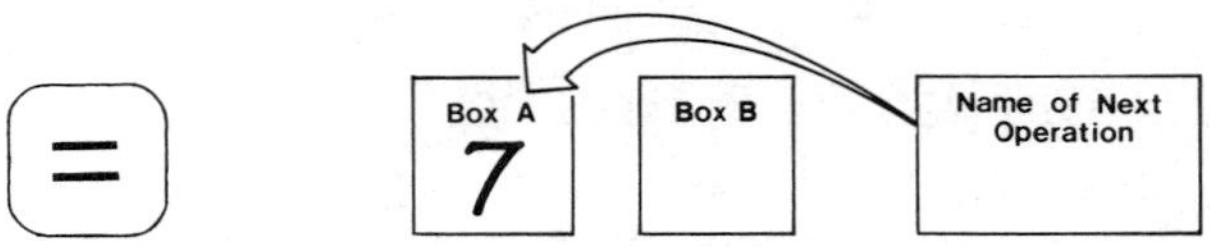

--the calculator performs the operation that is stored in the "Next Operation" Box on the contents of the number boxes and leaves the result in Box A.

Many calculators and computers approach arithmetic problems in a way similar to what we've just described. You may not be aware of it, but these machines are actually storing numbers in various locations and then performing operations on them.

In FORTH, there is <u>one</u> central location where numbers are temporarily stored before being operated on. That location is called the "stack." Numbers are "pushed onto the stack," and <u>then</u> operations work on the numbers on the stack.

The best way to explain the stack is to illustrate it. If you enter the following line at your terminal:

```
3 4 + . RETURN 7 ok
```

here's what happens, key by key.

Recall that when you enter a number at your terminal, the text interpreter hands it over to NUMBER, who runs it to some location. That location, it can now be told, is the stack. In short, when you enter the number three from the terminal, you push it onto the stack.

Now the four goes onto the "top" of the stack and pushes the three downward.

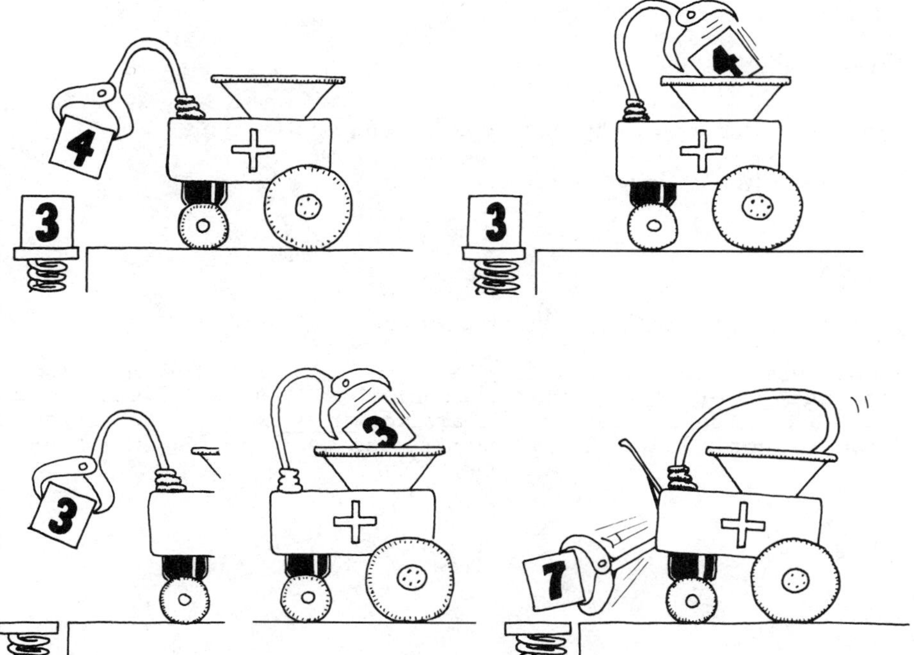

The next word in the input stream can be found in the dictionary. [+] has been previously defined to "take the top two numbers off the stack, add them, and push the result back onto the stack."

The next word, [.], is also found in the dictionary. It has been previously defined to take the number off the stack and print it at the terminal.

Postfix Power

Now wait, you say. Why does FORTH want you to type

```
3 4 +
```

instead of

```
3 + 4
```

which is more familiar to most people?

FORTH uses "postfix" notation (so called because the operator is affixed after the numbers) rather than "infix" notation (so called because the operator is affixed in-between the numbers) so that all words which "need" numbers can get them from the stack.†

---

†For Pocket-calculator Experts

Hewlett-Packard calculators feature a stack and postfix arithmetic.

For example:

> the word [+] gets two numbers from the stack and adds them;
>
> the word [.] gets one number from the stack and prints it;
>
> the word [SPACES] gets one number from the stack and prints that many spaces;
>
> the word [EMIT] gets a number that represents a character and prints that character;
>
> even the word STARS, which we defined ourselves, gets a number from the stack and prints that many stars.

When all operators are defined to work on the values that are already on the stack, interaction between many operations remains simple even when the program gets complex.

Earlier we pointed out that FORTH lets you execute a word in either of two ways: by simply naming it, or by putting it in the definition of another word and naming that word. Postfix is part of what makes this possible.

Just as an example, let's suppose we wanted a word that will always add the number 4 to whatever number is on the stack (for no other purpose than to illustrate our point). Let's call the word

```
FOUR-MORE
```

We could define it this way:

```
: FOUR-MORE   4 + ;RETURN
```

and test it this way:

```
3 FOUR-MORE .RETURN 7 ok
```

and again:

```
-10 FOUR-MORE .RETURN -6 ok
```

The "4" inside the definition goes onto the stack, just as it would if it were outside a definition. Then the [+] adds the two numbers on the stack. Since [+] always works on the stack, it doesn't care that the "4" came from inside the definition and the three from outside.

As we begin to give some more complicated examples, the value of the stack and of postfix arithmetic will become increasingly apparent to you. The more operators that are involved, the more important it is that they all be able to "communicate" with each other.

Keep Track of Your Stack

We've just begun to demonstrate the philosophy behind the stack and postfix notation. Before we continue, however, let's look more closely at the stack in action and get accustomed to its peculiarities.

FORTH's stack is described as "last-in, first-out" (LIFO). You can see from the earlier illustration why this is so. The three was pushed onto the stack first, then the four pushed on top of it. Later the adding machine took the four off first because it was on top. Hence "last-in, first-out."

In general, the only accessible value at any given time is the top value. Let's use another operation, the . to further demonstrate. Remember that each . removes one number from the stack and prints it. Four dots, therefore, remove four numbers and print them.

```
2 4 6 8 . . . . RETURN 8 6 4 2 ok
```

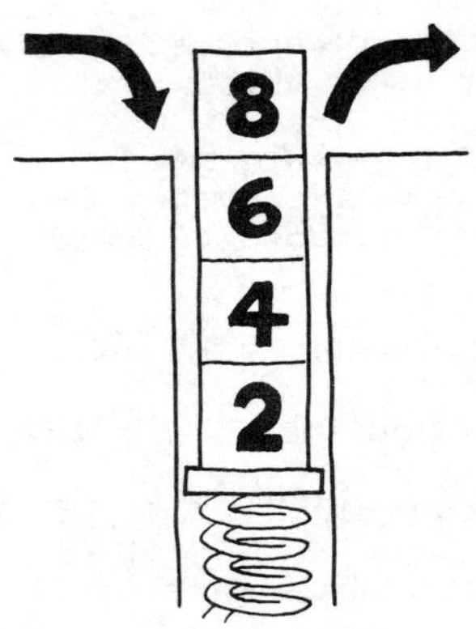

The system reads input from left to right and executes each word in turn.

> For input, the rightmost value on the screen will end up on <u>top</u> of the stack.
>
> For output, the rightmost value on the screen came from the <u>bottom</u> of the stack.

Let's see what kind of trouble we can get outselves into. Type:

```
10 20 30 . . . .
```

(that's <u>four</u> dots) then RETURN. What you get is:

10 20 30 . . . . RETURN 30 20 10 0 . STACK EMPTY†

Each dot removes one value. The fourth dot found that there was no value left on the stack to send to the terminal, and it told you so.

This error is called "stack underflow." (Notice that a stack underflow is not "ok.")

The opposite condition, when the stack completely fills up, is called "stack overflow." The stack is so deep, however, that this condition should never occur except when you've done something terribly wrong.

It's important to keep track of new words' "stack effects"; that is, the sort of numbers a word needs to have on the stack before you execute it, and the sort of numbers it will leave on the stack afterwards.

If you maintain a list of your newly created words with their meanings as you go, you or anyone else can easily understand the words' operations. In FORTH, such a list is called a "glossary."

To communicate stack effects in a visual way, FORTH programmers conventionally use a special stack notation in their glossaries or tables of words. We're introducing the stack notation now so that you'll have it under your belt when you begin the next chapter.

---

†For the Curious

Actually, dot always prints whatever is on the top, so if there is nothing on the stack, it prints whatever is just below the stack, which is usually zero. Only then is the error detected; the offending word (in this case dot) is returned to the screen, followed by the "error message."

Here's the basic form:

(before -- after)

The dash separates the things that should be on the stack (before you execute the word) from the things that will be left there afterwards. For example, here's the stack notation for the word [.]:

```
.        (n -- )
```

(The letter "n" stands for "number.") This shows that [.] expects one number on the stack (before) and leaves no number on the stack (after).

Here's the stack notation for the word [+].

```
+        (n1 n2 -- sum)
```

When there is more than one n, we number them n1, n2, n3, etc., consecutively. The numbers 1 and 2 do not refer to position on the stack. Stack position is indicated by the order in which the items are written; the rightmost item on either side of the arrow is the topmost item on the stack. For example, in the stack notation of [+], the n2 is on top:

```
+        (n1 n2 -- sum)
```

Since you probably have the hang of it by now, we'll be leaving out the RETURN symbol except where we feel it's needed for clarity. You can usually tell where to press "return" because the computer's response is always underlined.

Here's a list of the FORTH words you've learned so far, including their stack notations ("n" stands for number; "c" stands for character):

: xxx yyy ;	(--)	Creates a new definition with the name xxx, consisting of word or words yyy.
CR	(--)	Performs a carriage return and line feed at your terminal.
SPACES	(n --)	Prints the given number of blank spaces at your terminal.
SPACE	(--)	Prints one blank space at your terminal.
EMIT	(c --)	Transmits a character to the output device.
." xxx"	(--)	Prints the character string xxx at your terminal. The " character terminates the string.
+	(n1 n2 -- sum)	Adds.
.	(n --)	Prints a number, followed by one space.

In the next chapter we'll talk about getting the computer to perform some fancier arithmetic.

Review of Terms

Compile — to generate a dictionary entry in computer memory from source text (the written-out form of a definition). Distinct from "execute."

Dictionary — in FORTH, a list of words and definitions including both "system" definitions (predefined) and "user" definitions (which you invent). A dictionary resides in computer memory in compiled form.

Execute	to perform. Specifically, to execute a word is to perform the operations specified in the compiled definition of the word.
Extensibility	a characteristic of a computer language which allows a programmer to add new features or modify existing ones.
Glossary	a list of words defined in FORTH, showing their stack effects and an explanation of what they do, which serves as a reference for programmers.
Infix notation	the method of writing operators between the operands they affect, as in "2 + 5."
Input stream	the text to be read by the text interpreter. This may be text that you have just typed in at your terminal, or it may be text that is stored on disk.
Interpret	(when referring to FORTH's text interpreter) to read the input stream, then to find each word in the dictionary or, failing that, to convert it to a number.
LIFO	(last-in, first-out) the type of stack which FORTH uses. A can of tennis balls is a LIFO structure; the last ball you drop in is the one you must remove first.
Postfix notation	the method of writing operators after the operands they affect, as in "2 5 +" for "2 + 5." Also known as Reverse Polish Notation.
Stack	in FORTH, a region of memory which is controlled in such a way that data can be stored or removed in a last-in, first-out (LIFO) fashion.
Stack overflow	the error condition that occurs when the entire area of memory allowed for the stack is completely filled with data.
Stack underflow	the error condition that occurs when an operation expects a value on the stack, but there is no valid data on the stack.
Word	in FORTH, the name of a definition.

Problems -- Chapter 1

Note: before you work these problems, remember these simple rules:

Every [:] needs a [;].

and

Every [."] needs a ["].

1. Define a word called GIFT which, when executed, will type out the name of some gift. For example, you might try:

```
: GIFT   ." BOOKENDS " ;
```

Now define a word called GIVER which will print out a person's first name. Finally, define a word called THANKS which includes the new FORTH words GIFT and GIVER, and prints out a message something like this:

```
DEAR STEPHANIE,
     THANKS FOR THE BOOKENDS. ok
```

2. Define a word called TEN.LESS which takes a number on the stack, subtracts ten, and returns the answer on the stack. (Hint: you can use [+].)

3. After entering the words in Prob. 1, enter a new definition for GIVER to print someone else's name, then execute THANKS again. Can you explain why THANKS still prints out the first giver's name?

2 HOW TO GET RESULTS

In this chapter, we'll dive right into some specifics that you need to know before we go on. Specifically, we'll introduce some of the arithmetic instructions besides [+] and some special operators for rearranging the order of numbers on the stack, so that you'll be able to write mathematical equations in FORTH.

FORTH Arithmetic -- Calculator Style

Here are the four simplest integer-arithmetic operators in FORTH:†

			pronounced:
+	(n1 n2 -- sum)	Adds.	plus
-	(n1 n2 -- diff)	Subtracts (n1-n2).	minus
*	(n1 n2 -- prod)	Multiplies.	star
/	(n1 n2 -- quot)	Divides (n1/n2).	slash

Unlike calculators, computer terminals don't have special keys for multiplication and division. Instead we use [*] and [/].

---

†**If Math Is Not Your Thing**

Don't worry if this chapter looks a little like an algebra textbook. Solving math problems is only one of the things you can do with FORTH. Later we'll explore some of the other things FORTH can do.

Meanwhile, we'd like to remind you that integers are whole numbers, such as:

... -3, -2, -1, 0, 1, 2, 3, ...

Integer arithmetic (logically enough) is arithmetic that concerns itself only with integers, not with decimal-point numbers, such as 2.71.

In the first chapter, we learned that we can add two numbers by putting them both on the stack, then executing the word [+], then finally executing the word [.] (dot) to get the result printed at our terminal.

17 5 + . 22 ok

We can use this method with all of FORTH's arithmetic operators. In other words, we can use FORTH like a calculator to get answers, even without writing a "program." Try a multiplication problem:

7 8 * . 56 ok

By now we've seen that the operator comes after the numbers. In the case of subtraction and division, though, we must also consider the order of numbers ("7 - 4" is not the same as "4 - 7").

Just remember this rule:

> To convert to postfix, simply move the operator to the end of the expression:

Infix	Postfix
3 + 4	3 4 +
500 - 300	500 300 -
6 X 5	6 5 *
20 / 4	20 4 /

So to do this subtraction problem:

7 - 4 =

simply type in

7 4 - . 3 ok

For Adventuresome Newcomers Sitting at a Terminal

If you're one of those people who likes to fool around and figure things out for themselves without reading the book, then you're bound to discover a couple of weird things. First off, as we told you, these operators are integer operators. That not only means that you can't do calculations with decimal values, like

```
10.00 2.25 +
```

it also means that you can only get integer results, as in

```
21 4 / . 5 ok instead of 5.25 ok
```

Another thing is that if you try to multiply:

```
10000 10 *
```

or some such large numbers, you'll get a crazy answer. So we're telling you up front that with the operators introduced so far and with [.] to print the results, you can't have any numbers that are higher than 32767 or lower than -32768. Numbers within this range are called "single-length signed numbers."

+32767
0
-32768

Allowable range of single-length signed numbers.

Notice, in the list of FORTH words a few pages back, the letter "n," which stands for "number." Since FORTH uses single-length numbers more often than other types of numbers, the "n" signifies that the number must be single-length. And yes, there are other operators that extend this range ("double-length" operators, which are indicated by "d").

All of these mysteries will be explained in time, so stay tuned.

The order of numbers stays the same. Let's try a division problem:

```
20 4 / . 5 ok
```

The word [/] is defined to divide the second number on the stack by the top number:

What do you do if you have more than one operator in an expession, like:

```
4 + (17 * 12)
```

you ask? Let's take it step-by-step: the parentheses tell you to first multiply seventeen by twelve, <u>then</u> add four. So in FORTH you would write:

```
17 12 * 4 + . 208 ok
```
or 4 17 12 * +

and here's why:

17 and 12 go onto the stack. * multiplies them and returns the result.

Then the four goes onto the stack, on top of the 204. + rolls out the adding machine and adds them together, returning only the result.

Or suppose you want to add five numbers. You can do it in FORTH like this:

17 20 + 132 + 3 + 9 + . 181 ok

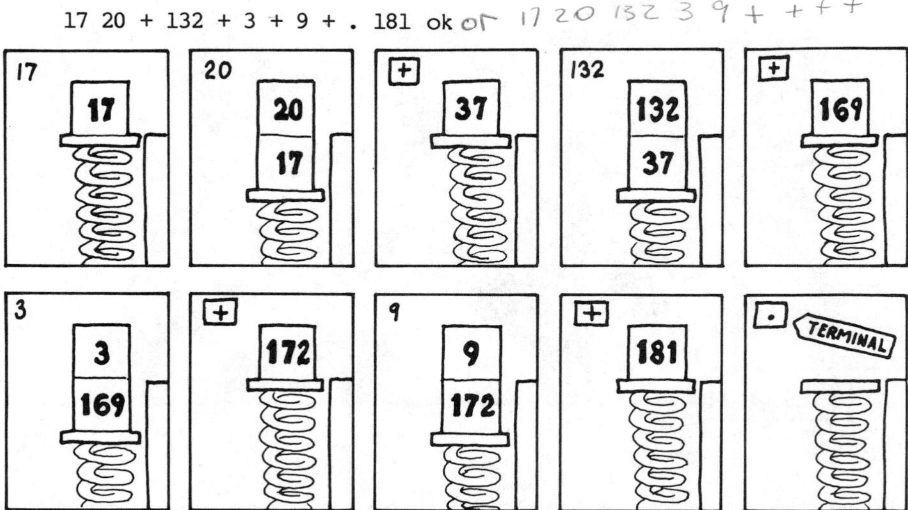

Now here's an interesting problem:

(3+9) * (4+6)

To solve it we have to add three to nine first, then add four to six, then finally multiply the two sums. In FORTH, we can write

3 9 + 4 6 + * . 120 ok

and here's what happens:

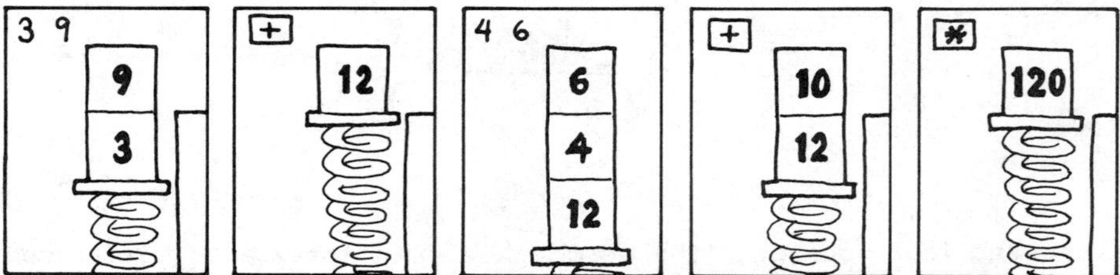

Notice that we very conveniently saved the sum twelve on the stack while we went on about the business of adding four to six.

Remember that we're not concerned yet with writing definitions. We are simply using FORTH as a calculator.

If you're like most beginners, you probably would like to try your hand at a few practice problems until you feel more comfortable with postfix.

Postfix Practice Problems (Quizzie 2-a)

Convert the following infix equations to postfix "calculator style." For example,

    ab + c

would become

    a b * c +

1. c(a + b)

2. $\frac{3a - b}{4} + c$

†3. $\frac{0.5\ ab}{100}$

4. $\frac{n + 1}{n}$

5. x(7x + 5)

Convert the following postfix expressions to infix:

6. a b - b a + /

7. a b 10 * /

---

†For Beginners

Remember, we're only using integer arithmetic, so you'll have to be clever.

Answers — Quizzie 2-a

1. a b + c * or c a b + *
2. 3 a * b - 4 / c +
3. a b * 100 / 2 / or a b * 200 /
4. n 1 + n /
5. 7 x * 5 + x *
6. $\frac{a - b}{b + a}$
7. $\frac{a}{10b}$

FORTH Arithmetic -- Definition Style

In Chap. 1 we saw that we could define new words in terms of numbers and other pre-defined words. Let's explore some further possibilities, using some of our newly-learned math operators.

Let's say we want to convert various measurements to inches. We know that

1 yard = 36 inches

and

1 foot = 12 inches

so we can define these two words:

```
: YARDS>IN   36 * ; ok
: FT>IN   12 * ; ok
```

where the names symbolize "yards-to-inches" and "feet-to-inches." Here's what they do:

```
10 YARDS>IN . 360 ok
2 FT>IN . 24 ok
```

If we always want our result to be in inches, we can define:

```
: YARDS   36 * ; ok
: FEET   12 * ; ok
: INCHES ; ok
```

so that we can use the phrase

```
10 YARDS 2 FEET + 9 INCHES + . 393 ok
```

Notice that the word INCHES doesn't do anything except remind the human user what the nine is there for. If we really want to get fancy, we can add these three definitions:

```
: YARD   YARDS ; ok
: FOOT   FEET ; ok
: INCH ; ok
```

so that the user can enter the singular form of any of these nouns and still get the same result:

```
1 YARD  2 FEET +  1 INCH + . 61 ok
2 YARDS  1 FOOT + . 84 ok
```

So far we have only defined words whose definitions contain a single math operator. But it's perfectly possible to put many operators inside a definition, if that's what you need to do.

Let's say we want a word that computes the sum of five numbers on the stack. A few pages back we summed five numbers like this:

```
17 20 + 132 + 3 + 9 + . 181 ok
```

But we can also enter

```
17 20 132 3 9 + + + + . 181 ok
```

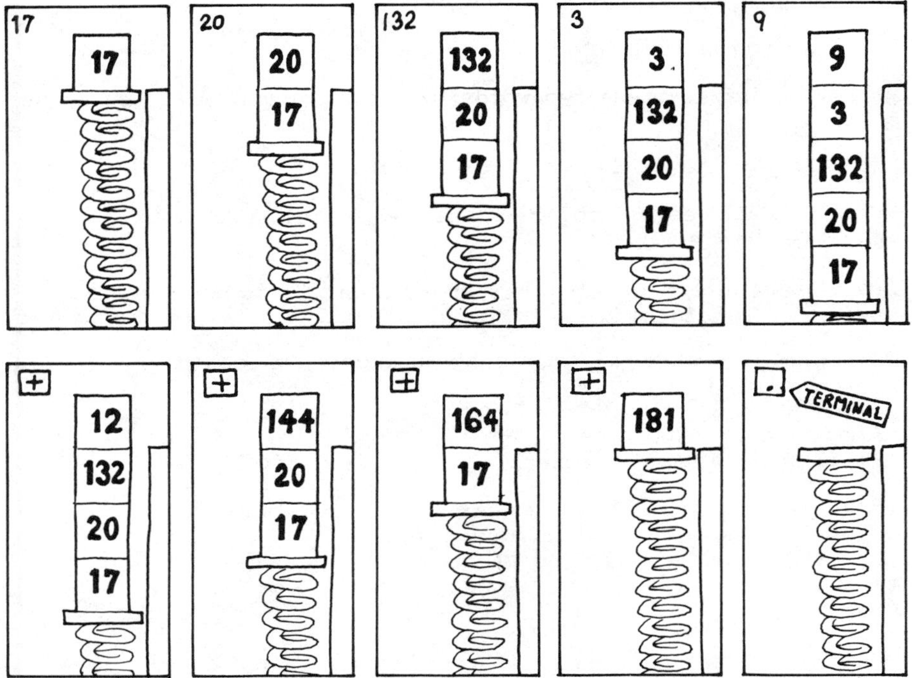

We get the same answer, even though we've clustered all the numbers into one group and all the operators into another group. We can write our definition like this:

```
: 5#SUM   + + + + ; ok
```

and execute it like this:

```
17 20 132 3 9 5#SUM . 181 ok
```

If we were going to keep 5#SUM for future use, we could enter it into our ever-growing glossary, along with a note that it "expects five arguments"† on the stack, which it will add together.

Here's another equation to write a definition for:‡

(a + b) * c

As we saw in Quizzie 2-a, this expression can be written in postfix as

c a b + *

Thus we could write our definition

```
: SOLUTION   + * ; ok
```

as long as we make sure that we enter the arguments in the proper order:

```
c a b SOLUTION
```

---

†For Semantic Freaks

In mathematics, the word "argument" refers to an independent variable of a function. Computer linguists have borrowed this term to refer to numbers being operated on by operators. They have also borrowed the word "parameters" to describe pretty much the same thing.

‡For Beginners Who Like Word-problems

If a jet plane flies at an average air speed of 600 mph and if it flies with a tail wind of 25 mph, how far will it travel in five hours?

If we define

```
: FLIGHT-DISTANCE   + * ;
```

we could enter

```
5 600 25 FLIGHT-DISTANCE . 3125 ok
```

Try it with different values, including head winds (negative values).

Definition-style Practice Problems (Quizzie 2-b)

Convert the following infix expressions into FORTH definitions and show the stack order required by your definitions. Since this is Quizzie 2-b, you can name your definitions 2B1, 2B2, etc. For example,

1. ab + c would become `: 2B1 * + ;`

   which expects this stack order: (c b a -- result)

2. $\frac{a - 4b}{6} + c$

3. $\frac{a}{8b}$

4. $\frac{0.5\ ab}{100}$

5. a(2a + 3)

6. $\frac{a - b}{c}$

Answers -- Quizzie 2-b

2. `: 2B2 4 * - 6 / + ;`
   (c a b -- result)
3. `: 2B3 8 * / ;`
   (a b -- result)
4. `: 2B4 * 200 / ;`
   (a b -- result)
5. `: 2B5 2 * 3 + * ;`
   (a a -- result)
6. If you said this one's impossible, you're right!--at least without the stack manipulation operators which we'll introduce very shortly.

The Division Operators

The word [/] is FORTH's simplest division operator. Slash supplies only the quotient; any remainder is lost. If you type:

```
22 4 / . 5 ok
```

you get only the quotient five, not the remainder two.

If you're thinking of a pocket calculator's per-cent operator, then five is not the full answer.

But [/] is only one of several division operators supplied by FORTH to give you the flexibility to tell the computer exactly what you want it to do.

For example, let's say you want to solve this problem: "How many dollar bills can I get in exchange for 22 quarters?" The real answer, of course, is exactly 5, not 5.5. A computerized money changer, for example, would not know how to give you 5.5 dollar bills.

Here are two more FORTH division operators:

			pronounced:
/MOD	(u1 u2 -- u-rem u-quot)	Divides. Returns the remainder and quotient.	slash-mod
MOD	(u1 u2 -- u-rem)	Returns the remainder from division.	mod

The "u" stands for "unsigned." We'll see what this means in the chapter on computer numbers. For now though, it means that the numbers can't be negative.

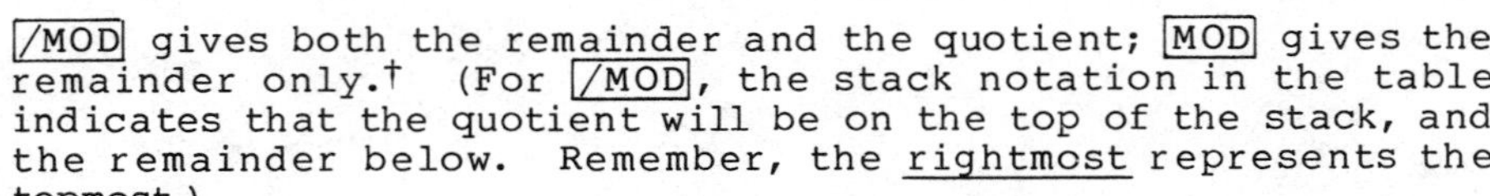

[/MOD] gives both the remainder and the quotient; [MOD] gives the remainder only.† (For [/MOD], the stack notation in the table indicates that the quotient will be on the top of the stack, and the remainder below. Remember, the rightmost represents the topmost.)

---

†For the Curious

MOD refers to the term "modulo," which basically means "remainder."

Let's try the first one:

```
22 4 /MOD . . 5 2 ok
```

Here /MOD performs the division and puts both the quotient and the remainder on the stack. The first dot prints the quotient because the quotient was on top.

SAMURAI /MOD (slash's older brother)

With what we've learned so far, we can easily define this word:

```
: QUARTERS   4 /MOD .  ." ONES AND "  .  ." QUARTERS " ;
```

So that you can type:

```
22 QUARTERS
```

with this result:

```
22 QUARTERS 5 ONES AND 2 QUARTERS ok
```

The second word in the table, MOD, leaves only the remainder. For example in:

```
22 4 MOD . 2 ok
```

the two is the remainder.

Stack Maneuvers

If you worked Prob. 6 in the last set, you discovered that the infix equation

$$\frac{a - b}{c}$$

cannot be solved with a definition unless there is some way to rearrange values on the stack.

Well, there *is* a way: by using a "stack manipulation operator" called SWAP.

SWAP

The word SWAP is defined to switch the order of the top two stack items:

As with the other stack manipulation operators, you can test SWAP at your terminal in "calculator style"; that is, it doesn't have to be contained within a definition.

First enter

```
1 2 . . 2 1 ok
```

then again, this time with SWAP:

```
1 2 SWAP . . 1 2 ok
```

Thus Prob. 6 can be solved with this phrase:

```
- SWAP /
```

with (c a b --) on the stack.

Let's give a, b, and c these test values:

a = 10   b = 4   c = 2

then put them on the stack and execute the phrase, like so:

```
2 10 4 - SWAP / . 3 ok
```

Here is a list of several stack manipulation operators, including SWAP.

Word	Stack effect	Description
SWAP	(n1 n2 -- n2 n1)	Reverses the top two stack items.
DUP	(n -- n n)	Duplicates the top stack item.
OVER	(n1 n2 -- n1 n2 n1)	Makes a copy of the second item and pushes it on top.
ROT	(n1 n2 n3 -- n2 n3 n1)	Rotates the third item to the top.
DROP	(n --)	Discards the top stack item.

DUP

The next stack manipulation operator on the list, DUP, simply makes a second copy (duplicate) of the top stack item.

For example, if we have "a" on the stack, we can compute:

a^2

as follows:

```
DUP *
```

in which the following steps occur:

Operation	Contents of Stack
	a
DUP	a a
*	a^2

OVER

Now somebody tells you to evaluate the expression:

a * (a + b)

given the following stack order:

(a b --)

But, you say, I'm going to need a new manipulation operator: I want two copies of the "a," and the "a" is under the "b." Here's the word you need: OVER. OVER simply makes a copy of the "a" and leapfrogs it over the "b":

(a b -- a b a)

Now the expression:

a * (a + b)

can easily be written:

OVER + *

Here's what happens:

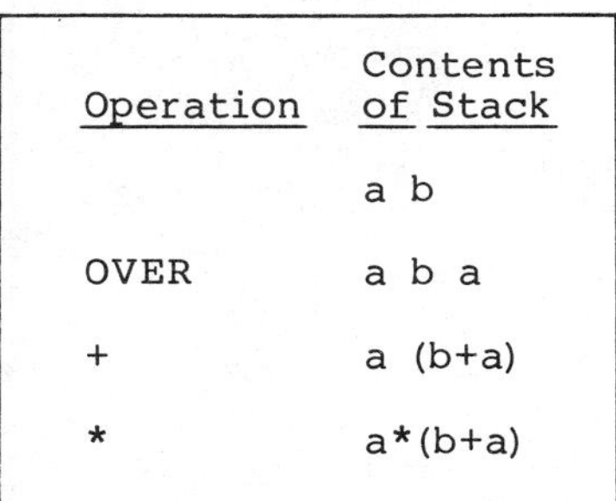

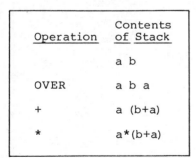

Operation	Contents of Stack
	a b
OVER	a b a
+	a (b+a)
*	a*(b+a)

When writing equations in FORTH, it's best to "factor them out" first. For example, if somebody asks you to evaluate:

a^2 + ab

in FORTH, you'll find it quite complicated (and maybe even impossible) using the words we've introduced so far ... unless you factor out the expression to read:

a * (a + b)

which is the expression we just evaluated so easily.

ROT

The fourth stack manipulator on the list is ROT (pronounced *rote*), which is short for "rotate." Here's what ROT does to the top three stack values:

For example, if we need to evaluate the expression:

ab - bc

we should first factor out the "b"s:

b * (a - c)

Now if our starting-stack order is this:

(c b a --)

we can use:

```
ROT - *
```

in which the following steps will occur:

Operation	Contents of Stack
	c b a
ROT	b a c
-	b (a-c)
*	(b*(a-c))

DROP

The final stack manipulation operator on the list is DROP. All it does is discard the top stack value.

Pretty simple, huh? We'll see some good uses for DROP later on.

A Handy Hint

A Non-destructive Stack Print

Beginners who are just learning to manipulate numbers on the stack in useful ways very often find themselves typing a series of dots to see what's on the stack after their manipulations. The problem with dots, though, is that they don't leave the numbers on the stack for future manipulations.

Here is the definition of a very useful word for such beginners. .S prints out all the values that happen to be on the stack "non-destructively"; that is, without removing them. Type the definition in as shown here, and don't worry about how it works.

```
: .S   CR  'S S0 @ 2- DO  I @ .  -2 +LOOP ; ok
```

Let's test it, first with nothing on the stack:

```
.S
0 ok
```

As you can see, in this version of .S, we always see at least one number as a reference for the bottom of the stack; that is, the same number we see when we type a [.] and get

```
.RETURN 0 . STACK EMPTY
```

Now let's try it with numbers on the stack:

```
1 2 3 .S
0 1 2 3 ok

ROT .S
0 2 3 1 ok
```

Stack Manipulation and Math Definitions (Quizzie 2-c)

1. Write a phrase which flips three items on the stack, leaving the middle number in the middle; that is,

   a b c   becomes   c b a

2. Write a phrase that does what OVER does, without using OVER.

3. Write a definition called <ROT, which rotates the top three stack items in the opposite direction from ROT; that is,

   a b c   becomes   c a b

Write definitions for the following equations, given the stack effects shown:

4. $\frac{n + 1}{n}$ (n -- result)

5. $x(7x + 5)$ (x -- result)

6. $9a^2 - ba$ (a b -- result)

Answers -- Quizzie 2-c

```
1.  SWAP ROT
2.  SWAP DUP ROT SWAP
3.  : <ROT   ROT ROT ;
4.  : 2C4    DUP 1 + SWAP / ;      or
    : 2C4    DUP 1+ SWAP / ;
5.  : 2C5    DUP 7 *  5 + * ;
6.  : 2C6    OVER 9 *  SWAP - * ;
```

Playing Doubles†

The next four stack manipulation operators should look vaguely familiar:

2SWAP	(d1 d2 -- d2 d1)	Reverses the top two pairs of numbers.
2DUP	(d -- d d)	Duplicates the top pair of numbers.
2OVER	(d1 d2 -- d1 d2 d1)	Makes a copy of the second pair of numbers and pushes it on top.
2DROP	(d --)	Discards the top pair of numbers.

two-swap
two-dupe
two-over
two-drop

The prefix "2" indicates that these stack manipulation operators handle numbers in pairs.‡ The letter "d" in the stack effects column stands for "double." "Double" has a special significance that we will discuss when we discuss "n" and "u."

The "2"-manipulators listed above are so straightforward, we won't even bore you with examples.

One more thing: there are still some stack manipulators we haven't talked about yet, so don't go crazy by trying too much fancy footwork on the stack.

Guess who.

---

†FORTH-79 Standard

These words are part of the Standard's "Double Number Word Set," which is optional in a Standard system. 2ROT is included.

‡For Old Hands

They can also be used to handle double-length (32-bit) numbers.

Here's a list of the FORTH words we've covered in this chapter:

Word	Stack effect	Description
+	(nl n2 -- sum)	Adds.
-	(nl n2 -- diff)	Subtracts (nl-n2).
*	(nl n2 -- prod)	Multiplies.
/	(nl n2 -- quot)	Divides (nl/n2).
/MOD	(ul u2 -- u-rem u-quot)	Divides. Returns the remainder and quotient.
MOD	(ul u2 -- u-rem)	Returns the remainder from division.
SWAP	(nl n2 -- n2 nl)	Reverses the top two stack items.
DUP	(n -- n n)	Duplicates the top stack item.
OVER	(nl n2 -- nl n2 nl)	Makes a copy of the second item and pushes it on top.
ROT	(nl n2 n3 -- n2 n3 nl)	Rotates the third item to the top.
DROP	(n --)	Discards the top stack item.
2SWAP	(dl d2 -- d2 dl)	Reverses the top two pairs of numbers.
2DUP	(d -- d d)	Duplicates the top pairs of numbers.
2OVER	(dl d2 -- dl d2 dl)	Makes a copy of the second pair of numbers and pushes it on top.
2DROP	(d --)	Discards the top pair of numbers.

Review of Terms

Double-length numbers
: integers which encompass a range of over -2 billion to +2 billion (and which we'll introduce officially in Chap. 7).

Single-length numbers
: integers which fall within the range of -32768 to +32767: the only numbers which are valid as the arguments or results of any of the operators we've discussed so far. (This seemingly arbitrary range comes from the way computers are designed, as we'll see later on.)

Problems -- Chapter 2

(answers in the back of the book)

1. What is the difference between DUP DUP and 2DUP?

2. Write a phrase which will reverse the order of the top four items on the stack; that is,

   (1 2 3 4 -- 4 3 2 1)

3. Write a definition called 3DUP which will duplicate the top three numbers on the stack; for example,

   (1 2 3 -- 1 2 3 1 2 3)

Write definitions for the following infix equations, given the stack effects shown:

4. $a^2 + ab + c$ (c a b -- result)

5. $\frac{a - b}{a + b}$ (a b -- result)

6. Write a set of words to compute prison sentences for hardened criminals such that the judge can enter:

   ```
   CONVICTED-OF ARSON HOMICIDE TAX-EVASION ok
   WILL-SERVE 35 YEARS ok
   ```

   or any series of crimes beginning with the word CONVICTED-OF and ending with WILL-SERVE. Use these sentences:

HOMICIDE	20 years
ARSON	10 years
BOOKMAKING	2 years
TAX-EVASION	5 years

7. You're the inventory programmer at Maria's Egg Ranch. Define a word called EGG.CARTONS which expects on the stack the total number of eggs laid by the chickens today and prints out the number of cartons that can be filled with a dozen each, as well as the number of left-over eggs.

3 THE EDITOR (AND STAFF)

Up till now you've been compiling new definitions into the dictionary by typing them at your terminal. This chapter introduces an alternate method, using disk storage.

Let's begin with some observations that specifically concern the dictionary.

Another Look at the Dictionary

If you've been experimenting at a real live terminal, you may have discovered some things we haven't mentioned yet. In any case, it's time to mention them.

> Discovery One: You can define the same word more than once in different ways--only the most recent definition will be executed.

For example, if you have entered:

```
: GREET  ." HELLO.  I SPEAK FORTH. " ; ok
```

then you should get this result:

```
GREET HELLO.  I SPEAK FORTH. ok
```

and if you redefine:

```
: GREET  ." HI THERE! " ; ok
```

you get the most recent definition:

```
GREET HI THERE! ok
```

Has the first GREET been erased? No, it's still there, but the most recent GREET is executed because of the search order. The text interpreter always starts at the "back of the dictionary" where the most recent entry is. The definition he finds first is the one you defined last. This is the one he shows to EXECUTE.

We can prove that the old GREET is still there. Try this:

```
FORGET GREET ok
```

and

```
GREET HELLO.  I SPEAK FORTH. ok
```

(the old GREET again!)

The word FORGET looks up the given word in the dictionary and, in effect, removes it from the dictionary along with anything you may have defined since that word. FORGET, like the interpreter, searches starting from the back; he only removes the most recently defined version of the word (along with any words that follow). So now when you type GREET at the terminal, the interpreter finds the original GREET.

FORGET is a good word to know; he helps you to weed out your dictionary so it won't overflow. (The dictionary takes up memory space, so as with any other use of memory, you want to conserve it.)

> Discovery Two: When you enter definitions from the terminal (as you have been doing), your source text† is not saved.

Only the compiled form of your definition is saved in the dic-

---

†For Beginners

The "source text" is the original version of the definition, such as:

```
: FOUR-MORE   4 + ;
```

which the compiler translates into a dictionary entry.

tionary. So, what if you want to make a minor change to a word you've already defined? This is where the EDITOR comes in. With the EDITOR, you can save your source text and modify it if you want to.

The EDITOR stores your source text on disk. So before we can really discuss the EDITOR, we'd better introduce the disk and the way the FORTH system uses it.

How FORTH Uses the Disk

Nearly all FORTH systems use disk memory. Even though disk memory is not absolutely necessary for a FORTH system, it's difficult to imagine FORTH without it.

To understand what disk memory does, compare it with computer memory (RAM). The difference is analogous to the difference between a filing cabinet and a rolling card-index.

So far you've been using computer memory, which is like the card index. The computer can access this memory almost instantaneously, so programs that are stored in RAM can run very fast. Unfortunately, this kind of memory is limited and relatively expensive.

On the other hand, the disk is called a "bulk memory" device because, like a filing cabinet, it can store a lot of information at a much cheaper price per unit of information than the memory inside the computer.

Both kinds of memory can be written to and read from.

The compiler compiles all dictionary entries into computer memory so that the definitions will be quickly accessible. The perfect place to store source text, however, is on the disk, which is what FORTH does. You can either send source text directly from the keyboard to the interpreter (as you have been doing), or you can save your source text on the disk and then later read it off the disk and send it to the text interpreter.

Disk memory is divided into units called "blocks." Many professional FORTH development systems have 500 blocks available (250 from each disk drive). Each block holds 1,024 characters of source text. The 1,024 characters are divided for display into 16 lines of 64 characters each, to fit conveniently on your terminal screen.

```
180 LIST

( LARGE LETTER-F)
: STAR   42 EMIT ;
: STARS   0 DO STAR LOOP ;
: MARGIN   CR 30 SPACES ;
: BLIP   MARGIN STAR ;
: BAR   MARGIN 5 STARS ;
: F   BAR BLIP BAR BLIP BLIP  CR ;


F
```

This is what a block looks like when it's listed on your terminal. To list a block for yourself, simply type the block-number and the word LIST, as in:

```
180 LIST
```

To give you a better idea of how the disk is used, we'll assume that your block 180 contains the sample definitions shown above. Except for line 0, everything should look familiar: these are the definitions you used to print a large letter "F" at your terminal.

Now if you were to type:

```
180 LOAD
```

you would send block 180 to the input stream and then on to the text interpreter. The text interpreter does not care where his text comes from. Recognizing the colons, he will have all the definitions compiled.

Notice that we've put our new word F on line 9. We've done this to show that when you load a block, you execute its contents. Simply by typing:

```
180 LOAD
```

all the definitions will be compiled and a letter "F" will be printed at your terminal.

Now for the unfinished business: line 0. The words inside the parentheses are for humans only; they are neither compiled nor executed. The word ((left parenthesis) tells the text interpreter to skip all the following text up to the terminating right parenthesis. Because (is a word, it must be set off with a space.†

It's good programming practice to identify your application blocks with comments, so that fellow programmers will understand them.

---

†For Beginners

The closing parenthesis is not a word, it is simply a character that is looked for by (, called a delimiter. (Recall that the delimiter for ." is the closing quote mark.)

Here are a few additional ways to make your blocks easy to read:

1. Separate the name from the contents of a definition by three spaces.

2. Break definitions up into phrases, separated by double spaces.

3. If the definition takes more than one line, indent all but the first line.

4. Don't put more than one definition on a single line unless the definitions are very short and logically related.

To summarize, the three commands we've learned so far that concern disk blocks are:

LIST	(n --)	Lists a disk block.
LOAD	(n --)	Loads a disk block (compiles or executes).
(xxx)	(--)	Causes the string xxx to be ignored by the text interpreter. The character) is the delimiter.

Dear EDITOR†

Now you're ready to learn how to put your text on the disk.

First find an empty block‡ and list it, using the form:

```
180 LIST
```

When you list an empty block, you'll see sixteen line numbers (0 - 15) running down the side of the screen, but nothing on any of the lines. The "ok" on the last line is the signal that the text interpreter has obeyed your command to list the block.

By listing a block, you also select that block as the one you're going to work on.

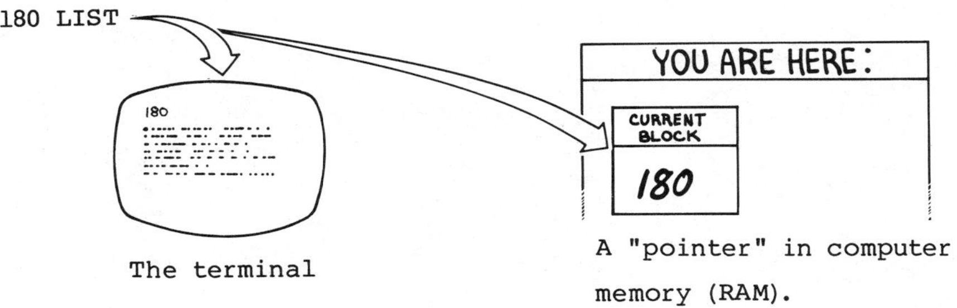

The terminal

A "pointer" in computer memory (RAM).

Now that you've made a block "current," you can list it by simply typing the word

```
L
```

Unlike LIST, L does not want to be preceded by a block number; instead, it lists the current block.

---

†**For Those Whose EDITOR Doesn't Follow These Rules**

The FORTH-79 Standard does not specify editor commands. Your system may use a different editor; if so, check your system documentation.

‡**For People at Terminals**

If you're using someone else's system, ask them which blocks are available. If you're using your own system, try 180. It should be free (empty).

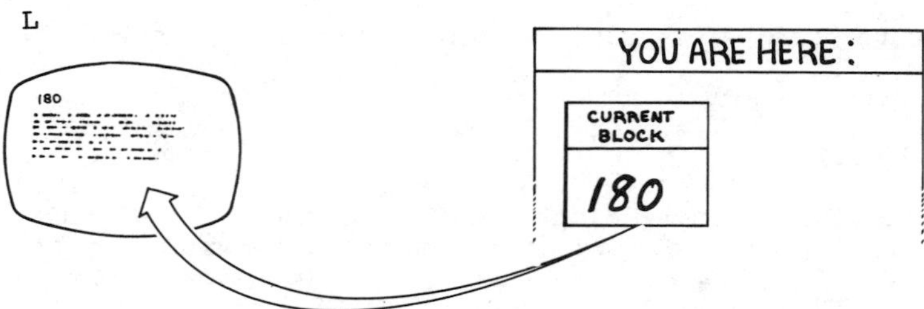

Now that you have a current block, it's time to select a current line by using the word [T]. Suppose we want to write something on line 3. Type:

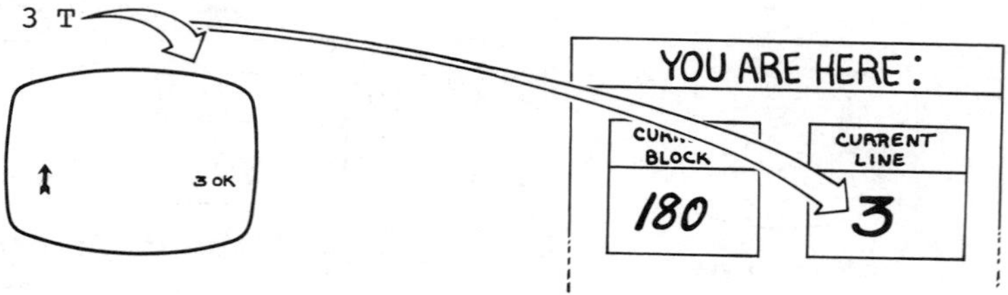

[T] lets you select the current line.† It also performs a carriage return, then types the given line (which so far contains nothing). At the end of the line, it reminds you which line you're on:

```
3 T
^                                              3 ok
```

(Remember, we're underlining the computer's output for the sake of clarity.) The caret at the beginning of the line is the EDITOR's cursor, which points to your current character position. On your terminal the caret might look like this: ↑

---

†For the Curious

Actually, the cursor position, not the line number, serves as the pointer. More on this in a future footnote.

Now that your sights are fixed, you can put some text in the current line by using [P].

P HERE IT IS RETURN ok

[P] puts the string that follows it (up to the carriage return) on the current line. It does not type out the line. If you don't believe the string is really there, you can type:

3 T

or simply:

L

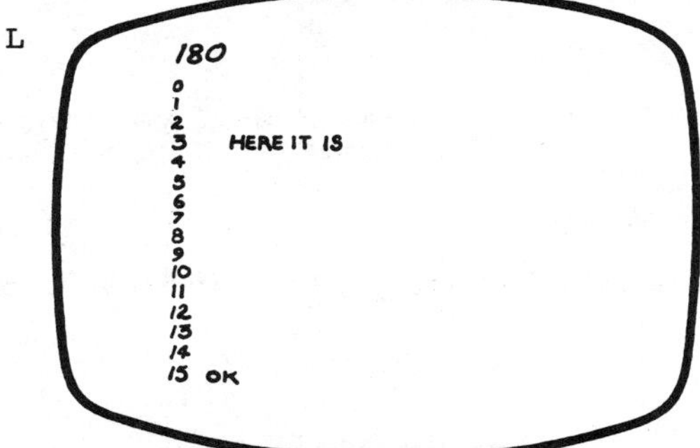

Remember that your current position remains the same, so if you were to now type

P THERE IT WENT RETURN ok

followed by [L], you'd see that the latter string had replaced the former on line 3.

Similarly, entering [P] followed by at least two blank spaces (one to separate the [P] from the string, the other as the string itself) causes the former string to be replaced by a blank space; in other words, it blanks the line.

In this chapter the symbol "b̸" means that you type a blank space. So to blank a line, type:

Pb̸b̸ RETURN

Character Editing Commands

In this section, we'll show you how to insert and delete text within a line.

F

Before you can insert or delete text, you must be able to position the EDITOR's cursor to the point of insertion or deletion. Suppose line 3 now contains:

    IF MUSIC BE THE FOD OF LOVE

and you want to insert the second "O" in "FOOD," you must first position the cursor after the "FO" like this:

    IF MUSIC BE THE FO^D OF LOVE

To position the cursor, use the command **F**, followed by a string, as in

    F FO RETURN

F searches forward from the current position of the cursor until it finds the given string (in this case "FO"), then places the cursor right after it.

F FO RETURN

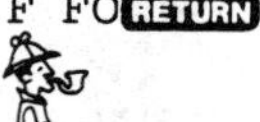

^IF MUSIC BE THE FOD OF LOVE

IF MUSIC BE THE FOD OF LOVE

IF MUSIC BE THE FO D OF LOVE

If you don't know the starting position of the cursor, first type "3 T" to reset the cursor to the start of the line. **F** then types the line, showing where the cursor is:

    IF MUSIC BE THE FO^D OF LOVE 3 ok

[I]

Now that the cursor is positioned where you want it, simply enter:

```
I O RETURN
```

and [I] will insert the character "O" just behind the cursor.

SQUIRT

```
IF MUSIC BE THE FOO^D OF LOVE
```

[I] then types the corrected line, including the cursor:

```
IF MUSIC BE THE FOO^D  OF LOVE                    3 ok
```

[E]

To erase a string (using the command [E]), you must first find the string, using [F]. For example, if you want to erase the word "MUSIC," first reset the cursor with:

```
3 T RETURN
```

then type:

```
F MUSIC RETURN
IF MUSIC^ BE THE FOOD OF LOVE                     3 ok
```

and then simply:

```
E RETURN
```

[E] erases the string you just found with [F].

Eberhart

```
IF MUSIC BE THE FOOD OF LOVE
```

[E] then types the line, including the cursor:

```
IF ^ BE THE FOOD OF LOVE                          3 ok
```

The cursor is now in a position where you can insert another word:

```
IF ROCK^ BE THE FOOD OF LOVE                              3 ok
```

[D]

The command [D] finds and deletes a string. It is a combination of [F] and [E], giving you two commands for the price of one. For example, if your cursor is here:

```
IF ROCK^ BE THE FOOD OF LOVE
```

then you can delete "FOOD" by simply typing:

```
D FOOD RETURN
IF ROCK BE THE ^ OF LOVE                                  3 ok
```

Once again, you can insert text at the new cursor position:

```
I CHEESEBURGERS RETURN
IF ROCK BE THE CHEESEBURGERS^ OF LOVE                     3 ok
```

Using [D] is a little more dangerous than using [F] and then [E]. With the two-step method, you know exactly what you're going to erase before you erase it.

[R]

The command [R] replaces a string that you've already found. It is a combination of [E] and [I]. For instance:

```
F NEED A RETURN
COMPUTERS NEED A^ TERMINAL                                2 ok
R CAN BE RETURN
COMPUTERS CAN BE^ TERMINAL                                2 ok
```

[R] is great when you want to make an insertion in front of a certain string. For example, if your line 0 is missing an "E":

```
( SAMPLE DEFINITIONS)                   MPTY              0 ok
```

then it's not easy to [F] your way through all those spaces to get the cursor over to the space before MPTY. Better you should use the following method:

```
F MPTY RETURN
```

then

```
R EMPTY RETURN
```

TILL

TILL is the most powerful command for deletion. It deletes everything from the current cursor position up till and including the given string. For example, if you have the line:

BREVITY IS THE SOUL^, THE ESSENCE, AND THE VERY SPARK OF WIT.

(note the cursor position), then the phrase:

    TILL SPARK RETURN

or even just

    TILL K RETURN

(since there's only one "K") will produce

    BREVITY IS THE SOUL ^OF WIT   5 ok

Has a nicer ring, doesn't it?

The Find Buffer and the Insert Buffer

In order to use the EDITOR effectively, you really have to understand the workings of its "find buffer" and its "insert buffer."

You may not have known it, but when you typed

    F MUSIC RETURN

the first thing F did was to move the string "MUSIC" into something called the "find buffer." A buffer, in computer parlance, is a temporary storage place for data. The find buffer is located in computer memory (RAM).

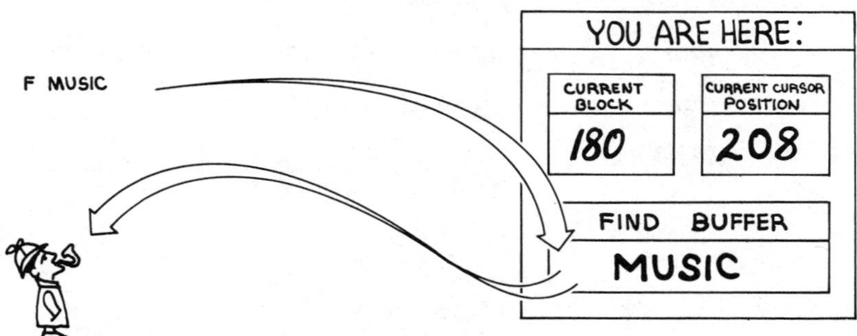

†

Then [F] proceeded to search the line for the contents of the find buffer.

Now you will be able to understand the following variation on [F]:

F RETURN

that is, [F] followed immediately by a return.

This variation causes [F] to search for the string that is already in the find buffer, left over from the last time you used [F].

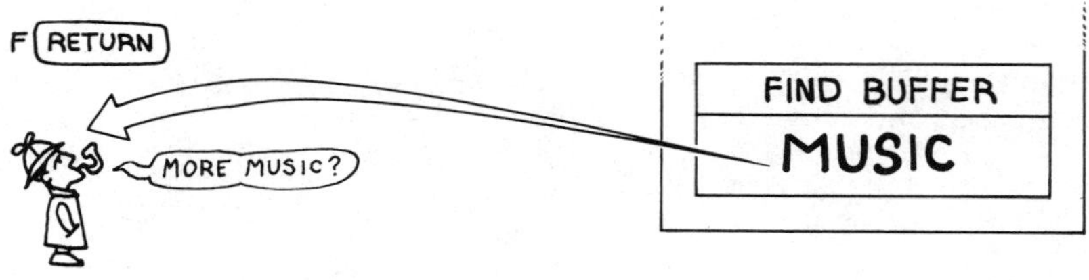

---

†For the Curious

By keeping the current cursor position, the editor doesn't need to keep a separate pointer for the current line. It simply uses the word [/MOD]. Since there are 64 characters per line, the phrase

```
208 64 /MOD . . 3 16 ok
```

shows the cursor is located at the 16th character in line 3.

What good is this? It lets you find numerous occurrences of the same string without retyping the string. For example, suppose line 8 contains the profundity:

```
^THE WISDOM OF THE FUTURE IS THE HOPE OF THE AGES
```

with the cursor at the beginning, and you want to erase the "THE" near the end. Start by typing

```
F THEb̸ RETURN
THE ^WISDOM OF THE FUTURE IS THE HOPE OF THE AGES 8 ok
```

Now that "THEb̸" is in the find buffer, you can simply type a series of single [F]s:

```
F RETURN
THE WISDOM OF THE ^FUTURE IS THE HOPE OF THE AGES 8 ok
F RETURN
THE WISDOM OF THE FUTURE IS THE ^HOPE OF THE AGES 8 ok
```

etc., until you find the "THE" you want, at which time you can erase it with [E].†

By the way, if you were to try entering [F] one more time, you'd get:

```
F THE NONE
```

This time [F] cannot find a match for the find buffer, so it returns the word "THE" to you, with the error message "NONE."

Remember we said that [D] is a combination of [F] and [E]? Well, that means that [D] also uses the find buffer.

With the cursor positioned at the beginning of the line and with "THEb̸" in the find buffer, you can delete all the "THE"s with single [D]s:

```
D RETURN
^WISDOM OF THE FUTURE IS THE HOPE OF THE AGES       8 ok
D RETURN
WISDOM OF ^FUTURE IS THE HOPE OF THE AGES           8 ok
D RETURN
WISDOM OF FUTURE IS ^HOPE OF THE AGES               8 ok
D RETURN
WISDOM OF FUTURE IS HOPE OF ^AGES                   8 ok
```

---

†For the Curious

[E] counts the number of characters in the find buffer and deletes that many characters preceding the cursor.

The other buffer is called the "insert buffer." It is used by [I]. Simply typing:

I RETURN

will insert the contents of the insert buffer at the current cursor position. The following experiment will demonstrate how you might use both buffers at the same time. Suppose line 14 contains

```
^THE YONDER, THE DANUBE, AND THE MAX                   14 ok
```

Now position the cursor:

```
F THEb RETURN
THE ^YONDER, THE DANUBE, AND THE MAX                   14 ok
```

and insert:

```
I BLUEb RETURN
THE BLUE ^YONDER, THE DANUBE, AND THE MAX              14 ok
```

You have now loaded both buffers like so:

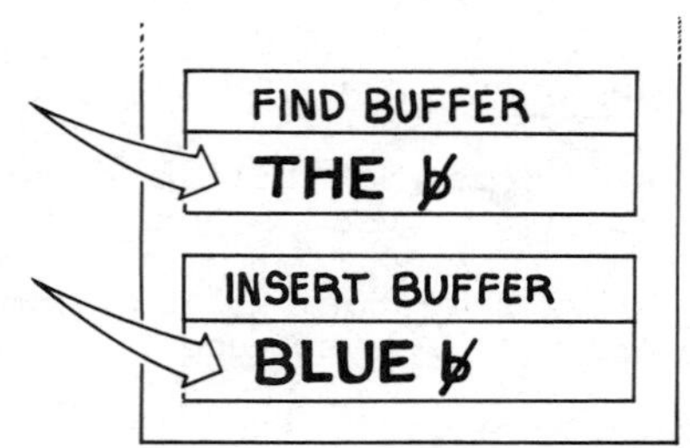

Now type:

```
F RETURN
THE BLUE YONDER, THE ^DANUBE, THE MAX                  14 ok
```

and:

```
I RETURN
THE BLUE YONDER, THE BLUE ^DANBUE, THE MAX             14 ok
```

and again:

```
F RETURN
THE BLUE YONDER, THE BLUE DANUBE, THE ^MAX             14 ok
I RETURN
THE BLUE YONDER, THE BLUE DANUBE, THE BLUE ^MAX  14 ok
```

This is what a computer scientist would call "spiffy."

Line Editing Commands

Now that we've shown you how to move letters and words around, we'll show you how to move whole lines around.

[P]

The word [P], which we introduced before, uses the very same insert buffer that [I] uses. Assuming that you still have "BLUE" in your insert buffer from the previous example and that line 14 is still your current line, then typing:

P RETURN

will replace the old line 14 with the contents of the insert buffer, so that line 14 now contains only the single word:

BLUE

To quickly review, you have now learned three ways to use [P]:

1) P ALL THIS TEXT RETURN	puts the string in the insert buffer, then in the current line.
2) Pb̸b̸ RETURN	blanks the insert buffer, then blanks the current line.
3) P RETURN	puts the contents of the insert buffer in the current line.

[U]

A very similar word is [U]. It places the contents of the insert buffer under the current line. For example, suppose your block contains:

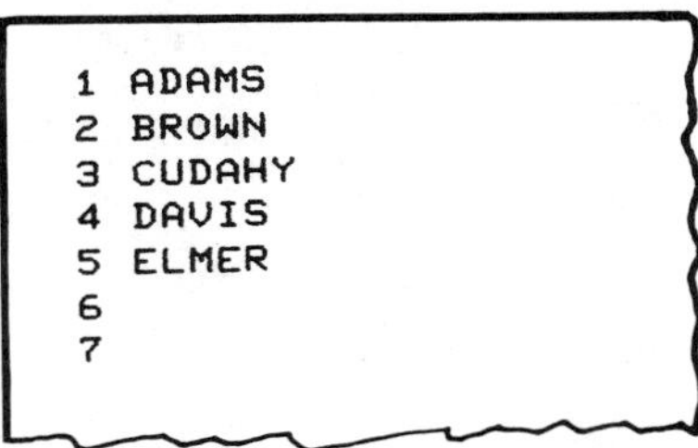

1 ADAMS
2 BROWN
3 CUDAHY
4 DAVIS
5 ELMER
6
7

If you move your cursor to line 2 with:

```
2 T
 ^BROWN                                        3 ok
```

and then type:

```
U CARLIN RETURN ok
U COOPER RETURN ok
```

you'll get:

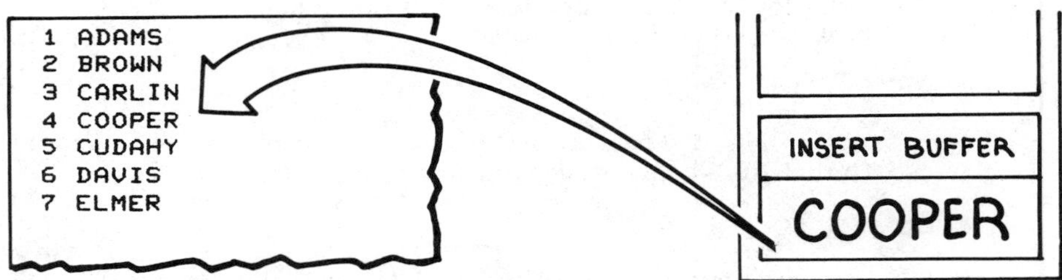

Instead of replacing the current line, [U] squeezes the contents of the insert buffer in below the current line, pushing all the lines below it down. If there were anything in line 15, it would roll off and disappear.

It's easier to use [U] than [P] when you're adding successive lines. For example:

```
1 T P ADAMS RETURN ok
U BROWN RETURN ok
U CUDAHY RETURN ok
U DAVIS RETURN ok
etc.
```

The three ways of using [P] also apply to [U].

[X]

[X] is the opposite of [U]; it extracts the current line. Using the above example, if you make line 3 current (with the phrase "3 T"), then by entering:

```
X RETURN
```

you extract line 3 and move the lower lines up.

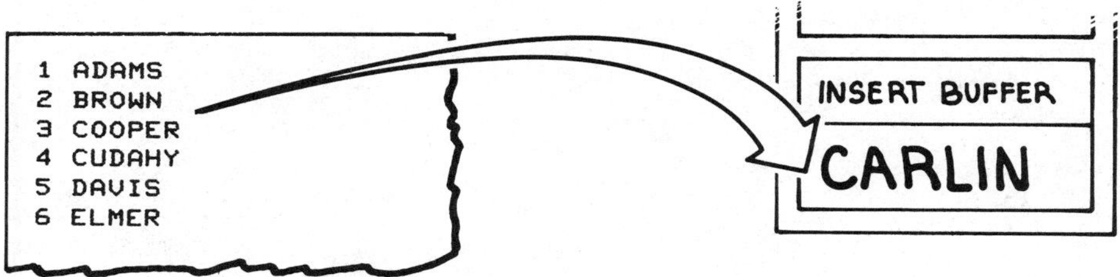

As you see, X also moves the extracted line into the insert buffer. This makes it easy to move the extracted line anywhere you want it. For example, the combination:

9 T RETURN

and:

P RETURN

would now put "CARLIN" on line 9.

Miscellaneous EDITOR Comands

WIPE

The word WIPE blanks an entire block. You can use WIPE to ensure that there will not be any strange characters which might keep a block from being loaded.

If your system doesn't have WIPE, another way to blank an entire block is this: first enter

0 T RETURN

then hit

X

sixteen times.

N and B

When you type the word N, you add one to the current block number.

Thus the combination:

```
N L
```

causes the next block to be listed.

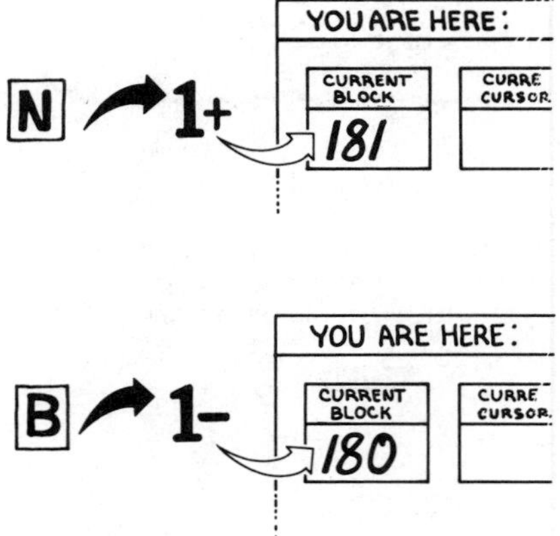

Similarly, the word B subtracts one from the current block number.

Thus the combination:

```
B L
```

lets you list one block back.

FLUSH

We can't say too much about this word until we discuss how the FORTH "operating system" converses with the disk, but for now you should know this: FLUSH† assures you that any change you've made to a block really gets written to the disk.

Say you've made some changes to a block, then you turn off the computer. When you come back tomorrow and list the block, it may seem as though you never made the changes at all. The operating system simply didn't get around to writing the corrected block to the disk before you turned off the computer. The same thing could happen if you were to load your application and then crash the system before it could write the changes to disk.

---

†FORTH-79 Standard

In the Standard, the name for this word is SAVE-BUFFERS.

So always enter FLUSH before removing the disk, cycling power, or trying something dangerous. Some programmers habitually FLUSH after every change without even thinking about it.

COPY

The word COPY lets you copy one block to another, displacing whatever was in the destination block. You use it in this form:

```
from to COPY
```

For example, entering:

```
153 200 COPY
```

will copy whatever is in block 153 into block 200.

Make it a habit to FLUSH after every COPY.

S

S is an expanded version of F. It lets you search for a given string in and beyond your current block into the following blocks, up to the block that you specify.

For example, if your current block is 180, and you type:

```
185 S TREASURE
```

then S will search for "TREASURE" in blocks 180 thru 184. If it finds "TREASURE" in, say, block 183, it will type:

```
THIS MOMENT THAT WE TREASURE^ TOGETHER          7 183 ok
```

giving both the block and the line number.

The block number with which you precede the word S represents the next block after the last one you want searched. There is a reason for this, but it won't make sense until a later chapter.

M

M lets you move an individual line (or group of lines) from one block to another. To move a line to another block, first make the line current with

```
182 LIST
```

then

```
7 T
 ^I SHOT A LINE INTO THE AIR                           7 ok
```

Then enter the destination block and the number of the line under which you want the line inserted, followed by the word M:

```
190 2 M
```

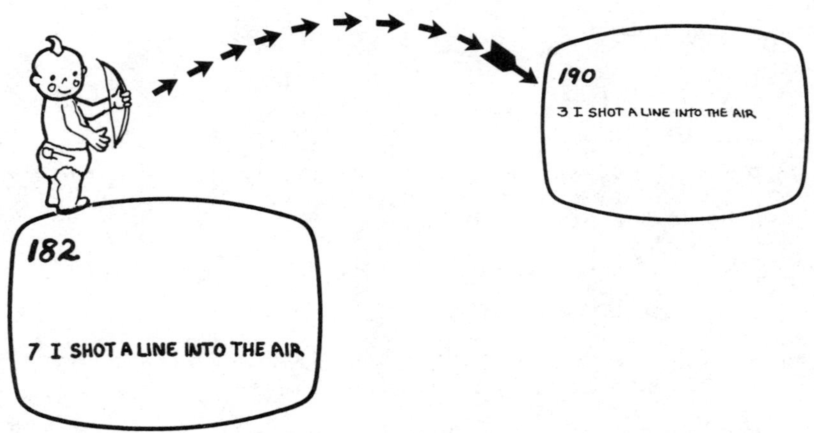

The line of text in the current block (block 182) moves down to the next line. So to move three consecutive lines, simply enter

```
190 2 M RETURN
190 3 M RETURN
190 4 M RETURN
```

^

You can type the caret character instead of RETURN to indicate the end of a character string, so that you can get more than one command on a line.

For example, you could type:

    D FRUIT^ I NUTS RETURN

all on the same line, and get the same result as if you had typed:

    D FRUIT RETURN

and:

    I NUTS RETURN

That's it for the EDITOR commands. Because FORTH is naturally flexible, and because users can define their own EDITOR commands if they want to, the set of EDITOR commands in your system may vary from the set presented here. This chapter closes with a review of all the commands we've talked about.

One final observation about the EDITOR: it is not a program, as it might be in another language. It is rather a collection of words. The EDITOR, in fact, is called a "vocabulary." We'll discuss the significance of vocabularies in a later chapter.

Getting LOADed

Now that you've learned to edit your definitions into a block, it's time to load them. But consider for a moment: each time you load definitions, you increase the size of your dictionary.

For example, let's say you write a definition for something you call 1FUNCTION, edit it into an available block, and load it. You test it and realize you forgot a SWAP. So you fix the source text with the EDITOR commands, then load the block again. It works!

Now in the same block you edit in a definition of something you call 2FUNCTION and load the block again. This time, you get it right on the first try. But what does your dictionary look like? From loading this block three times, you've got three versions of 1FUNCTION in there. The simplest way to avoid this problem is to use the word

EMPTY

EMPTY "forgets" all the definitions that you yourself have defined (not system definitions).† If you put EMPTY at the beginning of the block, you will start with a clean slate each time you load.

For example:

```
( SOLUTIONS -- QUIZZIE 2-B)       EMPTY
: 2B1    * + ;
: 2B2    4 * -   6 / + ;

```

Sometimes you don't want to get rid of your whole application, only part of it. Suppose you were to write a word processing application (so you can enter text, edit it in memory, then output it to a printer). After you've finished the basic application, you want to add variations, so it can use one format for correspondence, another format for magazine articles, and another format for address labels.

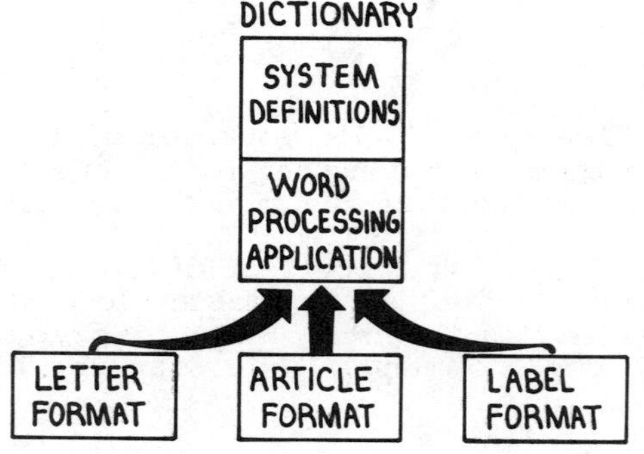

†For People on a Multiprogrammed System

EMPTY "forgets" your own personal extension of the dictionary, not anyone else's.

In FORTH these three variations are called "overlays" because they are mutually exclusive and can be made to replace each other. Here's how.

The basic word processing application should begin with EMPTY. The last definition should be a name only, such as

```
: VARIATIONS ;
```

This is called a "null definition" because it does nothing but mark a place in your portion of the dictionary.

Then at the beginning of each variation block, include the expression

```
FORGET VARIATIONS                  : VARIATIONS ;
```

Now when you load one variation, it FORGETs back to the null definition, compiles a new null definition, and then compiles the variation's definitions. When you load the other variation, you replace the first overlay with the second overlay.

One more trick: what if the source text for your application takes more than one block? The best solution is to let one block load the other blocks. For example, your "load block" might contain:

```
0 ( MY APPLICATION)
1
2 180 LOAD   181 LOAD   182 LOAD
```

It's much better to let a single load block LOAD all the related blocks than to let each block load the next one in a chain.

Now you know the ropes of disk storage. You'll probably want to edit most of the remaining examples and problems in this book into disk blocks rather than straight from the keyboard to the interpreter, especially the longer ones. It's just easier that way.

A Handy Hint -- When a Block Won't LOAD

On some FORTH systems, the following scenario may sometimes happen to you: you load some new definitions from a block, but when you try to execute them, FORTH doesn't seem to have ever heard of them (responding with a "?").

First you want to check whether any or all of your definitions were actually compiled into the dictionary. To do this, enter an apostrophe followed by a space, then the name of the word, then a ., as in

```
' THINGAMAJIG .RETURN
```

If . prints a number, then the definition is compiled, but if FORTH responds

```
THINGAMAJIG ?
```

then it isn't. There are two possible reasons for part of a block not getting compiled:

1) You made a typing error that keeps FORTH from being able to recognize a word. For instance, you may have typed

```
(COMMENT LINE)
```

without a space after (. This type of error is easy to find and correct because FORTH prints the name of any word it doesn't understand, like this:

```
180 LOADRETURN (COMMENT ?
```

2) There is a non-printing character (one you can't see)† somewhere in the block. To find a non-printing character, enter this:

```
0 TRETURN
1 TRETURN
2 TRETURN    etc.
```

If a line contains any non-printing characters, the "ok" at the end of the line will not line up with the "ok"s at the ends of the other lines, because non-printing characters don't print spaces. For any such line, reenter the entire line (using P).

---

†For Experts

The "null" character (ASCII 0) is the culprit. On most FORTH systems, null is actually a defined word, synonymous with EXIT, a word we will discuss in Chap. 9.

A Handy Hint

A Better Non-destructive Stack Print

Now that you know how to load longer definitions from a disk block, here's an improved version of .S which displays the contents of the stack non-destructively without displaying the "stack-empty" number.

This version uses an additional word called DEPTH, which returns the number of values on the stack. (Follow it with .)[†]

If you're a beginner, you might want to enter these two definitions into a special block all by themselves so you can load them any time you want them.

```
( NON-DESTRUCTIVE STACK PRINT)

: DEPTH   S0 @  'S - 2/ 2-  ;
: .S   CR  DEPTH  IF
     'S S0 @ 4 -  DO I @ . -2 +LOOP
        ELSE ." Empty " THEN ;
```

---

† FORTH-79 Standard

The Standard word set includes DEPTH.

Here's a list of the FORTH words we've covered in this chapter:

LIST	(n --)	Lists a disk block.
LOAD	(n --)	Loads a disk block (compiles or executes).
(xxx)	(--)	Causes the string xxx to be ignored by the text interpreter. The character) is the delimiter.
FLUSH	(--)	Forces any modifications that have been made to a block to be written to disk.
COPY	(source dest --)	Copies the contents of the source block to the destination block.
WIPE	(--)	Sets the contents of the current block to blanks.
FORGET xxx	(--)	Forgets all definitions back to and including xxx.
EMPTY	(--)	Forgets the entire contents of the user's dictionary.

Editing Commands -- Line Operators

T	(n --)	Types the line.
P Pb̸b̸ or P xxx	(--)	Copies the given string, if any, into the insert buffer, then puts a copy of the insert buffer in the current line.
U Ub̸b̸ or U xxx	(--)	Copies the given string, if any, into the insert buffer, then puts a copy of the insert buffer in the line under the current line.
M	(block line --)	Copies the current line into the insert buffer, and moves a copy of the insert buffer into the line under the specified line in the destination block.

X	(--)	Copies the current line into the insert buffer and <u>extracts</u> the line from the block.

Editing Commands -- String Operators

F or F xxx	(--)	Copies the given string, if any, into the find buffer, then <u>finds</u> the string in the current block.
S or S xxx	(n --)	Copies the given string, if any, into the find buffer, then <u>searches</u> the range of blocks, starting from the current block and ending with n-1, for the string.
E	(--)	To be used after F. <u>Erases</u> as many characters as are currently in the find buffer, going backwards from the cursor.
D or D xxx	(--)	Copies the given string, if any, into the find buffer, finds the next occurrence of the string within the current line, and <u>deletes</u> it.
TILL or TILL xxx	(--)	Copies the given string, if any, into the find buffer, then deletes all characters starting from the current cursor position up <u>till</u> and including the string.
I or I xxx	(--)	Copies the given string, if any, into the insert buffer, then <u>inserts</u> the contents of the insert buffer at the point just behind the cursor.
R or R xxx	(--)	Combines the commands E and I to <u>replace</u> a found string with a given string or the contents of the insert buffer.
↑ or ^	(--)	Indicates the end of the string to be placed in a buffer.

Review of Terms

Block — in FORTH, a division of disk memory containing up to 1024 characters of source text.

Buffer — a temporary storage area for data.

Disk — a disk that has been coated with a magnetic material so that, as in a tape recorder, a "head" can write or read data on its surface as the disk spins.

EDITOR — a vocabulary which allows a user to enter and modify text on the disk.

Find buffer — in FORTH's EDITOR, a memory location in which the string that is to be searched for is stored. Used by F, E, D, TILL, and S.

Insert Buffer — in FORTH's EDITOR, a memory location in which the string that is to be inserted is stored. Used by I, P, and U. In addition, X moves the line that it deletes into the insert buffer.

Load block — one block which, when loaded, itself loads the rest of the blocks for an application.

Null Definition — a definition that does nothing, written in the form:

```
: NAME ;
```

that is, a name only will be compiled into the dictionary. A null definition serves as a "bookmark" in the dictionary, for FORGET to find.

Overlay — a portion of an application which, when loaded, replaces another portion in the dictionary.

Pointer — a location in memory where a number can be stored (or changed) as a reference to something else.

Source text — in FORTH, the written-out form of a definition or definitions in English-like words and punctuation, as opposed to the compiled form that is entered into the dictionary.

Problems -- Chapter 3

1. a) Enter your definitions of GIFT, GIVER and THANKS from Probs. 1 and 3 of Chap. 1 into a block, then load and execute THANKS.

   b) Using the EDITOR, change the person's name in the definition of GIVER, then load and execute THANKS again. What happens this time?

2. Try loading some of your mathematical definitions from Chap. 2 into an available block, then load it. Fool around.

4 DECISIONS, DECISIONS, ...

In this chapter we'll learn how to program the computer to make "decisions." This is the moment when you turn your computer into something more than an ordinary calculator.

The Conditional Phrase

Let's see how to write a simple decision-making statement in FORTH. Imagine we are programming a mechanical egg-carton packer. Some sort of mechanical device has counted the eggs on the conveyor belt, and now we have the number of eggs on the stack. The FORTH phrase:

```
12 =  IF  FILL-CARTON  THEN
```

tests whether the number on the stack is equal to 12, and if it is, the word FILL-CARTON is executed. If it's not, execution moves right along to the words that follow THEN.

The word = takes two values off the stack

and compares them to see whether they are equal.

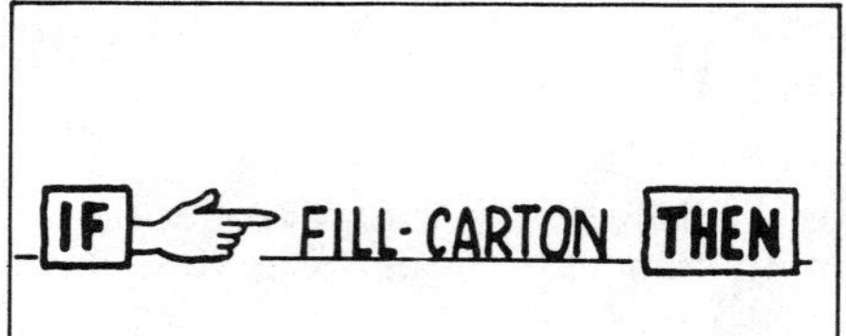

If the condition is true, IF allows the flow of execution to continue with the next word in the definition.

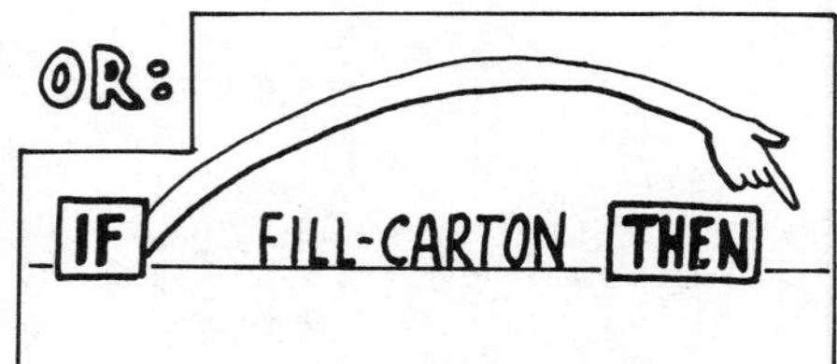

But if the condition is false, IF causes the flow of execution to skip to THEN, from which point execution will proceed.

Let's try it. Define this example word:

```
: ?FULL   12 =  IF ." IT'S FULL " THEN ; ok
11 ?FULL ok
12 ?FULL IT'S FULL ok
```

Notice: an IF...THEN statement must be contained within a colon definition. You can't just enter these words in "calculator style."

Don't be misled by the traditional English meanings of the FORTH words IF and THEN. The words that follow IF are executed if the condition is true. The words that follow THEN are always executed, as though you were telling the computer, "After you make the choice, then continue with the rest of the definition." (In this example, the only word after THEN is ;, which ends the definition.)

Let's look at another example. This definition checks whether the temperature of a laboratory boiler is too hot. It expects to find the temperature on the stack:

```
: ?TOO-HOT   220 > IF ." DANGER -- REDUCE HEAT " THEN ; ok
```

If the temperature on the stack is greater than 220, the danger message will be printed at the terminal. You can execute this one yourself, by entering the definition, then typing in a value just before the word.

```
290 ?TOO-HOT DANGER -- REDUCE HEAT ok
130 ?TOO-HOT ok
```

Remember that every IF needs a THEN to come home to. Both words must be in the same definition.

Here is a partial list of comparison operators that you can use before an IF...THEN statement:

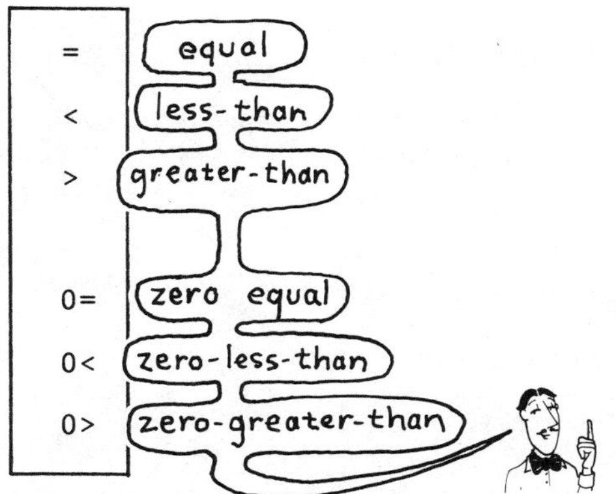

The words < and > expect the same stack order as the arithmetic operators, that is:

Infix		Postfix
2 < 10	is equivalent to	2 10 <
17 > -39	is equivalent to	17 -39 >

The words 0=, 0<, and 0> expect only one value on the stack. The value is compared with zero.

Another word, NOT, doesn't test any value at all; it simply reverses whatever condition has just been tested. For example, the phrase:

```
... = NOT IF ...
```

will execute the words after IF, if the two numbers on the stack are <u>not</u> equal.

The Alternative Phrase

FORTH allows you to provide an alternative phrase in an IF statement, with the word ELSE.

The following example is a definition which tests whether a given number is a valid day of the month:

```
: ?DAY   32 < IF ." LOOKS GOOD "  ELSE ." NO WAY " THEN ;
```

If the number on the stack is less than thirty-two, the message "LOOKS GOOD" will be printed. Otherwise, "NO WAY" will be printed.

Imagine that IF pulls a railroad-track switch, depending on the outcome of the test. Execution then takes one of two routes, but either way, the tracks rejoin at the word THEN.

By the way, in computer terminology, this whole business of rerouting the path of execution is called "branching."†

Here's a more useful example. You know that dividing any number by zero is impossible, so if you try it on a computer, you'll get an incorrect answer. We might define a word which only performs division if the denominator is not zero. The following definition expects stack items in this order:

---

†For Old Hands

FORTH has no GOTO statement. If you think you can't live without GOTO, just wait. By the end of this book you'll be telling your GOTO where to GOTO.

```
(numerator denominator -- )

: /CHECK   DUP 0= IF ." INVALID "  DROP
              ELSE / THEN ; †
```

Notice that we first have to DUP the denominator because the phrase

```
0= IF
```

will destroy it in the process.

Also notice that the word DROP removes the denominator if division won't be performed, so that whether we divide or not, the stack effect will be the same.

Nested IF...THEN Statements

It's possible to put an IF...THEN (or IF...ELSE...THEN) statement inside another IF...THEN statement. In fact, you can get as complicated as you like, so long as every IF has one THEN.

Consider the following definition, which determines the size of commercial eggs (extra large, large, etc.), given their weight in ounces per dozen:

```
: EGGSIZE    DUP  18 < IF ." REJECT "       ELSE
             DUP  21 < IF ." SMALL "        ELSE
             DUP  24 < IF ." MEDIUM "       ELSE
             DUP  27 < IF ." LARGE "        ELSE
             DUP  30 < IF ." EXTRA LARGE "  ELSE
                          ." ERROR "             ‡
                  THEN THEN THEN THEN THEN  DROP ;
```

---

†**For Experts**

There are better ways to do this, as we'll see.

‡**For People at Terminals**

Because this definition is fairly long, we suggest you load it from a disk block.

Once EGGSIZE has been loaded, here are some results you'd get:

```
23 EGGSIZE MEDIUM ok
29 EGGSIZE EXTRA LARGE ok
40 EGGSIZE ERROR ok †
```

We'd like to point out a few things about EGGSIZE:

The entire definition is a series of "nested" IF...THEN statements. The word "nested" does not refer to the fact that we're dealing with eggs, but to the fact that the statements nest inside one another, like a set of mixing bowls.

The five THENs at the bottom close off the five IFs in reverse order; that is:

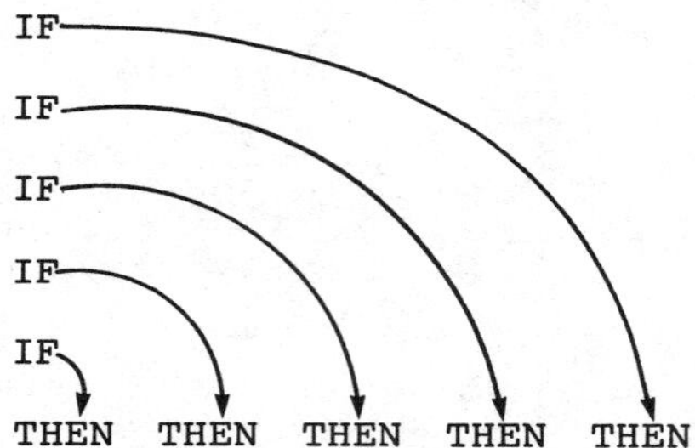

Also notice that a DROP is necessary at the end of the definition to get rid of the original value.

Finally, notice that the definition is visually organized to be read easily by human beings. Most FORTH programmers would rather waste a little space in a block (there are plenty of blocks) than let things get any more confused than they have to be.

---

†**For Trivia Buffs**

Here is the official table on which this definition is based:

Extra Large	27-30
Large	24-27
Medium	21-24
Small	18-21

A Closer Look at IF

How does the comparison operator (=, <, >, or whichever) let IF know whether the condition is true or false? By simply leaving a one or a zero on the stack. A one means that the condition is true; a zero means that the condition is false.

In computer jargon, when one piece of program leaves a value as a signal for another piece of program, that value is called a "flag."

Try entering the following phrases at the terminal, letting . show you what's on the stack as a flag.

```
5 4 > . 1 ok
5 4 < . 0 ok
```

(It's okay to use comparison operators directly at your terminal like this, but remember that an IF...THEN statement must be wholly contained within a definition because it involves branching.)

IF will take a one as a flag that means true and a zero as a flag that means false. Now let's take a closer look at NOT, which reverses the flag on the stack.

```
0 NOT . 1 ok
1 NOT . 0 ok
```

Now we'll let you in on a little secret: IF will take any non-zero value to mean true.† So what, you ask? Well, the fact

---

†**For the Doubting Few**

Just to prove it, try entering this test:

```
: TEST   IF ." NON-ZERO " ELSE ." ZERO " THEN ; ‡
```

Even though there is no comparison operator in the above definition, you'll still get

```
0 TEST ZERO ok
1 TEST NON ZERO ok
-400 TEST NON ZERO ok
```

‡**For Memory-Misers Who Read the above Footnote**

```
: TEST   IF ." NON-"  THEN ." ZERO " ;
```

that an arithmetic zero is identical to a flag that means "false" leads to some interesting results.

For one thing, if all you want to test is whether a number is zero, you don't need a comparison operator at all. For example, a slightly simpler version of /CHECK, which we saw earlier, could be

```
: /CHECK   DUP IF /  ELSE ." INVALID " DROP  THEN ;
```

Here's another interesting result. Say you want to test whether a number is an even multiple of ten, such as 10, 20, 30, 40, etc. You know that the phrase

```
10 MOD
```

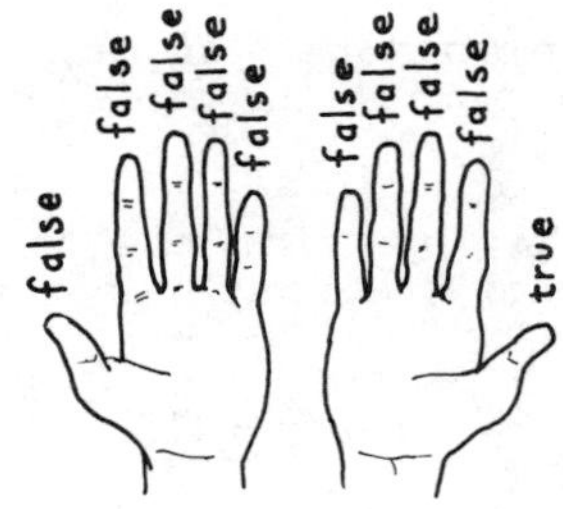

divides by ten and returns the remainder only. An even multiple of ten would produce a zero remainder, so the phrase

```
10 MOD 0=
```

gives the appropriate "true" or "false" flag.

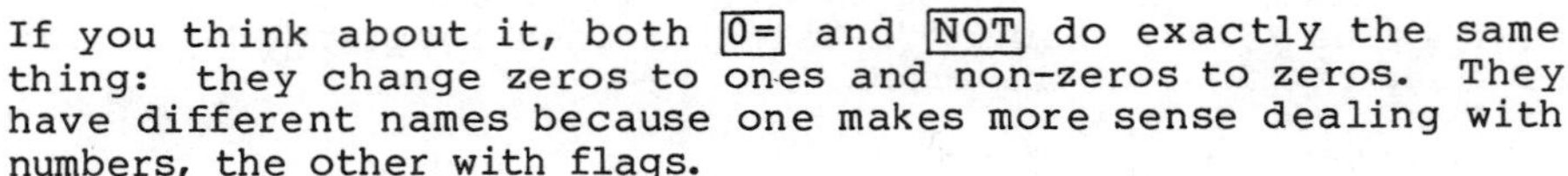
If you think about it, both 0= and NOT do exactly the same thing: they change zeros to ones and non-zeros to zeros. They have different names because one makes more sense dealing with numbers, the other with flags.

Still another interesting result is that you can use - (minus) as a comparison operator which tests whether two values are "not equal." When you subtract two equal numbers, you get zero (false); when you subtract two unequal numbers, you get a non-zero value (true).

And a final result is described in the next section.

A Little Logic

It's possible to take several flags from various tests and combine them into a single flag for one IF statement. You might combine them as an "either/or" decision, in which you make two comparison tests. If either or both of the tests are true, then the computer will execute something. If neither is true, it won't.

Here's a rather simple-minded example, just to show you what we mean. Say you want to print the name "ARTICHOKE" if an input number is either negative or a multiple of ten.

How do you do this in FORTH? Consider the phrase:

```
DUP 0<  SWAP  10 MOD 0= +
```

Here's what happens when the input number is, say, 30:

Operator	Contents of Stack		Operation
		30	
DUP	30	30	Duplicates it so we can test it twice.
0<	30	0	Is it negative? No (zero).
SWAP	0	30	Swaps the flag with the number.
10 MOD 0=	0	1	Is it evenly divisible by 10? Yes (one).
+		1	Adds the flags.

Adds the flags? What happens when you add flags? Here are four possibilities:

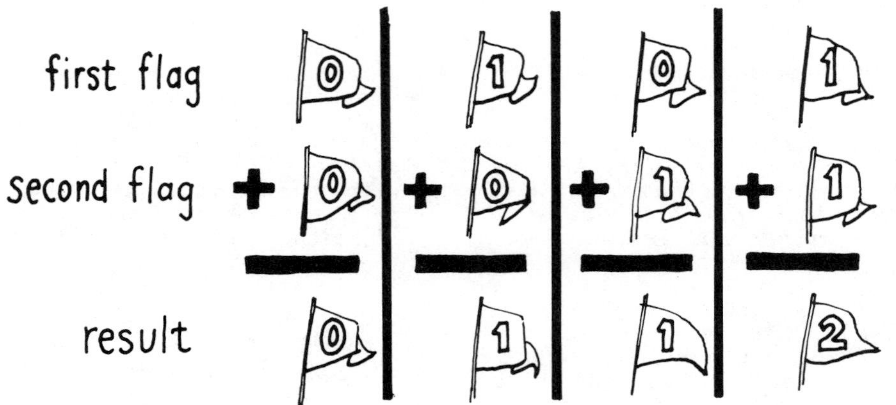

Lo and behold, the result flag is true if either or both conditions are true. In this example, the result is one, which means "true." If the input number had been -30, then both conditions would have been true and the sum would have been two. Two is, of course, non-zero. So as far as IF is concerned, two is as true as one.

Our simple-minded definition, then, would be:

```
: VEGETABLE   DUP 0<  SWAP  10 MOD 0=  +
     IF ." ARTICHOKE " THEN ;
```

Here's an improved version of a previous example called ?DAY.

The old ?DAY only caught entries over thirty-one. But negative numbers shouldn't be allowed either. How about this:

```
: ?DAY   DUP 1 <  SWAP 31 >  +
     IF ." NO WAY " ELSE ." THANK YOU " THEN ;
```

The above two examples will always work because any "true" flags will always be exactly "1." In some cases, however, a flag may be any non-zero value, not just "1," in which case it's dangerous to add them with +. For example,

```
1 -1 + . 0 ok
```

gives us a mathematically correct answer but not the answer we want if 1 and -1 are flags.

For this reason, FORTH supplies a word called OR, which will return the correct flag even in the case of 1 and -1. An "or decision" is the computer term for the kind of flag combination we've been discussing. For example, if either the front door or the back door is open (or both), flies will come in.

Another kind of decision is called an "and" decision. In an

"and" decision, both conditions must be true for the result to be true. For example, the front door and the back door must both be open for a breeze to come through. If there are three or more conditions, they must all be true.†

How can we do this in FORTH? By using the handy word AND. Here's what AND would do with the four possible combinations of flags we saw earlier:

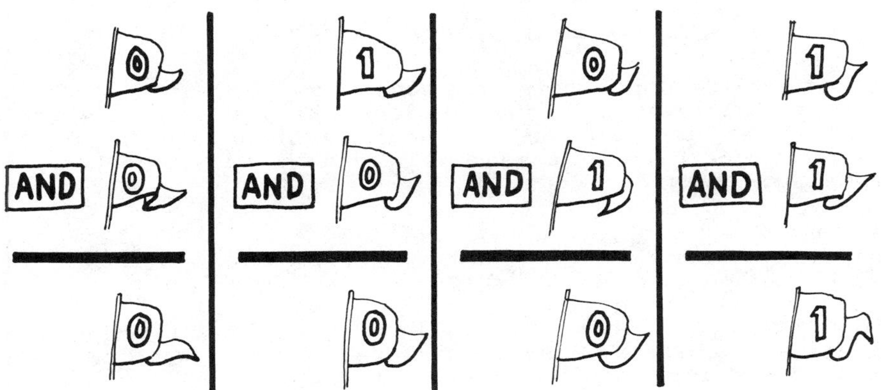

In other words, only the combination "1 1 AND" produces a result of one.

Let's say we're looking for a cardboard box that's big enough to fit a disk drive which measures:

height 6"

width 19"

length 22"

The height, width, and length requirements all must be satisfied for the box to be big enough. If we have the dimensions of a box on the stack, then we can define:

---

†**For the Curious Newcomer**

The use of words like "or" and "and" to structure part of an application is called "logic." A form of notation for logical statements was developed in the nineteenth century by George Boole; it is now called Boolean algebra. Thus the term "a Boolean flag" (or even just "a Boolean") simply refers to a flag that will be used in a logical statement.

```
: BOXTEST   ( length width height -- )
    6 >  ROT 22 >  ROT 19 >  AND AND
    IF ." BIG ENOUGH " THEN ;
```

Notice that we've put a comment inside the definition, to remind us of stack effects. This is particularly wise when the stack order is potentially confusing or hard to remember.

You can test BOXTEST with the phrase:

```
23 20 7 BOXTEST BIG ENOUGH ok
```

As your applications become more sophisticated, you will be able to write statements in FORTH that look like postfix English and are very easy to read. Just define the individual words within the definition to check some condition somewhere, then leave a flag on the stack.

An example is:

```
: SNAPSHOT   ?LIGHT ?FILM AND  IF PHOTOGRAPH THEN ;
```

which checks that there is available light and that there is film in the camera before taking the picture. Another example, which might be used in a computer-dating application, is:

```
: MATCH   HUMOROUS SENSITIVE AND
    ART.LOVING MUSIC.LOVING OR  AND  SMOKING NOT AND
    IF ." I HAVE SOMEONE YOU SHOULD MEET " THEN ;
```

where words like HUMOROUS and SENSITIVE have been defined to check a record in a disk file that contains information on other applicants of the appropriate sex.

question-dupe

abort-quote

Two Words with Built-in IFs

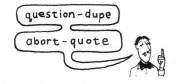

?DUP

The word ?DUP duplicates the top stack value only if it is non-zero. This can eliminate a few surplus words. For example, the definition

```
: /CHECK   DUP IF / ELSE DROP THEN ;
```

can be shortened to:

```
: /CHECK   ?DUP IF / THEN ;
```

ABORT"

It may happen that somewhere in a complex application an error might occur (such as division by zero) way down in one of the low-level words. When this happens you don't just want the computer to keep on going, and you also don't want it to leave anything on the stack.

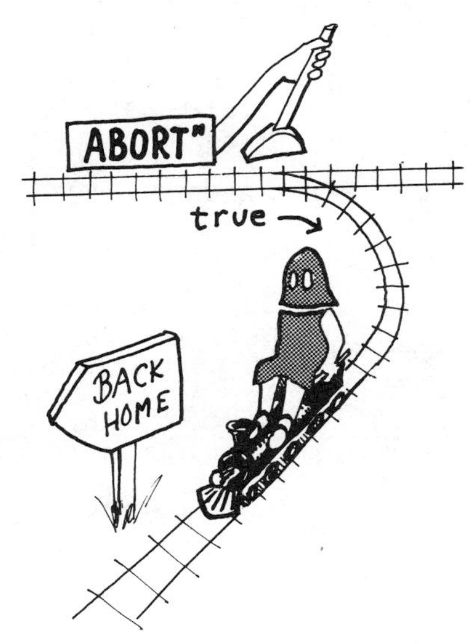

If you think such an error might occur, you can use the word ABORT". ABORT" expects a flag on the stack: a "true" flag tells it to "abort," which in turn clears the stack and returns execution to the terminal, waiting for someone to type something. ABORT" also prints the name of the last interpreted word, as well as whatever message you want.†

Let's illustrate. We hope you're not sick of /CHECK by now, because here is yet another version:

```
: /CHECK   DUP 0=  ABORT" ZERO DENOMINATOR " / ;
```

---

†**FORTH-79 Standard**

The Standard includes the word ABORT, which differs from ABORT" only in that it does not issue an error message.

In this version, if the denominator is zero, any numbers that happen to be on the stack will be dropped and the terminal will show:

```
8 0 /CHECK /CHECK ZERO DENOMINATOR
```

Just as an experiment, try putting /CHECK inside another definition:

```
: ENVELOPE   /CHECK  ." THE ANSWER IS " . ;
```

and try

```
8 4 ENVELOPE THE ANSWER IS 2 ok
8 0 ENVELOPE ENVELOPE ZERO DENOMINATOR
```

The point is that when /CHECK aborts, the rest of ENVELOPE is skipped. Also notice that the name ENVELOPE, not /CHECK, is printed.

A useful word to use in conjunction with ABORT" is ?STACK, which checks for stack underflow and returns a true flag if it finds it. Thus the phrase:

```
?STACK ABORT" STACK EMPTY "
```

aborts if the stack has underflowed.

FORTH uses the identical phrase, in fact. But it waits until all of your definitions have stopped executing before it performs the ?STACK test, because checking continuously throughout execution would needlessly slow down the computer.† You're free to insert a ?STACK ABORT" phrase at any critical or not-yet-tested portion of your application.

---

† **For Computer Philosophers**

FORTH provides certain error checking automatically. But because the FORTH operating system is so easy to modify, users can readily control the amount of error checking their system will do. This flexibility lets users make their own tradeoffs between convenience and execution speed.

Here's a list of the FORTH words we've covered in this chapter:

Word	Stack	Description
IF xxx ELSE yyy THEN zzz	IF: (f --)	If f is true (non-zero) executes xxx; otherwise executes yyy; continues with zzz regardless. The phrase ELSE yyy is optional.
=	(n1 n2 -- f)	Returns true if n1 and n2 are equal.
-	(n1 n2 -- n-diff)	Returns true (i.e., the non-zero difference) if n1 and n2 are not equal.
<	(n1 n2 -- f)	Returns true if n1 is less than n2.
>	(n1 n2 -- f)	Returns true if n1 is greater than n2.
0=	(n -- f)	Returns true if n is zero (i.e., reverses the truth value).
0<	(n -- f)	Returns true if n is negative.
0>	(n -- f)	Returns true if n is positive.
NOT	(f -- f)	Reverses the result of the previous test; equivalent to 0=.
AND	(n1 n2 -- and)	Returns the logical AND.
OR	(n1 n2 -- or)	Returns the logical OR.
?DUP	(n -- n n) or (0 -- 0)	Duplicates only if n is non-zero.
ABORT" xxx "	(f --)	If the flag is true, types out the last word interpreted, followed by the text. Also clears the user's stacks and returns control to the terminal. If false, takes no action.
?STACK	(-- f)	Returns true if a stack underflow condition has occurred.

Review of Terms

Abort — as a general computer term, to abruptly cease execution if a condition occurs which the program is not designed to handle, in order to avoid producing nonsense or possibly doing damage.

"And" decision — two conditions that are combined such that if both of them are true, the result is true.

Branching — breaking the normally straightforward flow of execution, depending on conditions in effect at the time of exection. Branching allows the computer to respond differently to different conditions.

Comparison operator — in general, a command that compares one value with another (for example, determines whether one is greater than the other) and sets a flag accordingly, which normally will be checked by a conditional operator. In FORTH, a comparison operator leaves the flag on the stack.

Conditional operator — a word, such as IF, which routes the flow of execution differently depending on some condition (true or false).

Flag — as a general computer term, a value stored in memory which serves as a signal as to whether some known condition is true or false. Once the "flag is set," any number of routines in various parts of a program may check (or reset) the flag, as necessary.

Logic — in computer terminology, the system of representing conditions in the form of "logical variables," which can be either true or false, and combining these variables using such "logical operators" as "and," "or," and "not," to form statements which may be true or false.

Nesting — placing a branching structure within an outer branching structure.

"Or" decision — two conditions that are combined such that if either of them is true, the result is true.

Problems -- Chapter 4

(answers in the back of the book)

1. What will the phrase

   ```
   0= NOT
   ```

   leave on the stack when the argument is

   ```
   1?
   0?
   200?
   ```

2. Explain what an artichoke has to do with any of this.

3. Define a word called CARD which, given a person's age on the stack, prints out either of these two messages (depending on the relevant laws in your area):

   ALCOHOLIC BEVERAGES PERMITTED or
   UNDER AGE

4. Define a word called SIGN.TEST that will test a number on the stack and print out one of three messages:

   POSITIVE or
   ZERO or
   NEGATIVE

5. In Chap. 1, we defined a word called STARS in such a way that it always prints at least one star, even if you say

   ```
   0 STARS * ok
   ```

   Using the word STARS, define a new version of STARS that corrects this problem.

6. Write the definition for a word called WITHIN which expects three arguments:

   (n low-limit hi-limit --)

   and leaves a "true" flag only if "n" is within the range

   low-limit $\leq$ n < hi-limit

7. Here's a number-guessing game (which you may enjoy writing more than anyone will enjoy playing). First you secretly enter a number onto the stack (you can hide your number after entering it by executing the word PAGE, which clears the terminal screen). Then you ask another player to enter a guess followed by the word GUESS, as in

```
100 GUESS
```

The computer will either respond "TOO HIGH," "TOO LOW," or "CORRECT!" Write the definition of GUESS, making sure that the answer-number will stay on the stack through repeated guessing until the correct answer is guessed, after which the stack should be clear.

8. Using nested tests and IF...ELSE...THEN statements, write a definition called SPELLER which will spell out a number that it finds on the stack, from -4 to 4. If the number is outside this range, it will print the message "OUT OF RANGE." For example:

```
2 SPELLER TWO ok
-4 SPELLER NEGATIVE FOUR ok
7 SPELLER OUT OF RANGE ok
```

Make it as short as possible. (Hint: the FORTH word ABS gives the absolute value of a number on the stack.)

9. Using your definition of WITHIN from Prob. 5, write another number-guessing game, called TRAP, in which you first enter a secret value, then a second player tries to home in on it by trapping it between two numbers, as in this dialogue:

```
0 1000 TRAP BETWEEN ok
330 660 TRAP BETWEEN ok
440 550 TRAP NOT BETWEEN ok
330 440 TRAP BETWEEN ok
```

and so on, until the player guesses the answer:

```
391 391 TRAP YOU GOT IT! ok
```

Hint: you may have to modify the arguments to WITHIN so that TRAP does not say "BETWEEN" when only one argument is equal to the hidden value.

5 THE PHILOSOPHY OF FIXED POINT

In this chapter we'll introduce a new batch of arithmetic operators. Along the way we'll tackle the problem of handling decimal points using only whole-number arithmetic.

Quickie Operators

Let's start with the real easy stuff. You should have no trouble figuring out what the words in the following table do.†

			pronounced:
1+	(n -- n+1)	Adds one.	one-plus
1-	(n -- n-1)	Subtracts one.	one-minus
2+	(n -- n+2)	Adds two.	two-plus
2-	(n -- n-2)	Subtracts two.	two-minus
2*	(n -- n*2)	Multiplies by two (arithmetic left shift).	two-star
2/	(n -- n/2)	Divides by two (arithmetic right shift).	two-slash

The reason they have been defined as words in your FORTH system is that they are used very frequently in most applications and even in the FORTH system itself.

---

†For Beginners

We'll explain what "arithmetic left shift" is later on.

There are three reasons to use a word such as 1+, instead of one and +, in your new definitions. First, you save a little dictionary space each time. Second, since such words have been specially defined in the "machine language" of each individual type of computer to take advantage of the computer's architecture, they execute faster than one and +. Finally, you save a little time during compilation.

Miscellaneous Math Operators

Here's a table of four miscellaneous math operators. Like the quickie operators, these functions should be obvious from their names.

Aunt Min and Uncle Max

Word	Stack effect	Description
ABS	(n -- |n|)	Returns the absolute value.
NEGATE	(n -- -n)	Changes the sign.
MIN	(nl n2 -- n-min)	Returns the minimum.
MAX	(nl n2 -- n-max)	Returns the maximum.

Here are two simple word problems, using ABS and MIN:

ABS

Write a definition which computes the difference between two numbers, regardless of the order in which the numbers are entered.

```
: DIFFERENCE   - ABS ;
```

This gives the same result whether we enter

```
52 37 DIFFERENCE . 15 ok      or
37 52 DIFFERENCE . 15 ok
```

MIN

Write a definition which computes the commission that furniture salespeople will receive if they've been promised $50 or 1/10 of the sale price, whichever is less, on each sale they make.

```
: COMMISSION   10 /  50 MIN ;
```

Three different values would produce these results:

```
600 COMMISSION . 50 ok
450 COMMISSION . 45 ok
50 COMMISSION . 5 ok
```

The Return Stack

We mentioned before that there were still some stack manipulation operators we hadn't discussed yet. Now it's time.

Up till now we've been talking about "the stack" as if there were only one. But in fact there are two: the "parameter stack" and the "return stack." The parameter stack is used more often by FORTH programmers, so it's simply called "the stack" unless there is cause for doubt.

As you've seen, the parameter stack holds parameters (or "arguments") that are being passed from word to word. The return stack, however, holds any number of "pointers" which the FORTH system uses to make its merry way through the maze of words that are executing other words. We'll elaborate later on.

You the user can employ the return stack as a kind of "extra hand" to hold values temporarily while you perform operations on the parameter stack.

The return stack is a last-in first-out structure, just like the parameter stack, so it can hold many values. But here's the catch: whatever you put on the return stack you must remove again before you get to the end of the definition (the semicolon), because at that point the FORTH system will expect to find a pointer there. You cannot use the return stack to pass parameters from one word to another.

The following table lists the words associated with the return stack. Remember, the stack notation refers to the parameter stack.

Word	Stack	Description	Pronounced
>R	(n --)	Takes a value off the parameter stack and pushes it onto the return stack.	to-R
R>	(-- n)	Takes a value off the return stack and pushes it onto the parameter stack.	R-from
I	(-- n)	Copies the top of the return stack without affecting it.	I
I'	(-- n)	Copies the second item of the return stack without affecting it.	I-prime
J	(-- n)	Copies the third item of the return stack without affecting it.	J

The words `>R` and `R>` transfer a value to and from the return stack, respectively. In the cartoon above, where the stack effect was:

    (2 3 1 -- 3 2 1)

This is the phrase that did it:

```
>R SWAP R>
```

Each `>R` and its corresponding `R>` must be used together in the same definition or, if executed interactively, in the same line of input (before you hit the RETURN key).

The other three words--`I`, `I'`, and `J`--only <u>copy</u> values from the return stack without removing them. Thus the phrase:

```
>R SWAP I
```

would produce the same result as far as it goes, but unless you clean up your trash† before the next semicolon (or return key), you will crash the system.

To see how `>R`, `R>`, and `I` might be used, imagine you are so unlucky as to need to solve the equation:

$$ax^2 + bx + c$$

with <u>all four</u> values on the stack in the following order:

    (a b c x --)

(remember to factor out first).

---

†You might call such an error in your program a "litter bug."

Operator	Parameter Stack	Return Stack
	a b c x	
>R	a b c	x
SWAP ROT	c b a	x
I	c b a x	x
*	c b ax	x
+	c (ax + b)	x
R> *	c x(ax+b)	
+	x(ax+b)+c	

Go ahead and try it. Load the following definition:

```
: QUADRATIC   ( a b c x -- n)
    >R SWAP ROT I *  + R> *  + ;
```

Now test it:

```
2 7 9 3 QUADRATIC 48 ok
```

One more note (it's a little off the subject, but this is the first chance we've had to note it): you have now learned two different words with the name [I] (remember the EDITOR's "insert" word?). The reason the same name can refer to two separate definitions, depending on the context, is that the words are in different vocabularies.

We briefly mentioned earlier that the EDITOR is a vocabulary. You can get into the EDITOR vocabulary automatically by using certain EDITOR commands, such as [T]. Another vocabulary is called FORTH, which contains all the other predefined words we've covered so far. You can get back into the FORTH vocabulary by starting to compile a new definition (that is, when the interpreter sees the word [:]).

We mention all this now simply to amaze and impress you. The real discussion of vocabularies comes in a future chapter.

An Introduction to Floating-Point Arithmetic

There are many controversies surrounding FORTH. Certain principles which FORTH programmers adhere to religiously are considered foolhardy by the proponents of more traditional languages. One such controversy is the question of "fixed-point representation" versus "floating-point representation."

If you already understand these terms, skip ahead to the next section, where we'll express our views on the controversy. If you're a beginner, you may appreciate the following explanation.

First, what does floating point mean? Take a pocket calculator, for example. Here's what the display looks like after each entry:

You enter:	Display reads:
1 . 5 0 x	1.5
2 . 2 3	2.23
=	3.345

The decimal point "floats" across the display as necessary. This is called a "floating point display."

"Floating point representation" is a way to store numbers in computer memory using a form of scientific notation. In scientific notation, twelve million is written:

$$12 \times 10^6$$

since ten to the sixth power equals one million. In many computers twelve million could be stored as two numbers: 12 and 6, where it is understood that 6 is the power of ten to be multiplied by 12, while 3.345 could be stored as 3345 and -3.

The idea of floating-point representation is that the computer can represent an enormous range of numbers, from atomic to astronomic, with two relatively small numbers.

What is fixed-point representation? It is simply the method of storing numbers in memory without storing the positions of each number's decimal point. For example, in working with dollars and cents, all values can be stored in cents. The <u>program</u>, rather than each individual <u>number</u>, can remember the location of the decimal point.

For example, let's compare fixed-point and floating-point representations of dollars-and-cents values.

Real-world Value	Fixed-point Representation	Floating-point Representation
1.23	123	123(-2)
10.98	1098	1098(-2)
100.00	10000	1(2)
58.60	5860	586(-1)

As you can see, with fixed-point all the values must conform to the same "scale." The decimal points must be properly "aligned" (in this case two places in from the right) even though they are not actually represented. With fixed-point, the computer treats all the numbers as through they were integers. If the program needs to print out an answer, however, it simply inserts the decimal point two places in from the right before it sends the number to the terminal or to the printer.

Why FORTH Programmers Advocate Fixed-Point

Many respectable languages and many distinguished programmers use floating-point arithmetic as a matter of course. Their opinion might be expressed like this: "Why should I have to worry about moving decimal points around? That's what computers are for."

That's a valid question--in fact it expresses the most significant advantage to floating-point implementation. For translating a mathematical equation into program code, having a floating-point language makes the programmer's life easier.

The typical FORTH programmer, however, perceives the role of a computer differently. A FORTH programmer is most interested in maximizing the efficiency of the machine. That means he or she wants to make the program run as fast as possible and require as little computer memory as possible.

To a FORTH programmer, if a problem is worth doing on a computer at all, it is worth doing on a computer well. The philosophy is, "If you just want a quick answer to a few calculations, you might as well use a hand-held calculator." You won't care if the calculator takes half a second to display the result. But if you have invested in a computer, you probably have to repeat the same set of calculations over and over and over again. Fixed-point arithmetic will give you the speed you need.

Is the extra speed that noticeable? Yes, it is. A floating-point multiplication or division can take three times as long as its equivalent fixed-point calculation. The difference is really noticeable in programs which have to do a lot of calculations before sending results to a terminal or taking some action.† Most mini- and microcomputers don't "think" in floating-point; you pay a heavy penalty for making them act as though they do.

Here are some of the reasons you might prefer to have floating-point capability.

1. You want to use your computer like a calculator on floating-point data.

2. You value the initial programming time more highly than the execution time spent every time the calculation is performed.

3. You want a number to be able to describe a very large dynamic range (greater than -2 billion to +2 billion).

4. Your system includes a discrete hardware floating-point multiply (a separate "chip" whose only job is to perform floating-point multiplication at super high speeds).

---

†For Experts

Many professional FORTH programmers who have been writing complex applications for years have never had to use floating-point. And their applications often involve solutions of differential equations, Fast Fourier Transforms, non-linear least squares fitting, linear regression, etc. Problems that traditionally required a main-frame have been done on slower minicomputers and microprocessors, in some cases with an overall <u>increase</u> in computation rate.

Most problems with physical inputs and outputs, including weather modeling, image reconstruction, automated electrical measurements, and the like all involve input and output variables that inherently have a dynamic range of no more than a few thousand to one, and thus fit comfortably into a 16-bit integer word. Intermediate calculation steps (such as summation) can be handled by the judicious use of scaling and double-length integers where required. For example, one common calculation step might involve multiplying each data point by a parameter (or by itself) and summing the result. In fixed point, this would be a 16 x 16-bit multiply and 32-bit summation. In floating-point, numbers are likely stored as 24-bit mantissa and 8-bit exponents. The 24-bit multiply will take about 1.5 times longer and the 32-bit addition 3-10 times longer than in fixed point. There is also the overhead of floating all the input data and fixing all the output data, approximately equal to one floating-point addition each. When these operations are performed thousands or millions of times, the overall saving by remaining in integer form is enormous.

All of these are valid reasons. Even Charles Moore, perhaps the staunchest advocate of simplicity in the programming community, has occasionally employed floating-point routines when the hardware supported it. Other FORTH programmers have written floating-point routines for their mini- and microcomputers. But the mainstream FORTH philosophy remains: "In most cases, you don't need to pay for floating-point."

FORTH backs its philosophy by supplying the programmer with a unique set of high-level commands called "scaling operators." We'll introduce the first of these commands in the next section. (The final example in Chap. 12 illustrates the use of scaling techniques.)

Star-slash the Scalar

Here's a math operator that is as useful as it is unusual: */.

*/	(n1 n2 n3 -- n-result)	Multiplies, then divides (n1*n2/n3). Uses a 32-bit intermediate result.

As its name implies, */ performs multiplication, then division. For example, let's say that the stack contains these three numbers:

```
(225 32 100 -- )
```

*/ will first multiply 225 by 32, then divide the result by 100.

This operator is particularly useful as an integer-arithmetic solution to problems such as percentage calculations.

For example, you could define the word % like this:

```
: %   100 */ ;
```

so that by entering the number 225 and then the phrase:

```
32 %
```

you'd end up with 32% of 225 (that is, 72) on the stack.†

[*/] is not just a [*] and a [/] thrown together, though. It uses a "double-length intermediate result." What does that mean, you ask?

Say you want to compute 34% of 2000. Remember that single-precision operators, like [*] and [/], only work with arguments and results within the range of -32768 to +32767. If you were to enter the phrase:

```
2000 34 *  100 /
```

you'd get an incorrect result, because the "intermediate result" (in this case, the result of multiplication) exceeds 32767, as shown in the left column in this pictorial simulation.

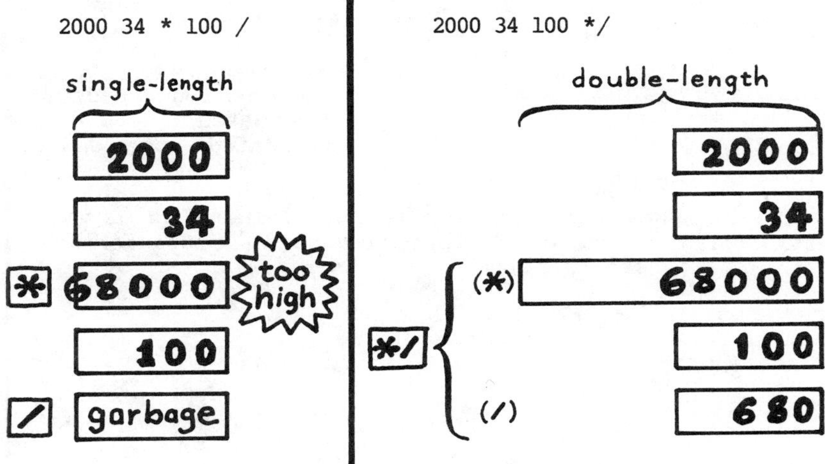

But [*/] uses a double-length intermediate result, so that its range will be large enough to hold the result of any two single-length numbers multiplied together. The phrase:

```
2000 34 100 */
```

returns the correct answer because the end result falls within the range of single-length numbers.

---

†For the curious

The method of first multiplying two integers, then dividing by 100 is identical to the approach most people take in solving such problems on paper.

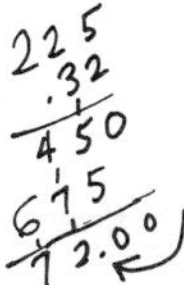

The previous example brings up another question: how to round off.

Let's assume that this is the problem:

> If 32% of the students eating at the school cafeteria usually buy bananas, how many bananas should be on hand for a crowd of 225? Naturally, we are only interested in whole bananas, so we'd like to round off any decimal remainder.

As our definition now stands, any value to the right of the decimal is simply dropped. In other words, the result is "truncated."

32% of:	Result:
225 = 72.00	72 -- exactly correct
226 = 72.32	72 -- correct, rounded down (truncated)
227 = 72.64	72 -- truncated, not rounded.

There is a way, however, with any decimal value of .5 or higher, to round upwards to the next whole banana. We could define the word R%, for "rounded percent," like this:

```
: R%   10 */  5 +  10 / ;
```

so that the phrase:

```
227 32 R% .
```

will give you 73, which is correctly rounded up.

Notice that we first divide by 10 rather than 100. This gives us an extra decimal place to work with, to which we can add five:

Operation	Stack Contents
	227 32 10
*/	726
5 +	731
10 /	73

The final division by ten sets the value to its rightful decimal position. Try it and see.†

A disadvantage to this method of rounding is that you lose one decimal place of range in the final result; that is, it can only go as high as 3,276 rather than 32,767. But if that's a problem, you can always use double-length numbers, which we'll introduce later, and still be able to round.

Some Perspective on Scaling

Let's back up for a minute. Take the simple problem of computing two-thirds of 171. Basically, there are two ways to go about it.

1. We could compute the value of the fraction 2/3 by dividing 2 by 3 to obtain the repeating decimal .666666, etc. Then we could multiply this value by 171. The result would be 113.9999999, etc., which is not quite right but which could be rounded up to 114.

2. We could multiply 171 by 2 to get 342. Then we could divide this by 3 to get 114.

Notice that the second way is simpler and more accurate.

Most computer languages support the first way. "You can't have a fraction like two-thirds hanging around inside a computer," it is believed, "you must express it as .666666, etc."

FORTH supports the second way. [*/] lets you have a fraction like two-thirds, as in:

```
171 2 3 */
```

Now that we have a little perspective, let's take a slightly more complicated example:

---

†For Experts

An even faster definition:

```
: R%   50 /  1+ 2/ ;
```

We want to distribute $150 in proportion to two values:†

```
  7,105      ?
  5,145      ?
 ------    ---
 12,250    150
```

Again, we could solve the problem this way:

(7,105 / 12,250) x 150

and

(5,145 / 12,250) x 150

but for greater accuracy; we should say:

(7,105 x 150) / 12,250

and

(5,145 x 150) / 12,250

which in FORTH is written:

```
7105 150 12250 */ . 87 ok
```

then

```
5145 150 12250 */ . 63 ok
```

It can be said that the values 87 and 63 are "scaled" to 7105 and 5145. Calculating percentages, as we did earlier, is also a form of scaling. For this reason, `*/` is called a "scaling operator."

---

†**For Beginners Who Like Word-problems**

Here's a word-problem for the above example:

The boss says he'll divide a $150 bonus between the two top-selling marketing representatives according to their monthly commissions. When the receipts are counted, the top two commissions are $7,105 and $5,145. How much of the bonus does each marketing rep get?

Another scaling operator in FORTH is */MOD:

*/MOD	(u1 u2 u3 — u-rem u-result)	Multiplies, then divides (u1*u2/u3). Returns the remainder and the quotient. Uses a double-length intermediate result.

We'll let you dream up a good example for */MOD yourself.

Using Rational Approximations†

So far we've only used scaling operations to work on rational numbers. They can also be used on rational approximations of irrational constants, such as pi or the square root of two. For example, the real value of pi is

3.14159265358, etc.

but to stay within the bounds of single-length arithmetic, we could write the phrase:

```
31416 10000 */
```

and get a pretty good approximation.

Now we can write a definition to compute the area of a circle, given its radius. We'll translate the formula:

$$\pi r^2$$

into FORTH. The value of the radius will be on the stack, so we DUP it and multiply it by itself, then star-slash the result:

---

†**For Math-block Victims:**

You can skip this section if it starts making your brain itch. But if you're feeling particularly smart today, we want you to know that ...

A rational number is a whole number or a fraction in which the numerator and denominator are both whole numbers. Seventeen is a rational number, as is 2/3. Even 1.02 is rational, because it's the same as 102/100. $\sqrt{2}$, on the other hand, is irrational.

```
: PI   DUP *  31416 10000 */ ;
```

Try it with a circle whose radius is ten inches:

```
10  PI  . 314 ok
```

But for even more accuracy, we might wonder if there is a pair of integers besides 31416 and 10000 that is a closer approximation to pi. Surprisingly, there is. The fraction:

```
355 113 */
```

is accurate to more than six places beyond the decimal, as opposed to less than four places with 31416.

Our new and improved definition, then, is:

```
: PI   DUP *  355 113 */ ;
```

It turns out that you can approximate nearly any constant by many different pairs of integers, all numbers less than 32768, with an error of less than 10^{-8}.†

---

†**For Really Dedicated Mathephiles**

Here's a handy table of rational approximations to various constants:

Number	Approximation	Error
π = 3.141 ...	355/ 113	8.5×10^{-8}
$\sqrt{2}$ = 1.414 ...	19601/13860	1.5×10^{-9}
$\sqrt{3}$ = 1.732 ...	18817/10864	1.1×10^{-9}
e = 2.718 ...	28667/10546	5.5×10^{-9}
$\sqrt{10}$ = 3.162 ...	22936/ 7253	5.7×10^{-9}
$\sqrt[12]{2}$ = 1.059 ...	26797/25293	1.0×10^{-9}
$\log_{10} 2/1.6384$ = 0.183 ...	2040/11103	1.1×10^{-8}
ln2/16.384 = 0.042 ...	485/11464	1.0×10^{-7}
.001° /22-bit rev = 0.858 ...	18118/21109	1.4×10^{-9}
arc-sec/22-bit rev = 0.309 ...	9118/29509	1.0×10^{-9}
c = 2.9979248	24559/ 8192	1.6×10^{-9}

Here's a list of the FORTH words we've covered in this chapter:

1+	(n -- n+1)	Adds one.
1-	(n -- n-1)	Subtracts one.
2+	(n -- n+2)	Adds two.
2-	(n -- n-2)	Subtracts two.
2*	(n -- n*2)	Multiplies by two (arithmetic left shift)
2/	(n -- n/2)	Divides by two (arithmetic right shift)
ABS	(n -- |n|)	Returns the absolute value.
NEGATE	(n -- -n)	Changes the sign.
MIN	(n1 n2 -- n-min)	Returns the minimum.
MAX	(n1 n2 -- n-max)	Returns the maximum.
>R	(n --)	Takes a value off the parameter stack and pushes it onto the return stack.
R>	(-- n)	Takes a value off the return stack and pushes it onto the parameter stack.
I	(-- n)	Copies the top of the return stack without affecting it.
I'	(-- n)	Copies the second item of the return stack without affecting it.
J	(-- n)	Copies the third item of the return stack without affecting it.
*/	(n1 n2 n3 -- n-result)	Multiplies, then divides (u1*n2/n3). Uses a 32-bit intermediate result.
*/MOD	(u1 u2 u3 -- u-rem u-result)	Multiplies, then divides (u1*u2/u3). Returns the remainder and the quotient. Uses a double-length intermediate result.

Review of Terms

Double-length intermediate result — a double-length value which is created temporarily by a two-part operator, such as `*/`, so that the "intermediate result" (the result of the first operation) is allowed to exceed the range of a single-length number, even though the initial arguments and the final result are not.

Fixed-point arithmetic — arithmetic which deals with numbers which do not themselves indicate the location of their decimal points. Instead, for any group of numbers, the program assumes the location of the decimal point or keeps the decimal location for all such numbers as a separate number.

Floating-point arithmetic — arithmetic which deals with numbers which themselves indicate the location of their decimal points. The program must be able to interpret the true value of each individual number before any arithmetic can be performed.

Parameter Stack — in FORTH, the region of memory which serves as common ground between various operations to pass arguments (numbers, flags, or whatever) from one operation to another.

Return stack — in FORTH, a region of memory distinct from the parameter stack which the FORTH system uses to hold "return addresses" (to be discussed in Chap. 9), among other things. The user may keep values on the return stack temporarily, under certain conditions.

Scaling — the process of multiplying (or dividing) a number by a ratio. Also refers to the process of multiplying (or dividing) a number by a power of ten so that all values in a set of data may be represented as integers with the decimal point assumed to be in the same place for all values.

Problems -- Chapter 5

1. Translate the following algebraic expression into a FORTH definition:

$$-\frac{ab}{c}$$

given (a b c --)

2. Given these four numbers on the stack:

(6 70 123 45 --)

write an expression that prints the largest value.

Practice in Scaling

3. In "calculator style," convert the following temperatures, using these formulas:

$$^{o}C = \frac{^{o}F - 32}{1.8}$$

$$^{o}F = (^{o}C \times 1.8) + 32$$

$$^{o}K = {}^{o}C + 273$$

(For now, express all arguments and results in whole degrees.)

a) 0° F in Centigrade
b) 212° F in Centigrade
c) -32° F in Centigrade
d) 16° C in Fahrenheit
e) 233° K in Centigrade

4. Now define words to perform the conversions in Prob. 3. Use the following names:

```
F>C   F>K   C>F   C>K   K>F   K>C
```

Test them with the above values.

6 THROW IT FOR A LOOP

In Chap. 4 we learned to program the computer to make "decisions" by branching to different parts of a definition depending on the outcome of certain tests. Conditional branching is one of the things that make computers as useful as they are.

In this chapter, we'll see how to write definitions in which execution can conditionally branch back to an earlier part of the same definition, so that some segment will repeat again and again. This type of control structure is called a "loop." The ability to perform loops is probably the most significant thing that makes computers as powerful as they are. If we can program the computer to make out one payroll check, we can program it to make out a thousand of them.

For now we'll write loops that do simple things like printing numbers at your terminal. In later chapters, we'll learn to do much more with them.

Definite Loops -- DO...LOOP

One type of loop structure is called a "definite loop." You, the programmer, specify the number of times the loop will loop. In FORTH, you do this by specifying a beginning number and an ending number (in reverse order) before the word DO. Then you put the words which you want to have repeated between the words DO and LOOP. For example

```
: TEST  10 0 DO  CR ." HELLO " LOOP ;
```

will print a carriage return and "HELLO" ten times, because zero from ten is ten.

```
TEST
HELLO
HELLO
HELLO
HELLO
HELLO
HELLO
HELLO
HELLO
HELLO
HELLO ok
```

Like an IF...THEN statement, which also involves branching, a DO...LOOP statement must be contained within a (single) definition.

The ten is called the "limit" and the zero is called the "index."

FORMULA:

limit index DO ... LOOP†

Here's what happens inside a DO...LOOP:

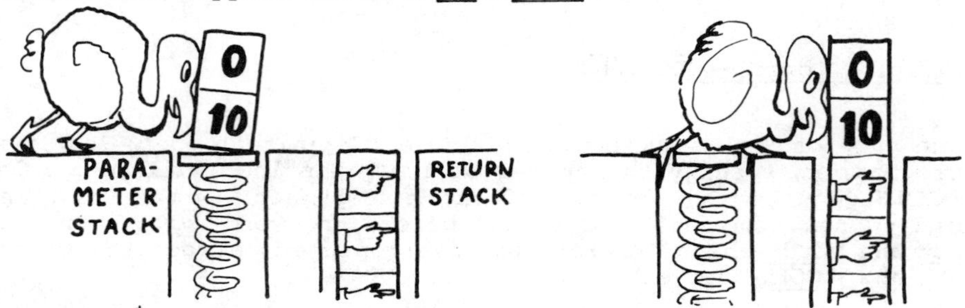

First DO‡ puts the index and the limit on the return stack.

---

† **For the Timid Beginner**

Go ahead! Nobody's looking.

```
: TEST   1000 0 DO  ." I'M GOING LOOPY! " LOOP ;
```

Go on, execute it! How often have you been able to tell anyone to do something a thousand times?

---

‡ half-brother of the DODO bird.

Then execution proceeds to the words inside the loop,

up till the word LOOP.[†]

If the index is less than the limit, LOOP reroutes execution back to DO,

and adds a one to the index.

LATER:

Eventually the index reaches ten, and LOOP lets execution move on to the next word in the definition.

[†](who just emerged from its loophole)

Remember that the FORTH word I copies the top of the return stack onto the parameter stack. You can use I to get hold of the current value of the index each time around. Consider the definition

```
: DECADE   10 0 DO  I .  LOOP ;
```

which executes like this:

```
DECADE 0 1 2 3 4 5 6 7 8 9 ok
```

Of course, you could pick any range of numbers (within the range of -32768 to +32767):

```
: SAMPLE   -243 -250 DO  I .  LOOP ;
SAMPLE -250 -249 -248 -247 -246 -245 -244 ok
```

Notice that even negative numbers increase by one each time. The limit is always higher than the index.

You can leave a number on the stack to serve as an argument to something inside a DO loop. For instance,

```
: MULTIPLICATIONS   CR  11 1 DO DUP I * . LOOP  DROP ;
```

will produce the following results:

```
7 MULTIPLICATIONS
7 14 21 28 35 42 49 56 63 70 ok
```

Here we're simply multiplying the current value of the index by seven each time around. Notice that we have to DUP the seven inside the loop so that a copy will be available each time and that we have to DROP it after we come out of the loop.

A compound interest problem gives us the opportunity to demonstrate some trickier stack manipulations inside a DO loop.

Given a starting balance, say $1000, and an interest rate, say 6%, let's write a definition to compute and print a table like this:

```
1000 6 COMPOUND
YEAR 1   BALANCE 1060
YEAR 2   BALANCE 1124
YEAR 3   BALANCE 1191
                        etc.
```

for twenty years.

First we'll load R%, our previously-defined word from Chap. 5, then we'll define

```
: COMPOUND   ( amt int -- )
    SWAP  21 1 DO ." YEAR " I .  3 SPACES
    2DUP R% +  DUP ." BALANCE " .  CR LOOP  2DROP ;
```

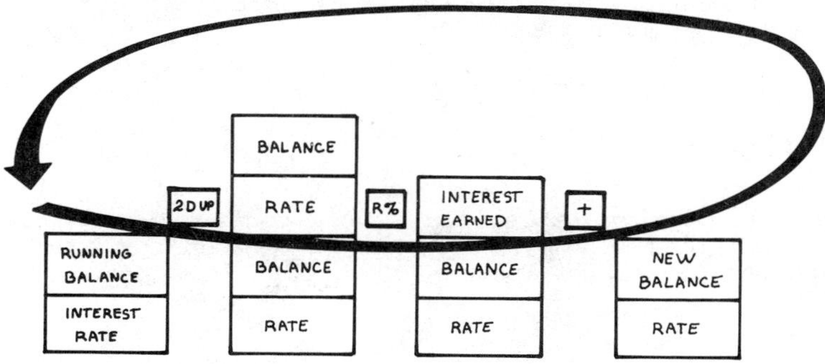

Each time through the loop, we do a [2DUP] so that we always maintain a running balance and an unchanged interest rate for the next go-round. When we're finally done, we [2DROP] them.

Getting [IF] fy

The index can also serve as a condition for an [IF] statement. In this way you can make something special happen on certain passes through the loop but not on others. Here's a simple example:

```
: RECTANGLE   256 0 DO I  16 MOD 0= IF
    CR THEN  ." *" LOOP ;
```

RECTANGLE will print 256 stars, and at every sixteenth star it will also perform a carriage return at your terminal. The result should look like this:

And here's an example from the world of nursery rhymes. We'll let you figure this one out.

```
: POEM   CR 11 1 DO I .  ." LITTLE "
     I 3 MOD 0= IF  ." INDIANS " CR  THEN LOOP
          ." INDIAN BOYS. " ;
```

Nested Loops

In the last section we defined a word called MULTIPLICATIONS, which contained a DO...LOOP. If we wanted to, we could put MULTIPLICATIONS inside another DO...LOOP, like this:

```
: TABLE   CR 11 1 DO I  MULTIPLICATIONS LOOP ;
```

Now we'll get a multiplication table that looks like this:

```
1 2 3 4 5 6 7 8 9 10
2 4 6 8 10 12 14 16 18 20
3 6 9 12 15 18 21 24 27 30
                                  etc.
10 20 30 40 50 60 70 80 90 100
```

because the I in the outer loop supplies the argument for MULTIPLICATIONS.

You can also nest DO loops inside one another all in the same definition:

```
: TABLE   CR 11 1 DO
     11 1 DO I J *  5 U.R  LOOP CR LOOP ;
```

Notice this phrase in the inner loop:

```
I J *
```

In Chap. 5 we mentioned that the word J copies the third item of the return stack onto the parameter stack. It so happens that in this case the third item on the return stack is the index of the outer loop.

Thus the phrase "I J *" multiplies the two indexes to create the values in the table.

Now what about this phrase?

```
5 U.R
```

This is nothing more than a fancy . that is used to print numbers in table form so that they line up vertically. The five represents the number of spaces we've decided each column in the table should be. The output of the new table will look like this:

```
    1    2    3    4    5    6    7    8    9   10
    2    4    6    8   10   12   14   16   18   20
    3    6    9   12   15   18   21   24   27   30    etc.
```

Each number takes five spaces, no matter how many digits it contains. (U.R stands for "unsigned number-print, right justified." The term "unsigned," you may recall, means you cannot use it for negative numbers.)

+LOOP

If you want the index to go up by some number other than one each time around, you can use the word +LOOP instead of LOOP.† +LOOP expects on the stack the number by which you want the index to change. For example, in the definition

```
: PENTAJUMPS   50 0 DO I .  5 +LOOP ;
```

the index will go up by five each time, with this result:

```
PENTAJUMPS 0 5 10 15 20 25 30 35 40 45 ok
```

while in

```
: FALLING   -10 0 DO I .  -1 +LOOP ;
```

the index will go down by one each time, with this result:

```
FALLING 0 -1 -2 -3 -4 -5 -6 -7 -8 -9 -10 ok
```

The argument for +LOOP, which is called the "increment," can come from anywhere, but it must be put on the stack each time around. Consider this experimental example:

```
: INC-COUNT   DO I .  DUP +LOOP  DROP ;
```

---

†For the Curious

A third DO loop ending word is introduced in Chap. 7.

There is no increment inside the definition; instead, it will have to be on the stack when INC-COUNT is executed, along with the limit and index. Watch this:

Step up by one:

```
1 5 0 INC-COUNT 0 1 2 3 4 ok
```

Step up by two:

```
2 5 0 INC-COUNT 0 2 4 ok
```

Step down by three:

```
-3 -10 10 INC-COUNT 10 7 4 1 -2 -5 -8 ok
```

Our next example demonstrates an increment that changes each time through the loop.

```
: DOUBLING   32767 1 DO  I .  I +LOOP ;
```

Here the index itself is used as the increment (I +LOOP), so that starting with one, the index doubles each time, like this:

```
DOUBLING
 1 2 4 8 16 32 64 128 256 512 1024 2048 4096 8192 16384 ok
```

(We chose 32767 as our limit because it is our highest allowable number in single-length.)

Notice that in this example we don't ever want the argument for +LOOP to be zero, because if it were we'd never come out of the loop. We would have created what is known as an "infinite loop."

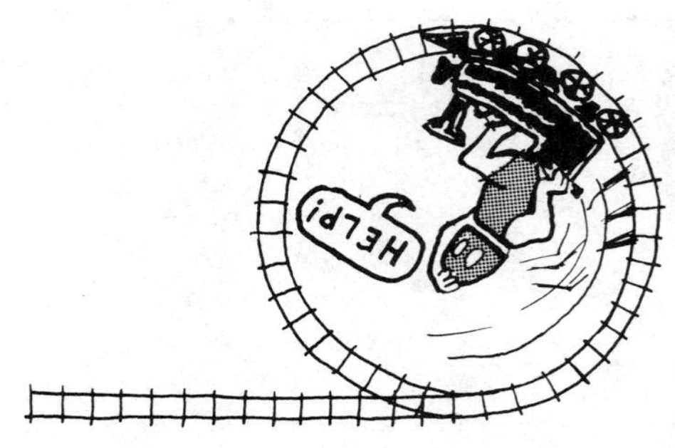

DOing It — FORTH style

There are a few things to remember before you go off and write some DO loops of your own.

First, keep this simple guide in mind:

Reasons for Termination

Execution makes its exit from a loop when ...

... the index has reached or passed the limit.

... the index has passed the limit—not when it has merely reached it.

But a DO loop always executes at least once:

```
: TEST   100 10 DO I . -1 +LOOP ;
TEST 10 ok
```

Second, remember that the words DO and LOOP are branching commands and that therefore they can only be executed inside a definition. This means that you cannot design/test your loop definitions in "calculator style" unless you simulate the loop yourself.

Let's see how a fledgling FORTH programmer might go about design/testing the definition of COMPOUND (from the first section of this chapter). Before adding the ." messages, the programmer might begin by jotting down this version on a piece of paper:

```
: COMPOUND   ( amt int -- )
     SWAP  21 1 DO I .  2DUP R% + DUP .  CR LOOP  2DROP ;
```

The programmer might test this version at the terminal, using . or .S to check the result of each step. The "conversation" might look like this:

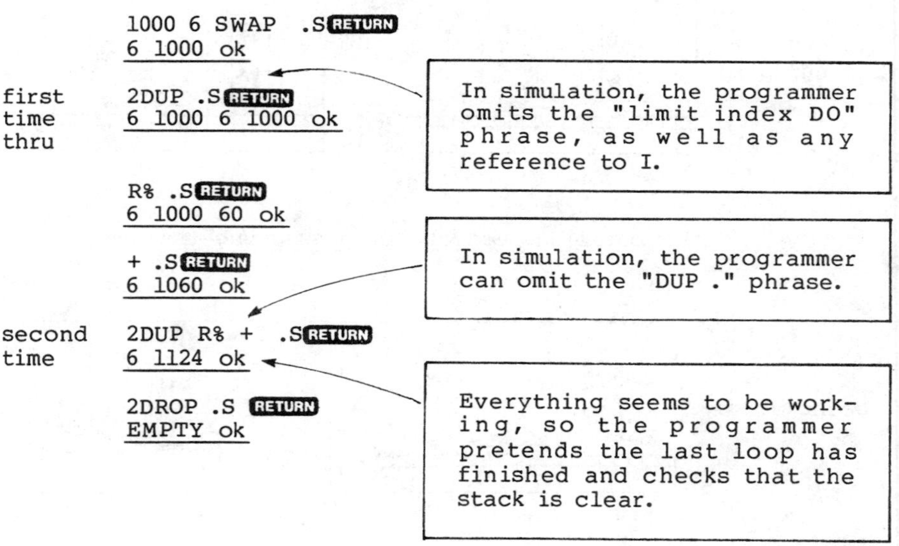

1000 6 SWAP .S RETURN
6 1000 ok
first time thru
2DUP .S RETURN
6 1000 6 1000 ok
In simulation, the programmer omits the "limit index DO" phrase, as well as any reference to I.
R% .S RETURN
6 1000 60 ok
+ .S RETURN
6 1060 ok
In simulation, the programmer can omit the "DUP ." phrase.
second time
2DUP R% + .S RETURN
6 1124 ok
2DROP .S RETURN
EMPTY ok
Everything seems to be working, so the programmer pretends the last loop has finished and checks that the stack is clear.

A Handy Hint

How to Clear the Stack

Sometimes a beginner will unwittingly write a loop which leaves a whole lot of numbers on the stack. For example

```
: FIVES   100 0 DO  I 5 . LOOP ;
```

instead of

```
: FIVES   100 0 DO  I 5 * .  LOOP ;
```

If you see this happen to anyone (surely it will never happen to you!) and if you see the beginner typing in an endless succession of dots to clear the stack, recommend typing in

```
XX
```

XX is not a FORTH word, so the text interpreter will execute the word ABORT", which among other things clears both stacks. The beginner will be endlessly grateful.

Indefinite Loops

While DO loops are called definite loops, FORTH also supports "indefinite" loops. This type of loop will repeat indefinitely or until some event occurs. A standard form of indefinite loop is

```
BEGIN ... UNTIL
```

The BEGIN...UNTIL loop repeats until a condition is "true."

The useage is

```
BEGIN xxx f UNTIL
```

where "xxx" stands for the words that you want to be repeated, and "f" stands for a flag. As long as the flag is zero (false), the loop will continue to loop, but when the flag becomes non-zero (true), the loop will end.

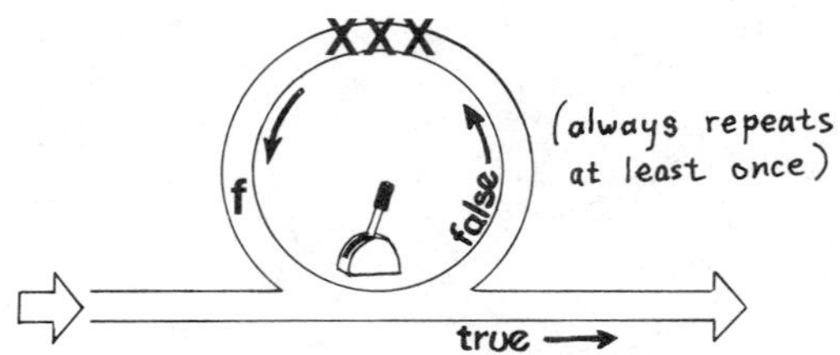

An example of a definition that uses a BEGIN...UNTIL statement is one we mentioned earlier, in our washing machine example:

```
: TILL-FULL   BEGIN  ?FULL UNTIL ;
```

which we used in the higher-level definition

```
: FILL   FAUCETS OPEN  TILL-FULL  FAUCETS CLOSE ;
```

?FULL will be defined to electronically check a switch in the washtub that indicates when the water reaches the correct level. It will return zero if the switch is not activated and a one if it is. TILL-FULL does nothing but repeatedly make this test over and over (thousands of times per second) until the switch is finally activated, at which time execution will come out of the loop. Then the ; in TILL-FULL will return the flow of execution to the remaining words in FILL, and the water faucets will be turned off.

Sometimes a programmer will deliberately want to create an infinite loop. In FORTH, the best way is with the form

```
BEGIN xxx 0 UNTIL
```

The zero supplies a "false" flag to the word UNTIL, so the loop will repeat eternally.

Beginners usually want to avoid infinite loops, because executing one means that they lose control of the computer (in the sense that only the words inside the loop are being executed). But infinite loops do have their uses. For instance, the text interpreter is part of an infinite loop called QUIT, which waits for input, interprets it, executes it, prints "ok," then waits for input once again. In most microprocessor-controlled machines, the highest-level definition contains an infinite loop that defines the machine's behavior.

Another form of indefinite loop is used in this format:

```
BEGIN xxx f WHILE yyy REPEAT
```

Here the test occurs halfway through the loop rather than at the end. As long as the test is true, the flow of execution continues with the rest of the loop, then returns to the beginning again. If the test is false, the loop ends.

Notice that the effect of the test is opposite that in the BEGIN...UNTIL construction. Here the loop repeats _while_ something is true (rather than _until_ it's true).

The indefinite loop structures lend themselves best to cases in which you're waiting for some external event to happen, such as the closing of a switch or thermostat, or the setting of a flag by another part of an application that is running simultaneously. So for now, instead of giving examples, we just want you to remember that the indefinite loop structures exist.

The Indefinitely Definite Loop

There is a way to write a definite loop so that it stops short of the prescribed limit if a truth condition changes state, by using the word LEAVE. LEAVE causes the loop to end on the very next LOOP or +LOOP.

Sometime during the course of the loop (while LOOP is asleep at the switch), the word LEAVE sets the limit to equal the index. Now the next time LOOP is executed, the loop will terminate.

Watch how we rewrite our earlier definition of COMPOUND. Instead of just letting the loop run twenty times, let's get it to quit after twenty times or as soon as our money has doubled, whichever occurs first.

We'll simply add this phrase:

```
2000 > IF LEAVE THEN
```

like this:

```
: DOUBLED   6 1000  21 1 DO  CR
    ." YEAR "  I 2 U.R
    2DUP R% +  DUP ."    BALANCE " .
    DUP 2000 > IF CR CR ." MORE THAN DOUBLED IN "
                   I . ." YEARS "  LEAVE  THEN
                                 LOOP 2DROP ;
```

The result will look like this:

```
DOUBLED
YEAR  1    BALANCE 1060
YEAR  2    BALANCE 1124
YEAR  3    BALANCE 1191
YEAR  4    BALANCE 1262
YEAR  5    BALANCE 1338
YEAR  6    BALANCE 1418
YEAR  7    BALANCE 1503
YEAR  8    BALANCE 1593
YEAR  9    BALANCE 1689
YEAR 10    BALANCE 1790
YEAR 11    BALANCE 1897
YEAR 12    BALANCE 2011

 MORE THAN DOUBLED IN 12 YEARS ok
```

One of the problems at the end of this chapter asks you to rework DOUBLED so that it expects the parameters of interest and starting balance, and computes by itself the doubled balance that LEAVE will try to reach.

Two Handy Hints: PAGE and QUIT

To give a neater appearance to your loop outputs (such as tables and geometric shapes), you might want to clear the screen first by using the word PAGE. You can execute PAGE interactively like this:

```
PAGE RECTANGLE
```

which will clear the screen before printing the rectangle that we defined earlier in this chapter. Or you could put PAGE at the beginning of the definition, like this:

```
: RECTANGLE   PAGE  256 0 DO
    I 16 MOD 0=  IF CR THEN ." *" LOOP ;
```

If you don't want the "ok" to appear upon completion of execution, use the word QUIT. Again, you can use QUIT interactively:

```
RECTANGLE QUIT
```

or you can make QUIT the last word in the definition (just before the semicolon).

Here's a list of the FORTH words we've covered in the chapter:

DO ... LOOP	DO: (limit index --) LOOP: (--)	Sets up a finite loop, given the index range.
DO ... +LOOP	DO: (limit index --) +LOOP: (n --)	Like DO ... LOOP except adds the value of n (instead of always one) to the index.
LEAVE	(--)	Terminates the loop at the next LOOP or +LOOP.
BEGIN ... UNTIL	UNTIL: (f --)	Sets up an indefinite loop which ends when f is true.
BEGIN xxx WHILE yyy REPEAT	WHILE: (f --)	Sets up an indefinite loop which always executes xxx and also executes yyy if f is true. Ends when f is false.
U.R	(u width --)	Prints the unsigned single-length number, right-justified within the field width.
PAGE	(--)	Clears the terminal screen and resets the terminal's cursor to the upper left-hand corner.
QUIT	(--)	Terminates execution for the current task and returns control to the terminal.

Review of Terms

Definite loop — a loop structure in which the words contained within the loop repeat a definite number of times. In FORTH, this number depends on the starting and ending counts (index and limit) which are placed on the stack prior to the execution of the word DO.

Infinite loop — a loop structure in which the words contained within the loop continue to repeat without any chance of an external event stopping them, except for the shutting down or resetting of the computer.

Indefinite loop — a loop structure in which the words contained within the loop continue to repeat until some truth condition changes state (true-to-false or false-to-true). In FORTH, the indefinite loops begin with the word BEGIN.

Problems -- Chapter 6

In Problems 1 through 6, you will create several words which will print out patterns of stars (asterisks). These will involve the use of DO loops and BEGIN...UNTIL loops.

1. First create a word named STARS which will print out n stars on the same line, given n on the stack:

   ```
   10 STARS RETURN ********** ok
   ```

2. Next define BOX which prints out a rectangle of stars, given the width and height (number of lines), using the stack order (width height --).

   ```
   10 3 BOX
   **********
   **********
   ********** ok
   ```

3. Now create a word named \STARS which will print a skewed array of stars (a rhomboid), given the height on the stack. Use a DO loop and, for simplicity, make the width a constant ten stars.

   ```
   3 \STARS
    **********
     **********
      ********** ok
   ```

4. Now create a word which slants the stars the other direction; call it /STARS. It should take the height as a stack input and use a constant ten width. Use a DO loop.

5. Now redefine this last word, using a BEGIN...UNTIL loop.

6. Write a definition called DIAMONDS which will print out the given number of diamonds shapes, as shown in this example:

2 DIAMONDS

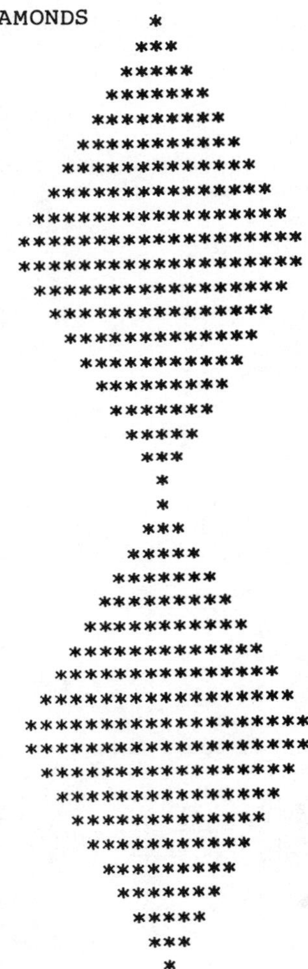

7. In our discussion of LEAVE we gave an example which computed 6% compound interest on a starting balance of $1000 for 20 years or until the balance had doubled, whichever came first. Rewrite this definition so that it will expect a starting balance and interest rate on the stack and will LEAVE when this starting balance has doubled.

8. Define a word called ** that will compute exponential values, like this:

   7 2 ** . 49 ok
   (seven squared)

   2 4 ** . 16 ok
   (two to the fourth power)

   For simplicity, assume positive exponents only (but make sure ** works correctly when the exponent is one--the result should be the number itself).

7 A NUMBER OF KINDS OF NUMBERS

So far we've only talked about signed single-length numbers. In this chapter we'll introduce unsigned numbers and double-length numbers, as well as a whole passel of new operators to go along with them.

The chapter is divided into two sections:

For beginners--this section explains how a computer looks at numbers and exactly what is meant by the terms signed or unsigned and by single-length or double-length.

For everyone--this section continues our discussion of FORTH for beginners and experts alike, and explains how FORTH handles signed and unsigned, single- and double-length numbers.

SECTION I -- FOR BEGINNERS

Signed vs. Unsigned Numbers

All digital computers store numbers in binary form.† In FORTH, the stack is sixteen bits wide (a "bit" is a "binary digit"). Below is a view of sixteen bits, showing the value of each bit:

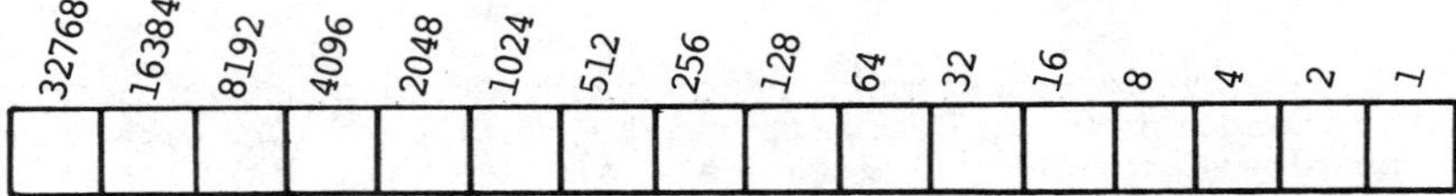

If every bit were to contain a 1, the total would be 65535. Thus in 16 bits we can express any value between 0 and 65535. Because this kind of number does not let us express negative values, we call it an "unsigned number." We have been indicating unsigned numbers with the letter "u" in our tables and stack notations.

But what about negative numbers? In order to be able to express a positive or negative number, we need to sacrifice one bit that will essentially indicate sign. This bit is the one at the far left, the "high-order bit." In 15 bits we can express a number as high as 32767. When the sign bit contains 1, then we can go an equal distance back into the negative numbers. Thus within 16 bits we can represent any number from -32768 to +32767. This should look familiar to you as the range of a single-length number, which we have been indicating with the letter "n."

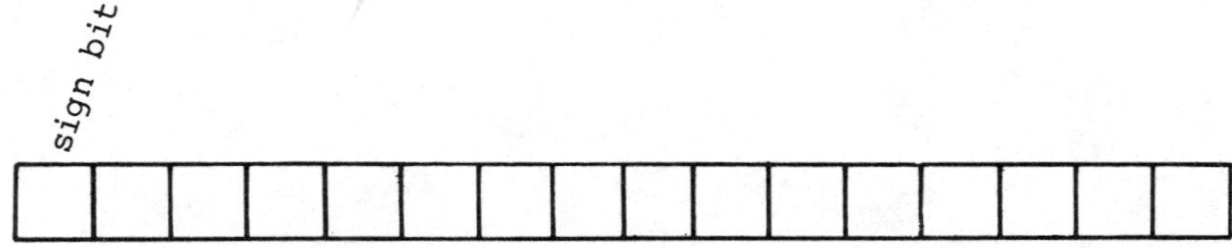

---

†For Beginner Beginners

If you are unfamiliar with binary notation, ask someone you know who likes math, or find a book on computers for beginners.

Before we leave you with any misconceptions, we'd better clarify the way negative numbers are represented. You might think that it's a simple matter of setting the sign bit to indicate whether a number is positive or negative, but it doesn't work that way.

To explain how negative numbers are represented, let's return to decimal notation and examine a counter such as that found on many tape recorders.

Let's say the counter has three digits. As you wind the tape forward, the counter-wheels turn and the number increases. Starting once again with the counter at 0, now imagine you're winding the tape backwards. The first number you see is 999, which, in a sense, is the same as -1. The next number will be 998, which is the same as -2, and so on.

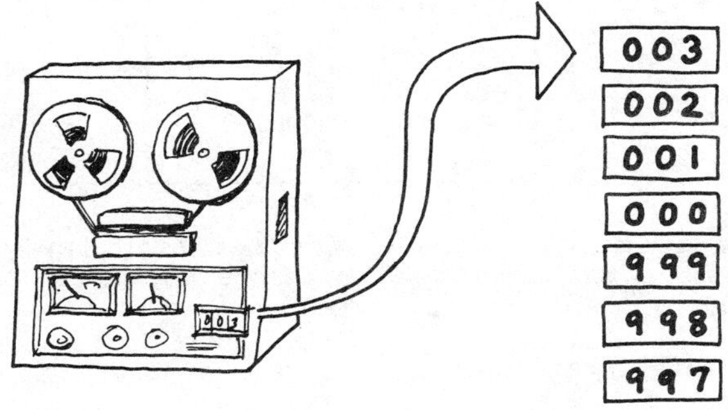

The representation of signed numbers in a computer is similar.

Starting with the number

    0000000000000000

and going backwards one number, we get

    1111111111111111   (sixteen ones)

which stands for 65535 in unsigned notation as well as for -1 in signed notation. The number

    1111111111111110

which stands for 65534 in unsigned notation, represents -2 in signed notation.

Here's a chart that shows how a binary number on the stack can be used either as an unsigned number or as a signed number:

as an unsigned number		as a signed number
65535	1111111111111111	
...	...	
32768	1000000000000000	
32767	0111111111111111	32767
...	...	...
0	0000000000000000	0
	1111111111111111	-1
	...	...
	1000000000000000	-32768

This bizarre-seeming method for representing negative values makes it possible for the computer to use the same procedures for subtraction as for addition.

To show how this works, let's take a very simple problem:

```
 2
-1
```

Subtracting one from two is the same as adding two plus negative one. In single-length binary notation, the two looks like this:

```
0000000000000010
```

while negative-one looks like this:

```
1111111111111111
```

The computer adds them up the same way we would on paper; that is when the total of any column exceeds one, it carries a one into the next column. The result looks like this:

```
  0000000000000010
+ 1111111111111111
 10000000000000001
```

As you can see, the computer had to carry a one into every column all the way across, and ended up with a one in the seventeenth place. But since the stack is only sixteen bits wide, the result is simply

    0000000000000001

which is the correct answer, one.

We needn't explain how the computer converts a positive number to negative, but we will tell you that the process is called "two's complementing."

Arithmetic Shift

While we're on the subject of how a computer performs certain mathematical operations, we'll explain what is meant by the mysterious phrases back in Chap. 5: "arithmetic left shift" and "arithmetic right shift."

A FORTH Instant Replay:

2*	(n -- n*2)	Multiplies by two (arithmetic left shift).
2/	(n -- n/2)	Divides by two (arithmetic right shift).

To illustrate, let's pick a number, say six, and write it in binary form:

    0000000000000110

(4 + 2). Now let's shift every digit one place to the left, and put a zero in the vacant place in the one's column.

    0000000000001100

This is the binary representation of twelve (8 + 4), which is exactly double the original number. This works in all cases, and it also works in reverse. If you shift every digit one place to the right and fill the vacant digit with a zero, the result will always be half of the original value.

In arithmetic shift, the sign bit does not get shifted. This means that a positive number will stay positive and a negative number will stay negative when you divide or multiply it by two. (When the high-order bit shifts with all the other bits, the term is "logical shift.")

The important thing for you to know is that a computer can shift digits much more quickly than it can go through all the folderol of normal division or multiplication. When speed is critical, it's much better to say

```
2*
```

than

```
2 *
```

and it may even be better to say

```
2* 2* 2*
```

than

```
8 *
```

depending on your particular model of computer, but this topic is getting too technical for right now.

An Introduction to Double-length Numbers

A double-length number is just what you probably expected it would be: a number that is represented in thirty-two bits instead of sixteen. Signed double-length numbers have a range of ±2,147,483,647 (a range of over four billion).

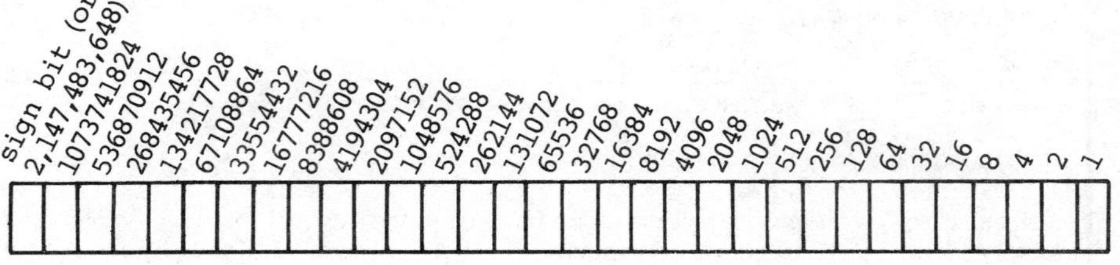

In FORTH, a double-length number takes the place of two single-length numbers on the stack. Operators like 2SWAP and 2DUP are useful either for double-length numbers or for pairs of single-length numbers.

One more thing we should explain: to the non-FORTH-speaking computer world, the term "word" means a 16-bit value, or two bytes. But in FORTH, "word" means a defined command. So in order to avoid confusion, FORTH programmers refer to a 16-bit value as a "cell." A double-length number requires two cells.

Other Number Bases

As you get more involved in programming, you'll need to employ other number bases besides decimal and binary, particularly hexadecimal (base 16) and octal (base 8). Since we'll be talking about these two number bases later on in this chapter, we think you might like an introduction now.

Computer people began using hexadecimal and octal numbers for one main reason: computers think in binary and human beings have a hard time reading long binary numbers. For people, it's much easier to convert binary to hexadecimal than binary to decimal, because sixteen is an even power of two, while ten is not. The same is true with octal. So programmers usually use hex or octal to express the binary numbers that the computer uses for things like addresses and machine codes. Hexadecimal (or simply "hex") looks strange at first since it uses the letters A through F.

Decimal	Binary	Hexadecimal
0	0000	0
1	0001	1
2	0010	2
3	0011	3
4	0100	4
5	0101	5
6	0110	6
7	0111	7
8	1000	8
9	1001	9
10	1010	A
11	1011	B
12	1100	C
13	1101	D
14	1110	E
15	1111	F

Let's take a single-length binary number:

0111101110100001

To convert this number to hexadecimal, we first subdivide it into four units of four bits each:

| 0111 | 1011 | 1010 | 0001 |

then convert each 4-bit unit to its hex equivalent:

| 7 | B | A | 1 |

or simply 7BA1.

Octal numbers use only the numerals 0 through 7. Because nowadays most computers use hexadecimal representation, we'll skip an octal conversion example

We'll have more on conversions in the section titled "Number Conversions" later in this chapter.

The ASCII Character Set

If the computer uses binary notation to store numbers, how does it store characters and other symbols? Binary, again, but in a special code that was adopted as an industry standard many years ago. The code is called the American Standard Code for Information Interchange code, usually abbreviated ASCII.

Table 7-1 shows each character in the system and its numerical equivalent, both in hexadecimal and in decimal form.

The characters in the first column (ASCII codes 0-1F hex) are called "control characters" because they indicate that the terminal or computer is supposed to do something like ring its bell, backspace, start a new line, etc. The remaining characters are called "printing characters" because they produce visible characters including letters, the numerals zero through nine, all available symbols and even the blank space (hex 20). The only exception is DEL (hex 7F) which is a signal to the computer to ignore the last character sent.

In Chap. 1 we introduced the word EMIT. EMIT takes an ASCII code on the stack and sends it to the terminal so that the terminal will print it as a character. For example,

```
65 EMIT A ok
66 EMIT B ok
```

etc. (We're using the decimal, rather than the hex, equivalent because that's what your computer is most likely expecting right now.)†

Why not test EMIT on *every* printing character, "automatically"?

```
: PRINTABLES   127 32 DO I EMIT SPACE LOOP ;
```

---

†For Experts

Why are you snooping on the beginner's section?

TABLE 7-1 -- ASCII CHARACTERS & EQUIVALENTS

Char	Hex	Dec	Char	Hex	Dec	Char	Hex	Dec	Char	Hex	Dec
NUL	00	0	SP	20	32	@	40	64	`	60	96
SOH	01	1	!	21	33	A	41	65	a	61	97
STX	02	2	"	22	34	B	42	66	b	62	98
ETX	03	3	#	23	35	C	43	67	c	63	99
EOT	04	4	$	24	36	D	44	68	d	64	100
ENQ	05	5	%	25	37	E	45	69	e	65	101
ACK	06	6	&	26	38	F	46	70	f	66	102
BEL	07	7	'	27	39	G	47	71	g	67	103
BS	08	8	(	28	40	H	48	72	h	68	104
HT	09	9	)	29	41	I	49	73	i	69	105
LF	0A	10	*	2A	42	J	4A	74	j	6A	106
VT	0B	11	+	2B	43	K	4B	75	k	6B	107
FF	0C	12	,	2C	44	L	4C	76	l	6C	108
CR	0D	13	-	2D	45	M	4D	77	m	6D	109
SM	0E	14	.	2E	46	N	4E	78	n	6E	110
SI	0F	15	/	2F	47	O	4F	79	o	6F	111
DLE	10	16	0	30	48	P	50	80	p	70	112
DC1	11	17	1	31	49	Q	51	81	q	71	113
DC2	12	18	2	32	50	R	52	82	r	72	114
DC3	13	19	3	33	51	S	53	83	s	73	115
DC4	14	20	4	34	52	T	54	84	t	74	116
NAK	15	21	5	35	53	U	55	85	u	75	117
SYN	16	22	6	36	54	V	56	86	v	76	118
ETB	17	23	7	37	55	W	57	87	w	77	119
CAN	18	24	8	38	56	X	58	88	x	78	120
EM	19	25	9	39	57	Y	59	89	y	79	121
SUB	1A	26	:	3A	58	Z	5A	90	z	7A	122
ESC	1B	27	;	3B	59	[	5B	91	{	7B	123
FS	1C	28	<	3C	60	\	5C	92	|	7C	124
GS	1D	29	=	3D	61	]	5D	93	}	7D	125
RS	1E	30	>	3E	62	^	5E	94	~	7E	126
US	1F	31	?	3F	63	_	5F	95	DEL (RB)	7F	127

The "Char" columns list the ASCII characters (some of which are control characters); the "Hex" columns give the hexadecimal equivalents; and the "Dec" columns present the decimal equivalents.

PRINTABLES will emit every printable character in the ASCII set; that is, the characters from decimal 32 to decimal 126. (We're using the ASCII codes as our DO loop index.)

```
PRINTABLES  ! " # $ % & ' ( ) * + ... ok
```

Beginners may be interested in some of the control characters as well. For instance, try this:

```
7 EMIT ok
```

You should have heard some sort of beep, which is the video terminal's version of the mechanical printer's "typewriter bell."

Other control characters that are good to know include the following:

name	operation	decimal equivalent
BS	backspace	8
LF	line feed	10
CR	carriage return	13

Experiment with these control characters, and see what they do.

ASCII is designed so that each character can be represented by one byte. The tables in this book use the letter "c" to indicate a byte value that is being used as a coded ASCII character.

Bit Logic

The words AND and OR (which we introduced in Chap. 4) use "bit logic"; that is, each bit is treated independently, and there are no "carries" from one bit-place to the next. For example, let's see what happens when we AND these two binary numbers:

```
0000000011111111
0110010110100010  AND
----------------
0000000010100010
```

For any result-bit to be "1," the respective bits in both arguments must be "1." Notice in this example that the argument on top contains all zeroes in the high-order byte and all ones in the low-order byte. The effect on the second argument in this example is that the low-order eight bits are kept but the high-order eight bits are all set to zero. Here the first argument is being used as a "mask," to mask out the high-order byte of the second argument.

The word [OR] also uses bit logic. For example,

```
1000100100001001
0000001111001000  [OR]
----------------
1000101111001001
```

a "1" in either argument produces a "1" in the result. Again, each column is treated separately, with no carries.

By clever use of masks, we could even use a 16-bit value to hold sixteen separate flags. For example, we could find out whether this bit

```
1011101010011100
           ▲
```

is "1" or "0" by masking out all other flags, like this:

```
1011101010011100
0000000000010000  [AND]
----------------
0000000000010000
```

Since the bit was "1," the result is "true." Had it been "0," the result would have been "0" or "false."

We could set the flag to "0" without affecting the other flags by using this technique:

```
1011101010011100
1111111111101111  [AND]
----------------
1011101010001100
           ▲
```

We used a mask that contains all "1"s except for the bit we wanted to set to "0." We can set the same flag back to "1" by using this technique:

```
1011101010001100
0000000000010000  [OR]
----------------
1011101010011100
           ▲
```

SECTION II -- FOR EVERYBODY

Signed and Unsigned Numbers

Back in Chap. 1 we introduced the word NUMBER.

If the word INTERPRET can't find an incoming string in the dictionary, it hands it over to the word NUMBER. NUMBER then attempts to convert the string into a number expressed in binary form. If NUMBER succeeds, it pushes the binary equivalent onto the stack.

NUMBER does not do any range-checking.† Because of this, NUMBER can convert either signed or unsigned numbers.

For instance, if you enter any number between 32768 and 65535, NUMBER will convert it as an unsigned number. Any value between -32768 and -1 will be stored as a two's-complement integer.

This is an important point: the stack can be used to hold either signed or unsigned integers. Whether a binary value is interpreted as signed or unsigned depends on the operators that you apply to it. You decide which form is better for a given situation, then stick to your choice.

---

†For Beginners

This means that NUMBER does not check whether the number you've entered as a single-length number exceeds the proper range. If you enter a giant number, NUMBER converts it but only saves the least significant sixteen digits.

We've introduced the word [.], which prints a value on the stack as a <u>signed</u> number:

```
65535 . -1 ok
```

The word [U.] prints the same binary representation as an <u>unsigned</u> number:

```
65535 U. 65535 ok
```

U.	(u --)	Prints the unsigned single-length number, followed by one space.	u-dot

In this book the letter "n" signifies <u>signed</u> single-length numbers, while the letter "u" signifies <u>unsigned</u> single-length numbers. (We've already introduced [U.R], which prints an unsigned number right-justified within a given column width.)

Here is a table of additional words that use unsigned numbers:

U*	(u1 u2 -- ud)	Multiplies two 16-bit numbers. Returns a 32-bit result. All values are unsigned.	u-star
U/MOD	(ud u1 -- u2 u3)	Divides a 32-bit by a 16-bit number. Returns a 16-bit quotient and remainder. All values are unsigned.	u-slash-mod
U<	(u1 u2 -- f)	Leaves true if u1 < u2, where both are treated as 16-bit unsigned integers.	u-less-than
DO ... /LOOP†	DO: (u-limit u-index --) /LOOP: (u --)	Like DO ... +LOOP except uses an unsigned limit, index, and increment.	slash-loop

---

†FORTH-79 Standard

[/LOOP] is included in the optional Reference Word Set.

/LOOP is similar to +LOOP, in that it terminates a DO loop and that it takes an incrementing value. The difference is that with /LOOP, the index and limit may range from zero to 65535, and the increment must be positive. /LOOP executes somewhat faster than +LOOP.

Number Bases

When you first load FORTH, all number conversions use base ten (decimal) for both input and output.

You can easily change the base by executing one of the following comands:

HEX	(--)	Sets the base to sixteen.
OCTAL	(--)	Sets the base to eight (available on some systems).†
DECIMAL	(--)	Returns the base to ten.

---

†For Experts

OCTAL is omitted unless the design of the particular processor compels its use.

When you change the number base, it stays changed until you change it again. So be sure to declare DECIMAL as soon as you're done with another number base.†

These commands make it easy to do number conversions in "calculator style."

For example, to convert decimal 100 into hexadecimal, enter

```
DECIMAL 100 HEX . 64 ok
```

To convert hex F into decimal (remember you are already in hex), enter

```
0F DECIMAL . 15 ok
```

Make it a habit, starting right now, to precede each hexadecimal value with a zero, as in

```
0A  0B  0F
```

This practice avoids mix-ups with such predefined words as B, D, or F in the EDITOR vocabulary.

A Handy Hint

A Definition of BINARY -- or Any-ARY

Beginners who want to see what numbers look like in binary notation may enter this definition:

```
: BINARY   2 BASE ! ;
```

The new word BINARY will operate just like OCTAL or HEX but will change the number base to two. On systems which do not have the word OCTAL, experimenters may define

```
: OCTAL   8 BASE ! ;
```

---

†For People Using Multiprogrammed Systems

When you change the number base, you change it for your terminal task only. Every terminal task uses a separate number base.

Double-length Numbers

Double-length numbers provide a range of ±2,147,483,647. Most FORTH systems support double-length numbers to some degree.†‡ Normally, the way to enter a double-length number onto the stack (whether from the keyboard or from a block) is to punctuate it with one of these five punctuation marks:

, . / - :

For example, when you type

200,000 RETURN

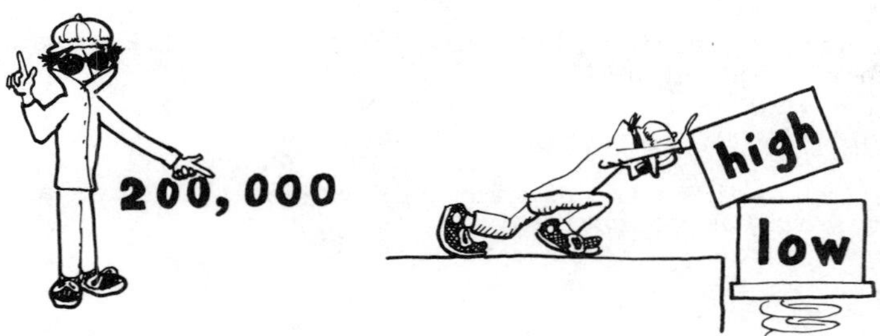

NUMBER recognizes the comma as a signal that this value should be converted to double-length. NUMBER then pushes the value onto the stack as two consecutive "cells" (cell is the FORTH term for sixteen bits), the high order cell on top.

---

†**For polyFORTH Users:**

polyFORTH includes double-length routines, but they are "electives," which means that they are written in the group of blocks which you must load each time the system is booted. This arrangement gives you the flexibility to either load these routines or delete them from your load block, according to the needs of your application.

‡**FORTH-79 Standard**

The Standard requires only three double-length arithmetic primitives. The optional Double Number Word Set includes many more double-length operators.

The FORTH word D. prints a double-length number without any punctuation.

D.	(d --)	Prints the signed double-length number, followed by one space.

d-dot

In this book, the letter "d" stands for a double-length signed integer.

For example, having entered a double-length number, if you were now to execute D., the computer would respond:

```
D. 200000 ok
```

Notice that all of the following numbers are converted in exactly the same way:

```
12345. D. 12345 ok
123.45 D. 12345 ok
1-2345 D. 12345 ok
1/23/45 D. 12345 ok
1:23:45 D. 12345 ok
```

But this is not the same:

```
-12345
```

because this value would be converted as a negative, single-length number. (This is the only case in which a hyphen is interpreted as a minus sign and not as punctuation.)

In the next section we'll show you how to define your own equivalents to D. which will print whatever punctuation you want along with the number.

Number Formatting -- Double-length Unsigned†

$200.00   12/31/80   372-8493   6:32:59   98.6

The above numbers represent the kinds of output you can create by defining your own "number-formatting words" in FORTH. This section will show you how.

The simplest number-formatting definition we could write would be

```
: UD.   <#  #S  #>  TYPE ;
```

UD. will print an unsigned double-length number. The words <# and #> (respectively pronounced bracket-number and number-bracket) signify the beginning and the end of the number-conversion process. In this definition, the entire conversion is being performed by the single word #S (pronounced numbers). #S converts the value on the stack into ASCII characters. It will only produce as many digits as are necessary to represent the number; it will not produce leading zeroes. But it always produces at least one digit, which will be zero if the value was zero. For example:

```
12,345 UD. 12345ok
12. UD. 12ok
0 UD. 0ok
```

The word TYPE prints the characters that represent the number at your terminal. Notice that there is no space between the number and the "ok." To get a space, you would simply add the word SPACE, like this:

```
: UD.   <# #S #>  TYPE SPACE ;
```

Now let's say we have a phone number on the stack, expressed as a 32-bit unsigned integer. For example, we may have typed in

```
372-8493
```

(remember that the hyphen tells NUMBER to treat this as a double-length value). We want to define a word which will format this value back as a phone number. Let's call it .PH# (for "print the phone number") and define it thus:

---

†For Those Whose Systems Do Not Have Double-length Routines Loaded

The examples used in this and the next section won't do what you expect. The principles remain the same, however, so read these two sections carefully, then read the note on page 172.

```
: .PH#   <#  # # # # 45 HOLD  #S  #>  TYPE SPACE ;
```

Our definition of .PH# has everything that UD. has, and more. The FORTH word # (pronounced number) produces a single digit only. A number-formatting definition is reversed from the order in which the number will be printed, so the phrase

```
# # # #
```

produces the right-most four digits of the phone number.

Now it's time to insert the hyphen. Looking up the ASCII value for hyphen in the table in the beginner's section of this chapter, we find that a hyphen is represented by decimal 45. The FORTH word HOLD takes this ASCII code and inserts it into the formatted number character string.

We now have three digits left. We might use the phrase

```
# # #
```

but it's easier to simply use the word #S, which will automatically convert the rest of the number for us.

If you are more familiar with ASCII codes represented in hexadecimal form, you can use this definition instead:

```
HEX   : .PH#   <#  # # # # 2D HOLD  #S  #>  TYPE SPACE ;
DECIMAL
```

Either way, the compiled definition will be exactly the same.

Now let's format an unsigned double-length number as a date, in the following form:

```
7/15/80
```

Here is the definition:

```
: .DATE   <#  # # 47 HOLD  # # 47 HOLD  #S  #>   TYPE SPACE ;
```

Let's follow the above definition, remembering that it is written in reverse order from the output. The phrase

```
# # 47 HOLD
```

produces the right-most two digits (representing the year) and the right-most slash. The next occurrence of the same phrase produces the middle two digits (representing the day) and the left-most slash. Finally, #S produces the left-most two digits (representing the month).

We could have just as easily defined

```
# # 47 HOLD
```

as its own word and used this word twice in the definition of .DATE.

Since you have control over the conversion process, you can actually convert different digits in different number bases, a feature which is useful in formatting such numbers as hours and minutes. For example, let's say that you have the time in seconds on the stack, and you want a word that will print hh:mm:ss. You might define it this way:

```
: SEXTAL   6 BASE ! ; †
: :00   #  SEXTAL #  DECIMAL  58 HOLD ;
: SEC   <#  :00 :00 #S  #>  TYPE SPACE ;
```

We will use the word :00 to format the seconds and the minutes. Both seconds and minutes are modulo-60, so the right digit can go as high as nine, but the left digit can only go up to five. Thus in the definition of :00 we convert the first digit (the one on the right) as a decimal number, then go into "sextal" (base 6) and convert the left digit. Finally, we return to decimal and insert the colon character. After :00 converts the seconds and the minutes, #S converts the remaining hours.

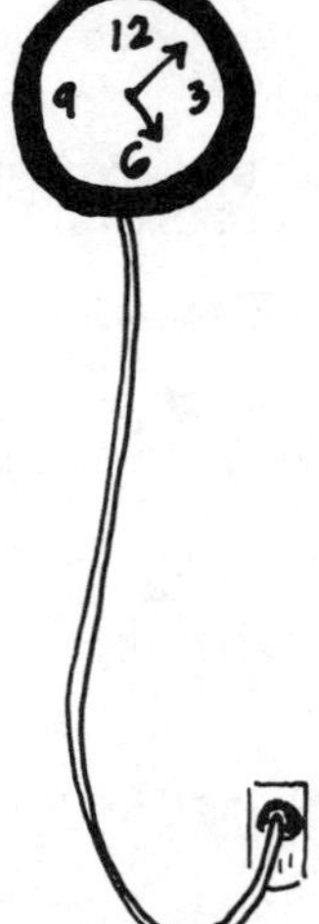

For example, if we had 4500 seconds on the stack, we would get

```
4500. SEC 1:15:00 ok
```

Table 7-2 summarizes the FORTH words that are used in number formatting. (Note the "KEY" at the bottom, which serves as a reminder of the meanings of "n," "d," etc.)

---

†For Beginners

See the Handy Hint on page 163.

TABLE 7-2 -- NUMBER FORMATTING

<#	Begins the number conversion process. Expects an unsigned double-length number on the stack.	bracket-number
#	Converts one digit and puts it into an output character string. # always produces a digit--if you're out of significant digits, you'll still get a zero for every #.	number
#S	Converts the number until the result is zero. Always produces at least one digit (0 if the value is zero).	numbers
c HOLD	Inserts, at the current position in the character string being formatted, a character whose ASCII value is on the stack. HOLD (or a word that uses HOLD) must be used between <# and #>.	
SIGN	Inserts a minus sign in the output string if the third number on the stack is negative. Usually used immediately before #> for a leading minus sign.	
#>	Completes number conversion by leaving the character count and address on the stack (these are the appropriate arguments for TYPE).	number-bracket

Stack effects for number formatting

phrase	stack	type of arguments
<# ... #>	(d -- adr u) or (u 0 -- adr u)	32-bit unsigned 16-bit unsigned
<# ... SIGN #>	(n |d| -- adr u) or	32-bit signed (where n is the high-order cell of d and |d| is the absolute value of d).
	(n |n| 0 -- adr u)	16-bit signed (where |n| is the absolute value).

KEY

n, nl ...	16-bit signed numbers	adr	address
d, dl, ...	32-bit signed numbers	c	ASCII character value
u, ul, ...	16-bit unsigned numbers		

Number Formatting -- Signed and Single-length

So far we have formatted only unsigned double-length numbers. The <# ... #> form expects only unsigned double-length numbers, but we can use it for other types of numbers by making certain arrangements on the stack.

For instance, let's look at a simplified version of the system definition of D. (which prints a signed double-length number):

```
: D.   SWAP OVER DABS  <#  #S SIGN  #>  TYPE SPACE ;
```

The word SIGN, which must be situated within the <# ... #> phrase, inserts a minus sign in the character string only if the third number on the stack is negative. So we must put a copy of the high-order cell (the one with the sign bit) at the bottom of the stack, by using the phrase

```
SWAP OVER
```

Because <# expects only unsigned double-length numbers, we must take the absolute value of our double-length signed number, with the word DABS. We now have the proper arrangement of arguments on the stack for the <# ... #> phrase. The word SIGN, like HOLD, will insert the minus sign at whatever point within the character string we situate it. Since we want our minus sign to appear at the left, we include SIGN at the right of our <# ... #> phrase. In some cases, such as accounting, we may want a negative number to be written

```
12345-
```

in which case we would place the word SIGN at the left side of our <# ... #> phrase, like this:

```
<#  SIGN #S  #>
```

Let's define a word which will print a signed double-length number with a decimal point and two decimal places to the right of the decimal. Since this is the form most often used for writing dollars and cents, let's call it .$ and define it like this:

```
: .$   SWAP OVER DABS
     <#  # # 46 HOLD  #S SIGN  36 HOLD  #>  TYPE SPACE ;
```

Let's try it:

```
2000.00 .$ $2000.00 ok
```

or even

```
2,000.00 .$ $2000.00 ok
```

We recommend that you save .$, since we'll be using it in some future examples.

You can also write special formats for single-length numbers. For example, if you want to use an unsigned single-length number, simply put a zero on the stack before the word <#. This effectively changes the single-length number into a double-length number which is so small that it has nothing (zero) in the high-order cell.

To format a signed single-length number, again you must supply a zero as a high-order cell. But you also must leave a copy of the signed number in the third stack position for SIGN, and you must leave the absolute value of the number in the second stack position. The phrase to do all of this is

```
DUP ABS 0
```

Here are the "set-up" phrases that are needed to print various kinds of numbers:

Number to be printed	Precede <# by
32-bit, unsigned	(nothing needed)
31-bit, plus sign	SWAP OVER DABS (to save the sign in the third stack position for SIGN)
16-bit, unsigned	0 (to give a dummy high-order part)
15-bit, plus sign	DUP ABS 0 (to save the sign)

If Your System Does Not Have Double-length Routines Loaded

In this case the set-up phrases are different, as follows:

Number to be printed	Precede <# by
16-bit, unsigned	DUP
15-bit, plus sign	DUP ABS DUP

Even though # still expects two cells on the stack, in this case the significant cell must be on top (where normally the high-order cell is found). The contents of the second stack position are not used.

Double-length Operators

Here is a list of double-length math operators:† ‡

D+	(d1 d2 -- d-sum)	Adds two 32-bit numbers.	d-plus
D-	(d1 d2 -- d-diff)	Subtracts two 32-bit numbers (d1-d2).	d-minus
DNEGATE	(d -- -d)	Changes the sign of a 32-bit number.	d-negate
DABS	(d -- |d|)	Returns the absolute value of a 32-bit number.	d-absolute
DMAX	(d1 d2 -- d-max)	Returns the maximum of two 32-bit numbers.	d-max
DMIN	(d1 d2 -- d-min)	Returns the minimum of two 32-bit numbers.	d-min
D=	(d1 d2 -- f)	Returns true if d1 and d2 are equal.	d-equal
D0=	(d -- f)	Returns true if d is zero.	d-zero-equal
D<	(d1 d2 -- f)	Returns true if d1 is less than d2.	d-less-than
DU<	(ud1 ud2 -- f)	Returns true if ud1 is less than ud2. Both numbers are unsigned.	d-u-less-than
D.R	(d width --)	Prints the signed 32-bit number, right-justified within the field width.	d-dot-r

---

†**For polyFORTH Users**

The double-length routines must be loaded.

‡**FORTH-79 Standard**

Except for D+, D<, and DNEGATE, which are required, these words are part of the optional Double Number Word Set.

The initial "D" signifies that these operators may only be used for double-length operations, whereas the initial "2," as in 2SWAP and 2DUP, signifies that these operators may be used either for double-length numbers or for pairs of single-length numbers.

Here's an example using D+:

```
200,000 300,000  D+ D. 500000 ok
```

A warning for experimenters: you can write definitions that contain double-precision operators, but you cannot include a punctuated, double-precision number inside a definition. In the next chapter we'll explain what to do instead.

Mixed-Length Operators

Here's a table of very useful FORTH words which operate on a combination of single- and double-length numbers:†

M+	(d n -- d-sum)	Adds a 32-bit number to a 16-bit number. Returns a 32-bit result.
M/	(d n -- n-quot)	Divides a 32-bit number by a 16-bit number. Returns a 16-bit result. All values are signed.
M*	(n1 n2 -- d-prod)	Multiplies two 16-bit numbers. Returns a 32-bit result. All values are signed.
M*/	(d n n -- d-result)	Multiplies a 32-bit number by a 16-bit number and divides the triple-length result by a 16-bit number (d*n/n). Returns a 32-bit result. All values are signed.

---

†**FORTH-79 Standard**

The mixed-length operators are not included in either the Required or the Double Number Word Set.

Here's an example using M+:

```
200,000 7 M+ D. 200007 ok
```

Or, using M*/, we can redefine our earlier version of % so that it will accept a double-length argument:

```
: %   100 M*/ ;
```

as in

```
200.50 15 % D. 3007 ok
```

If you have loaded the definition of .$ which we gave in the last Handy Hint, you can enter

```
200.50 15 % .$ $30.07 ok
```

We can redefine our earlier definition of R% to get a rounded double-length result, like this:

```
: R%   10 M*/  5 M+  10 M/ ;
```

then

```
987.65 15 R% .$ $30.08 ok
```

Notice that M*/ is the only ready-made FORTH word which performs multiplication on a double-length argument. To multiply 200,000 by 3, for instance, we must supply a "1" as a dummy denominator:

```
200,000 3 1 M*/ D. 600000 ok
```

since

$$\frac{3}{1}$$

is the same as 3.

M*/ is also the only ready-made FORTH word that performs division with a double-length result. So to divide 200,000 by 4, for instance, we must supply a "1" as a dummy numerator:

```
200,000 1 4 M*/ D. 50000 ok
```

Numbers in Definitions

When a definition contains a number, such as

```
: SCORE-MORE   20 + ;
```

the number is compiled into the dictionary in binary form, just as it looks on the stack.

The number's binary value depends on the number base at the time you compile the definition. For example, if you were to enter

```
HEX   : SCORE-MORE   14 + ;   DECIMAL
```

the dictionary definition would contain the hex value 14, which is the same as the decimal value 20 (16 + 4). Henceforth, SCORE-MORE will always add the equivalent of decimal 20 to the value on the stack, regardless of the current number base.

If, on the other hand, you were to put the word HEX inside the definition, then you would change the number base when you execute the definition.

For example, if you were to define:

```
DECIMAL
: EXAMPLE   HEX 20 .  DECIMAL ;
```

the number would be compiled as the binary equivalent of decimal 20, since DECIMAL was current at compilation time.

At execution time, here's what happens:

```
EXAMPLE 14 ok
```

The number is output in hexadecimal.

For the record, a number that appears inside a definition is called a "literal." (Unlike the words in the rest of the definition which allude to other definitions, a number must be taken literally.)

Here is a list of the FORTH words we've covered in this chapter:

Unsigned operators

U.	(u --)	Prints the unsigned single-length number, followed by one space.
U*	(u1 u2 -- ud)	Multiplies two 16-bit numbers. Returns a 32-bit result. All values are unsigned.
U/MOD	(ud u1 -- u2 u3)	Divides a 32-bit by a 16-bit number. Returns a 16-bit quotient and remainder. All values are unsigned.
U<	(u1 u2 -- f)	Leaves true if u1 < u2, where both are treated as 16-bit unsigned integers.
DO ... /LOOP	DO: (u-limit u-index --) /LOOP: (u --)	Like DO ... +LOOP except uses an unsigned limit, index, and increment.

Number bases

HEX	(--)	Sets the base to sixteen.
OCTAL	(--)	Sets the base to eight (available on some systems).
DECIMAL	(--)	Returns the base to ten.

Number formatting operators

<#	Begins the number conversion process. Expects an unsigned double-length number on the stack.
#	Converts one digit and puts it into an output character string. # always produces a digit--if you're out of significant digits, you'll still get a zero for every #.

#S	Converts the number until the result is zero. Always produces at least one digit (0 if the value is zero).
c HOLD	Inserts, at the current position in the character string being formatted, a character whose ASCII value is on the stack. HOLD (or a word that uses HOLD) must be used between <# and #>.
SIGN	Inserts a minus sign in the output string if the third number on the stack is negative. Usually used immediately before #> for a leading minus sign.
#>	Completes number conversion by leaving the character count and address on the stack (these are the appropriate arguments for TYPE).

Stack effects for number formatting

phrase	stack	type of arguments
<# ... #>	(d -- adr u) or	32-bit unsigned
	(u 0 -- adr u)	16-bit unsigned
<# ... SIGN #>	(n |d| -- adr u) or	32-bit signed (where n is the high-order cell of d and |d| is the absolute value of d).
	(n |n| 0 -- adr u)	16-bit signed (where |n| is the absolute value).

Double-length operators (Optional in FORTH-79 Standard)

D+	(d1 d2 -- d-sum)	Adds two 32-bit numbers.
D-	(d1 d2 -- d-diff)	Subtracts two 32-bit numbers (d1-d2).
DNEGATE	(d -- -d)	Changes the sign of a 32-bit number.
DABS	(d -- |d|)	Returns the absolute value of a 32-bit number.
DMAX	(d1 d2 -- d-max)	Returns the maximum of two 32-bit numbers.

DMIN	(dl d2 -- d-min)	Returns the minimum of two 32-bit numbers.
D=	(dl d2 -- f)	Returns true if dl and d2 are equal.
D0=	(d -- f)	Returns true if d is zero.
D<	(dl d2 -- f)	Returns true if dl is less than d2.
DU<	(udl ud2 -- f)	Returns true if udl is less than ud2. Both numbers are unsigned.
DU<		Prints the signed 32-bit number, followed by one space.
D.R	(d width --)	Prints the signed 32-bit number, right-justified within the field width.

Mixed-length operators (Not required by FORTH-79 Standard)

M+	(d n -- d-sum)	Adds a 32-bit number to a 16-bit number. Returns a 32-bit result.
M/	(d n -- n-quot)	Divides a 32-bit number by a 16-bit number. Returns a 16-bit result. All values are signed.
M*	(nl n2 -- d-prod)	Multiplies two 16-bit numbers. Returns a 32-bit result. All values are signed.
M*/	(d n n -- d-result)	Multiplies a 32-bit number by a 16-bit number and divides the triple-length result by a 16-bit number (d*n/n). Returns a 32-bit result. All values are

KEY

n, nl ...	16-bit signed numbers	b	8-bit byte
d, dl, ...	32-bit signed numbers	f	Boolean flag
u, ul, ...	16-bit unsigned numbers	c	ASCII character value
ud, udl, ...	32-bit unsigned numbers	adr	address

Review of Terms

Arithmetic left and right shift	the process of shifting all bits in a number, except the sign bit, to the left or right, in effect doubling or halving the number, respectively.
ASCII	a standardized system of representing input/output characters as byte values. Acronym for American Standard Code for Information Interchange. (Pronounced ask-key.)
Binary	number base 2.
Byte	the standard term for an 8-bit value.
Cell	the FORTH term for a 16-bit value.
Decimal	number base 10.
Hexadecimal	number base 16.
Literal	in general, a number or symbol which represents only itself; in FORTH, a number that appears inside a definition.
Mask	a value which can be "superimposed" over another, hiding certain bits and revealing only those bits that we are interested in.
Number formatting	the process of printing a number, usually in a special form such as 3/13/81 or $47.93.
Octal	number base 8.
Sign bit, high-order bit	the bit which, for a signed number, indicates whether it is positive or negative and, for an unsigned number, represents the bit of the highest magnitude.
Two's complement	for any number, the number of equal absolute value but opposite sign. To calculate 10 - 4, the computer first produces the two's complement of 4 (i.e., -4), then computes 10 + (-4).
Unsigned number	a number which is assumed to be positive.

Unsigned single-length number	an integer which falls within the range 0 to 65535.
Word	in FORTH, a defined dictionary entry; elsewhere, a term for a 16-bit value.

Problems -- Chapter 7

FOR BEGINNERS

1. Veronica Wainwright couldn't remember the upper limit for a signed single-length number, and she had no book to refer to, only a FORTH terminal. So she wrote a definition called N-MAX, using a BEGIN...UNTIL loop. When she executed it, she got

   32767 ok

   What was her definition?

2. Since you now know that AND and OR employ bit logic, explain why the following example *must* use OR instead of +:

```
: MATCH   HUMOROUS SENSITIVE AND
     ART-LOVING MUSIC-LOVING OR  AND  SMOKING NOT  AND
        IF ." I HAVE SOMEONE YOU SHOULD MEET "  THEN ;
```

3. Write a definition that "rings" your terminal's bell three times. Make sure that there is enough of a delay between the bells so that they are distinguishable. Each time the bell rings, the word "BEEP" should appear on the terminal screen.

(Problems 4 and 5 are practice in double-length math.)

4. a. Rewrite the temperature conversion definitions which you created for the problems in Chap. 5. This time assume that the input and resulting temperatures are to be double-length signed integers which are scaled (i.e., multiplied) by ten. For example, if 10.5 degrees is entered, it is a 32-bit integer with a value of 105.

   b. Write a formatted output word named .DEG which will display a 32-bit signed integer scaled by ten as a string of digits, a decimal point, and one fractional digit.

   For example:

   12.3 .DEG RETURN 12.3 ok

Problem 4, continued

c. Solve the following conversions:

```
   0.0° F in Centigrade
 212.0° F in Centigrade
  20.5° F in Centigrade
  16.0° C in Fahrenheit
 -40.0° C in Fahrenheit
 100.0° K in Centigrade
 100.0° K in Fahrenheit
 233.0° K in Centigrade
 233.0° K in Fahrenheit
```

5. a. Write a routine which evaluates the quadratic equation

$$7x^2 + 20x + 5$$

given x, and returns a double-length result.

b. How large an x will work without overflowing thirty-two bits as a signed number?

FOR EVERYONE

6. Write a word which prints the numbers 0 through 16 (decimal) in decimal, hexadecimal, and binary form in three columns. E.g.,

```
DECIMAL  0   HEX  0   BINARY     0
DECIMAL  1   HEX  1   BINARY     1
DECIMAL  2   HEX  2   BINARY    10
        ...
DECIMAL 16   HEX 10   BINARY 10000
```

7. If you enter

.. RETURN

(two periods not separated by a space) and the system responds "ok," what does this tell you?

8. Write a definition for a phone-number formatting word that will also print the area code with a slash if and only if the number includes an area code. E.g.,

```
555-1234 .PH# 555-1234 ok
213/372-8493 .PH# 213/372-8493 ok
```

8 VARIABLES, CONSTANTS, AND ARRAYS

As we have seen throughout the previous seven chapters, FORTH programmers use the stack to store numbers temporarily while they perform calculations or to pass arguments from one word to another. When programmers need to store numbers more permanently, they use variables and constants.

In this chapter, we'll learn how FORTH treats variables and constants, and in the process we'll see how to directly access locations in memory.

Variables

Let's start with an example of a situation in which you'd want to use a variable--to store the day's date.† First we'll create a variable called DATE. We do this by saying

```
VARIABLE DATE
```

If today is the twelfth, we now say

```
12 DATE !
```

that is, we put a twelve on the stack, then give the name of the variable, then finally execute the word [!], which is pronounced <u>store</u>. This phrase stores the number twelve into the variable DATE.

Conversely, we can say

---

†For Beginners

Suppose your computer generates bank statements all day, and every statement must show the date. You don't want to keep the date on the stack all the time, and you don't want the date to be part of a definition that you'd have to redefine every day. You want to use a variable.

```
DATE @
```

that is, we can name the variable, then execute the word @, which is pronounced fetch. This phrase fetches the twelve and puts it on the stack. Thus the phrase

```
DATE @ . 12 ok
```

prints the date.

To make matters even easier, there is a FORTH word whose definition is this:

```
: ?  @ . ;
```

So instead of "DATE-fetch-dot," we could simply type

```
DATE ? 12 ok
```

The value of DATE will be twelve until we change it. To change it, we simply store a new number:

```
13 DATE ! ok
DATE ? 13 ok
```

Conceivably we could define additional variables for the month and year:

```
VARIABLE DATE  VARIABLE MONTH  VARIABLE YEAR
```

then define a word called !DATE (for "store-the-date") like this:

```
: !DATE   YEAR !  DATE !  MONTH ! ;
```

to be used like this:

```
7 31 80 !DATE ok
```

then define a word called .DATE (for "print-the-date") like this:

```
: .DATE   MONTH ?  DATE ?  YEAR ? ;
```

Your FORTH system already has a number of variables defined; one is called BASE. BASE contains the number base that you're currently working in. In fact, the definitions of HEX and DECIMAL (and OCTAL, if your system has it) are simply

```
: DECIMAL   10 BASE ! ;
: HEX   16 BASE ! ;
: OCTAL   8 BASE ! ;
```

You can work in any number base by simply storing it into [BASE].†

Somewhere in the definitions of the system words which perform input and output number conversions, you will find the phrase

```
BASE @
```

because the current value of [BASE] is used in the conversion process. Thus a single routine can convert numbers in <u>any</u> base. This leads us to make a formal statement about the use of variables:

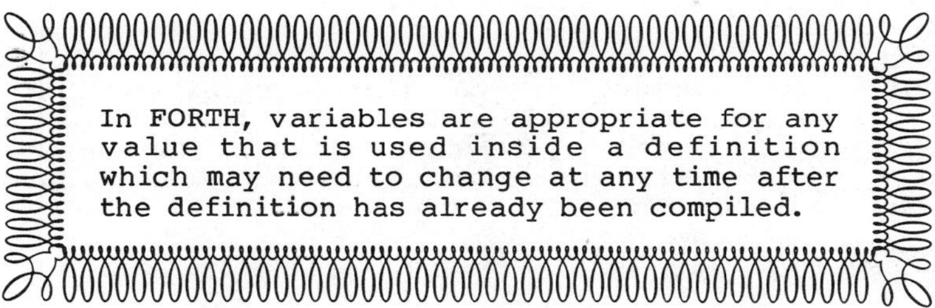

In FORTH, variables are appropriate for any value that is used inside a definition which may need to change at any time after the definition has already been compiled.

A Closer Look at Variables

When you create a variable such as DATE by using the phrase

```
VARIABLE DATE
```

you are really compiling a new word, called DATE, into the dictionary. A simplified view would look like this:

---

†**For Experts**

A three-letter code such as an airport terminal name, can be stored as a single-length unsigned number in base 36. For example:

```
: ALPHA   36 BASE ! ; ok
ALPHA ok
ZAP U. ZAP ok
```

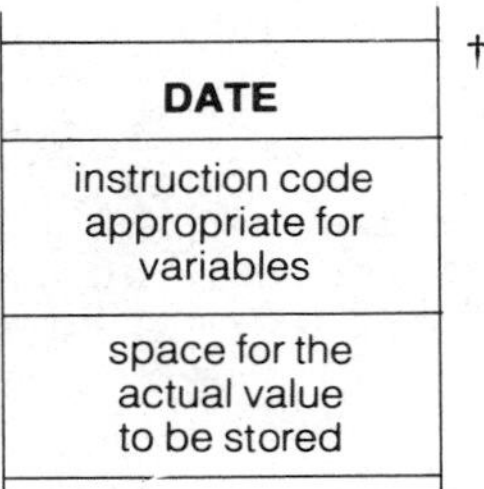

DATE is like any other word in your dictionary except that you defined it with the word VARIABLE instead of the word :. As a result, you didn't have to define what your definition would do; the word VARIABLE itself spells out what is supposed to happen. And here is what happens:

When you say

```
12 DATE !
```

Twelve goes onto the stack, then the text interpreter looks up DATE in the dictionary and, finding it, points it out to EXECUTE.

---

†For Experts

In the next chapter we'll show you what a dictionary entry really looks like in memory.

EXECUTE executes a variable by copying the address of the variable's "empty" cell (where the value will go) onto the stack.†

The word ! takes the address (on top) and the value (underneath), and stores the value into that location. Whatever number used to be at that address is replaced by the new number.

(To remember what order the arguments belong in, think of setting down your parcel, then sticking the address label on top.)

---

†**For Beginners**

In computer terminology, an address is a number which identifies a location in computer memory. For example, at address 2076 (addresses are usually expressed as hexadecimal, unsigned numbers), we can have a 16-bit representation of the value 12. Here 2076 is the "address"; 12 is the "contents."

The word @ expects one argument only: an address, which in this case is supplied by the name of the variable, as in

```
DATE @
```

Using the value on the stack as an address, the word @ pushes the contents of that location onto the stack, "dropping" the address. (The contents of the location remain intact.)

Using a Variable as a Counter

In FORTH, a variable is ideal for keeping a count of something. To reuse our egg-packer example, we might keep track of how many eggs go down the conveyor belt in a single day. (This example will work at your terminal, so enter it as we go.)

First we can define

```
VARIABLE EGGS
```

to keep the count in. To start with a clean slate every morning, we would store a zero into EGGS by executing a word whose definition looks like this:

```
: RESET   0 EGGS ! ;
```

Then somewhere in our egg-packing application, we would define a word which executes the following phrase every time an egg passes an electric eye on the conveyor:

```
1 EGGS +!
```

The word [+!] adds the given value to the contents of the given address.† (It doesn't bother to tell you what the contents are.) Thus the phrase

```
1 EGGS +!
```

increments the count of eggs by one. For purposes of illustration, let's put this phrase inside a definition like this:

```
: EGG   1 EGGS +! ;
```

At the end of the day, we would say

```
EGGS ?
```

to find out how many eggs went by since morning.

Let's try it:

```
RESET ok
EGG ok
EGG ok
EGG ok
EGGS ? 3 ok
```

Here's a review of the words we've covered in the chapter so far:

---

†For the Curious

[+!] is usually defined in assembly language, but an equivalent high-level definition is

```
: +!   DUP @ ROT  + SWAP ! ;
```

VARIABLE xxx	(--) xxx: (-- adr)	Creates a variable named xxx; the word xxx returns its address when executed.	variable
!	(n adr --)	Stores a 16-bit number into the address.	store
@	(adr -- n)	Replaces the address with its contents.	fetch
?	(adr --)	Prints the contents of the address, followed by one space.	question
+!	(n adr --)	Adds a 16-bit number to the contents of the address.	plus-store

Constants

While variables are normally used for values that may change, constants are used for values that won't change. In FORTH, we create a constant and set its value at the same time, like this:

```
220 CONSTANT LIMIT
```

LIMIT
instruction code appropriate for constants
220

Here we have defined a constant named LIMIT, and given it the value 220. Now we can use the word LIMIT in place of the value, like this:

```
: ?TOO.HOT   LIMIT > IF ." DANGER -- REDUCE HEAT " THEN ;
```

If the number on the stack is greater than 220, then the warning message will be printed.

Notice that when we say

```
LIMIT
```

we get the value, not the address. We don't need the "fetch."

This is an important difference between variables and constants.† The reason for the difference is that with variables, we need the address to have the option of fetching or storing. With constants, we always want the value; we almost never store.

One use for constants is to name a hardware address. For example, a microprocessor-controlled camera application might contain this definition:

```
: PHOTOGRAPH   SHUTTER OPEN  TIME EXPOSE  SHUTTER CLOSE ;
```

Here the word SHUTTER has been defined as a constant so that execution of SHUTTER returns the hardware address of the camera's shutter. It might, for example, be defined:

```
HEX
3E27 CONSTANT SHUTTER
DECIMAL
```

The words OPEN and CLOSE might be defined simply as

```
: OPEN    1 SWAP ! ;
: CLOSE   0 SWAP ! ;
```

so that the phrase

```
SHUTTER OPEN
```

writes a "1" to the shutter address, causing the shutter to open.

Here are some situations when it's good to define numbers as constants:

1. When it's important that you make your application more readable. One of the elements of FORTH style is that definitions should be self-documenting, as is the definition of PHOTOGRAPH above.

---

†For People Who Intend to Use polyFORTH's Target Compiler T.M.

In your case the difference is more profound. A constant's <u>value</u> will be compiled into PROM; a variable compiles into PROM a reference to a location in RAM.

2. When it's more convenient to use a name instead of the number. For example, if you think you may have to change the value (because, for instance, the hardware might get changed) you will only have to change the value once--in the block where the constant is defined--then recompile your application.

3. When you are using the same value many times in your application. In the compiled form of a definition, reference to a constant requires less memory space.†

CONSTANT xxx	(n --) xxx: (-- n)	Creates a constant named xxx with the value n; the word xxx returns n when executed.

---

†For polyFORTH Users

Because of reason 3, polyFORTH includes constant-definitions of two often-used numbers:

```
0 CONSTANT 0
1 CONSTANT 1
```

Double-length Variables and Constants†

You can define a double-length variable by using the word 2VARIABLE. For example,

```
2VARIABLE DATE
```

Now you can use the FORTH words 2! (pronounced two-store) and 2@ (two-fetch) to access this double-length variable. You can store a double-length number into it by simply saying

```
800,000 DATE 2!
```

and fetch it back with

```
DATE 2@ D. 800000 ok
```

Or you can store the full month/date/year into it, like this:

```
7/16/81 DATE 2!
```

and fetch it back with

```
DATE 2@ .DATE 7/16/81 ok
```

assuming that you've loaded the version of .DATE we gave in the last chapter.‡

You can define a double-length constant by using the FORTH word 2CONSTANT, like this:

```
200,000 2CONSTANT APPLES
```

Now the word APPLES will place the double-length number on the stack.

```
APPLES D. 200000 ok
```

---

†FORTH-79 Standard

The words described in this section are not required except in the Double Number Word Set.

‡For polyFORTH Users

polyFORTH uses an even-more-clever arrangement to store the date as one single-length integer.

Use of 2CONSTANT becomes necessary when you need to include a double-length value inside a definition. In FORTH the only way to do this is by first defining the double-length value as a 2CONSTANT. For example, to define a word which adds 400,000 to a double-length value on the stack, we must define

```
400,000 2CONSTANT MUCH
: MUCH-MORE   MUCH D+ ;
```

in order to be able to say

```
APPLES MUCH-MORE D. 600000 ok †
```

As the prefix "2" reminds us, we can also use 2CONSTANT to define a pair of single-length numbers. The reason for putting two numbers under the same name is a matter of convenience and of saving space in the dictionary.

As an example, recall (from Chap. 5) that we can use the phrase

```
355 113 */
```

to multiply a number by an approximation of pi. We could store these two integers as a 2CONSTANT as follows:

```
355 113 2CONSTANT PI
```

then simply use the phrase

```
PI */
```

as in

```
10000 PI */ . 31415 ok
```

Here is a review of the double-length data-structure words:

---

† For polyFORTH Users

polyFORTH includes the following definition for a double-length zero for convenient use inside a colon definition:

```
0. 2CONSTANT 0.
```

2VARIABLE xxx	(--)	Creates a double-length variable named xxx;	two-variable
	xxx: (-- adr)	the word xxx returns its address when executed.	
2CONSTANT xxx	(d --)	Creates a double-length constant named xxx with the value d;	two-constant
	xxx: (-- d)	the word xxx returns the value d when executed.	
2!	(d adr --)	Stores a double-length number into the address.	two-store
2@	(adr -- d)	Returns the double-length contents of the address.	two-fetch

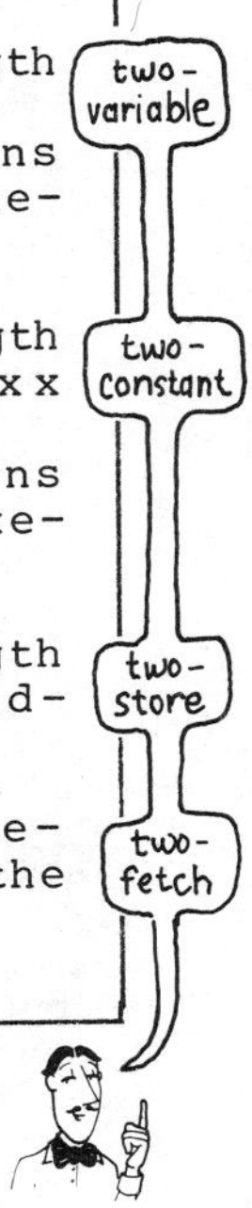

Arrays

As you know, the phrase

```
VARIABLE DATE
```

creates a definition which conceptually looks like this:

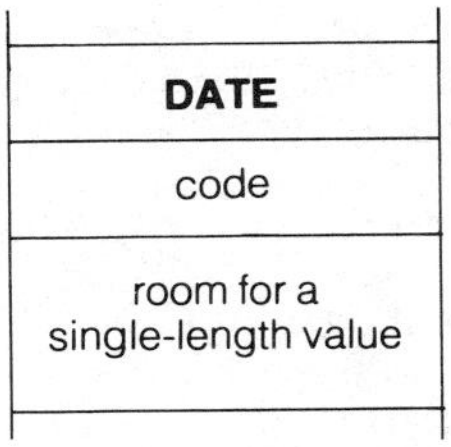

DATE
code
room for a single-length value

Now if you say

```
2 ALLOT
```

an additional two bytes are allotted in the definition, like this:

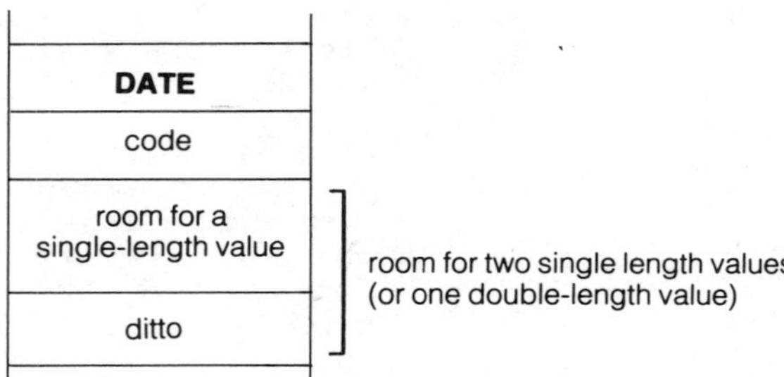

The result is the same as if you had used 2VARIABLE. By changing the argument to ALLOT, however, you can define any number of variables under the same name. Such a group of variables is called an "array."

For example, let's say that in our laboratory, we have not just one, but five burners that heat various kinds of liquids.

We can make our word ?TOO-HOT check that all five burners have not exceeded their individual limit if we define LIMIT using an array rather than a constant.

Let's give the array the name LIMITS, like this:

```
VARIABLE LIMITS  8 ALLOT
```

The phrase "8 ALLOT" gives the array an extra eight bytes or four cells (five cells in all).

LIMITS	addresses
code	↓
room for burner-0's limit	3162
room for burner-1's limit	3164
room for burner-2's limit	3166
room for burner-3's limit	3168
room for burner-4's limit	316A

Suppose we want the limit for burner 0 to be 220. We can store this value by simply saying

```
220 LIMITS !
```

because LIMITS returns the address of the first cell in the array. Suppose we want the limit for burner 1 to be 340. We can store this value by adding 2 bytes to the address of the original cell, like this:

```
340 LIMITS 2+ !
```

We can store limits for burners 2, 3, and 4 by adding the "offsets" 4, 6, and 8, respectively, to the original address. Since the offset is always double the burner number, we can define the convenient word

```
: LIMIT   2* LIMITS + ;
```

to take a burner number on the stack and compute an address that reflects the appropriate offset.†

Now if we want the value 170 to be the limit for burner 2, we simply say

```
170 2 LIMIT !
```

or similarly, we can fetch the limit for burner 2 with the phrase

```
2 LIMIT ? 170 ok
```

This technique increases the usefulness of the word LIMIT, so that we can redefine ?TOO.HOT as follows:

```
: ?TOO.HOT   ( burner# temp -- )
    LIMIT @ >  IF ." DANGER -- REDUCE HEAT " THEN ;
```

which works like this:

```
210 0 ?TOO.HOT ok
230 0 ?TOO.HOT DANGER -- REDUCE HEAT ok
300 1 ?TOO.HOT ok
350 1 ?TOO.HOT DANGER -- REDUCE HEAT ok

etc.
```

---

†For Beginners

a) Some people call the "offset" an "index," and some people say that one uses an offset to "index into" an array.

b) The reason we number our burners 0 through 4 instead of 1 through 5 is so that we can use the burner number itself (doubled for byte addressing) as the offset.

   A thing which most people would call the "first" in a series, programmers think of as the "zeroth." Still, if you need to call the burner on the left "burner 1," you can simply change LIMIT to say

```
: LIMIT   1- 2* LIMITS + ;
```

Another Example -- Using an Array for Counting

Meanwhile, back at the egg ranch:

Here's another example of an array. In this example, each element of the array is used as a separate counter. Thus we can keep track of how many cartons of "extra large" eggs the machine has packed, how many "large," and so forth.

Recall from our previous definition of EGGSIZE (in Chap. 4) that we used four categories of acceptable eggs, plus two categories of "bad eggs."

```
0 REJECT
1 SMALL
2 MEDIUM
3 LARGE
4 EXTRA LARGE
5 ERROR
```

So let's create an array that is six cells long:

```
VARIABLE COUNTS  10 ALLOT
```

The counts will be incremented using the word +!, so we must be able to set all the elements in the array to zero before we begin counting. The phrase

```
COUNTS 12 0 FILL
```

will fill twelve bytes, starting at the address of COUNTS, with zeros. If your FORTH system includes the word ERASE,† it's better to use it in this situation. ERASE fills the given number of bytes with zeroes. Use it like this:

```
COUNTS 12 ERASE
```

FILL	(adr n b --)	Fills n bytes of memory, beginning at the address, with value b.
ERASE	(adr n --)	Fills n bytes of memory, beginning at the address, with zeroes.

---

† FORTH-79 Standard

ERASE is included in the optional Reference Word Set.

For convenience, we can put the phrase inside a definition, like this:

```
: RESET   COUNTS  12 ERASE ;
```

Now let's define a word which will give us the address of one of the counters, depending on the category number it is given (0 through 5), like this:

```
: COUNTER   2*  COUNTS + ;
```

and another word which will add one to the counter whose number is given, like this:

```
: TALLY   COUNTER  1 SWAP +! ;
```

The "1" serves as the increment for +!, and SWAP puts the arguments for +! in the order they belong, i.e., (n adr --).

Now, for instance, the phrase

```
3 TALLY
```

will increment the counter that corresponds to large eggs.

Now let's define a word which converts the weight per dozen into a category number:

```
: CATEGORY   DUP 18 < IF 0 ELSE
             DUP 21 < IF 1 ELSE
             DUP 24 < IF 2 ELSE
             DUP 27 < IF 3 ELSE
             DUP 30 < IF 4 ELSE
                         5
          THEN THEN THEN THEN THEN  SWAP DROP ;†
```

(By the time we get to the phrase "SWAP DROP," we will have two values on the stack: the weight which we have been DUPing and the category number, which will be on top. We want only the category number; "SWAP DROP" eliminates the weight.)

---

† For Experts

We'll see a simpler definition at the end of this chapter.

For instance, the phrase

```
25 CATEGORY
```

will leave the number 3 on the stack. The above definition of CATEGORY resembles our old definition of EGGSIZE, but, in the true FORTH style of keeping words as short as possible, we have removed the output messages from the definition. Instead, we'll define an additional word which expects a category number and prints an output message, like this:

```
: LABEL   DUP  0= IF ." REJECT "        ELSE
          DUP 1 = IF ." SMALL "         ELSE
          DUP 2 = IF ." MEDIUM "        ELSE
          DUP 3 = IF ." LARGE "         ELSE
          DUP 4 = IF ." EXTRA LARGE "   ELSE
                     ." ERROR "
          THEN THEN THEN THEN THEN DROP ; †
```

For example:

```
1 LABEL SMALL ok
```

Now we can define EGGSIZE using three of our own words:

```
: EGGSIZE   CATEGORY  DUP LABEL  TALLY ;
```

Thus the phrase

```
23 EGGSIZE
```

will print

```
MEDIUM ok
```

at your terminal and update the counter for medium eggs.

How will we read the counters at the end of the day? We could check each cell in the array separately with a phrase such as

```
3 COUNTER ?
```

(which would tell us how many "large" cartons were packed). But let's get a little fancier and define our own word to print a table of the day's results in this format:

---

†**For Experts**

We'll see a more elegant version of this definition in the next chapter.

QUANTITY	SIZE
1	REJECT
112	SMALL
132	MEDIUM
143	LARGE
159	EXTRA LARGE
0	ERROR

Since we have already devised category numbers, we can simply use a DO loop and index on the category number, like this:

```
: REPORT   PAGE   ." QUANTITY     SIZE"  CR CR
     6 0 DO  I COUNTER  @  5 U.R
                7 SPACES  I LABEL CR        LOOP ;
```

(The phrase

```
I COUNTER @  5 U.R
```

takes the category number given by I, indexes into the array, and prints the contents of the proper element in a five-column field.)

Factoring Definitions

This is a good time to talk about factoring as it applies to FORTH definitions. We've just seen an example in which factoring simplified our problem.

Our first definition of EGGSIZE, from Chap. 4, categorized eggs by weight and printed the name of the categories at the terminal. In our present version we factored out the "categorizing" and the "printing" into two separate words. We can use the word CATEGORY to provide the argument either for the printing word or the counter-tallying word (or both). And we can use the printing word, LABEL, in both EGGSIZE and REPORT.

As Charles Moore, the inventor of FORTH, has written:

> A good FORTH vocabulary contains a large number of small words. It is not enough to break a problem into small pieces. The object is to isolate words that can be reused.

For example, in the recipe:

Get can of tomato sauce.
Open can of tomato sauce.
Pour tomato sauce into pan.
Get can of mushrooms.
Open can of mushrooms.
Pour mushrooms into pan.

you can "factor out" the getting, opening, and pouring, since they are common to both cans. Then you can give the factored-out process a name and simply write:

```
TOMATOES ADD
MUSHROOMS ADD
```

and any chef who's graduated from the Postfix School of Cookery will know exactly what you mean.

Not only does factoring make a program easier to write (and fix!), it saves memory space, too. A reusable word such as ADD gets defined only once. The more complicated the application, the greater the savings.

Here's another thought about FORTH style before we leave the egg ranch. Recall our definition of EGGSIZE

```
: EGGSIZE   CATEGORY DUP LABEL  TALLY ;
```

CATEGORY gave us a value which we wanted to pass on to both LABEL and TALLY, so we include the DUP. To make the definition "cleaner," we might have been tempted to take the DUP out and put it inside the definition of LABEL, at the beginning. Thus we might have written

```
: EGGSIZE   CATEGORY LABEL  TALLY ;
```

where CATEGORY passes the value to LABEL, and LABEL passes it on to TALLY. Certainly this approach would have worked. But then, when we defined REPORT, we would have had to say

```
I LABEL DROP
```

instead of simply

```
I LABEL
```

FORTH programmers tend to follow this convention: when possible, words should destroy their own parameters. In general, it's better to put the DUP inside the "calling definition" (EGGSIZE, here) than in the "called" definition (LABEL, here).

Another Example -- "Looping" through an Array

We'd like to introduce a little technique that is relevant to arrays. We can best illustrate this technique by writing our own definition of a FORTH word called DUMP.† DUMP is used to print out the contents of a series of memory addresses. The usage is

```
adr count DUMP
```

For instance, we could enter

```
COUNTS 12 DUMP
```

to print out the contents of our egg-counting array called COUNTS. Since DUMP is primarily designed as a programming tool to print out the contents of memory locations, it prints either byte-by-byte or cell-by-cell, depending on the type of addressing the computer uses. Our version of DUMP will print cell-by-cell.

Obviously our DUMP will involve a DO loop. The question is: what should we use for an index? Although we might use the count itself (0 - 6) as the loop index, it's better to use the address as the index.

The address of COUNTS will be the starting index for the loop, while the address plus the count will serve as the limit, like this:

```
: DUMP   OVER + SWAP  DO CR I @  5 U.R  2 /LOOP ; ‡
```

The key phrase here is

```
OVER + SWAP
```

which immediately precedes the DO.

---

†FORTH-79 Standard

The Standard does not require DUMP.

‡For Those Whose Systems Do Not Have /LOOP

Substitute +LOOP.

The ending and starting addresses are now on the stack, ready to serve as the limit and index for the DO loop. Since we are "indexing on the addresses," once we are inside the loop we merely have to say

```
I @  5 U.R
```

to print the contents of each element in the array. Since we are examining bytes in pairs (because @ fetches a 16-bit value), we increment the index by two each time, by using

```
2 /LOOP
```

Byte Arrays

FORTH lets you create an array in which each element consists of a single byte rather than a full cell. This is useful any time you are storing a series of numbers whose range fits into that which can be expressed within eight bits.

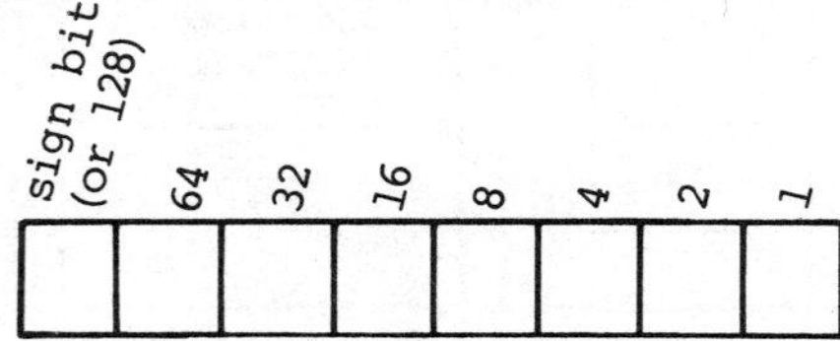

The range of an unsigned 8-bit number is 0 to 255. Byte arrays are also used to store ASCII character strings. The benefit of using a byte array instead of a cell array is that you can get the same amount of data in half the memory space.

The mechanics of using a byte array are the same as using a cell array except that

1. you don't have to double the offset, since each element corresponds to one address, and

2. you must use the words C! and C@ instead of ! and @. These words, which operate on byte values only, have been given the prefix "C" because their typical use is accessing ASCII characters.

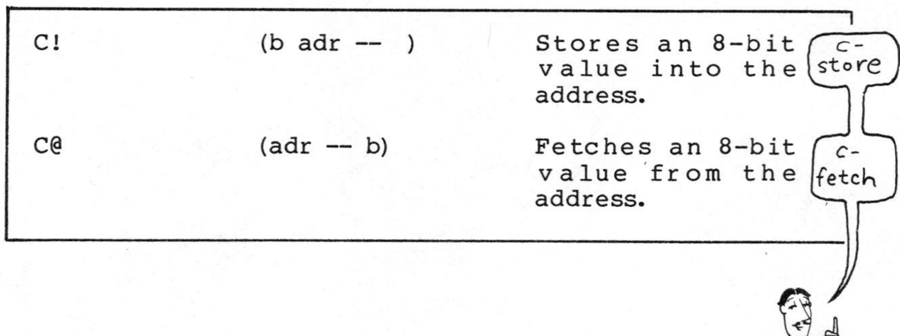

C!	(b adr --)	Stores an 8-bit value into the address.
C@	(adr -- b)	Fetches an 8-bit value from the address.

Initializing an Array

Many situations call for an array whose values never change during the operation of the application and which may as well be stored into the array at the same time that the array is created, just as CONSTANTs are. FORTH provides the means to accomplish this through the two words CREATE and , (pronounced create and comma).

Suppose we want permanent values in our LIMITS array. Instead of saying

```
VARIABLE LIMITS  8 ALLOT
```

we can say

```
CREATE LIMITS 220 ,  340 ,  170 ,  100 ,  190 ,
```

Usually the above line would be loaded from a disk block, but it also works interactively.

Like the word VARIABLE, CREATE puts a new name in the dictionary at compile time and returns the address of that definition when it is executed. But it does not "allot" any bytes for a value.

The word , takes a number off the stack and stores it into the array. So each time you express a number and follow it with ,, you add one cell to the array.†

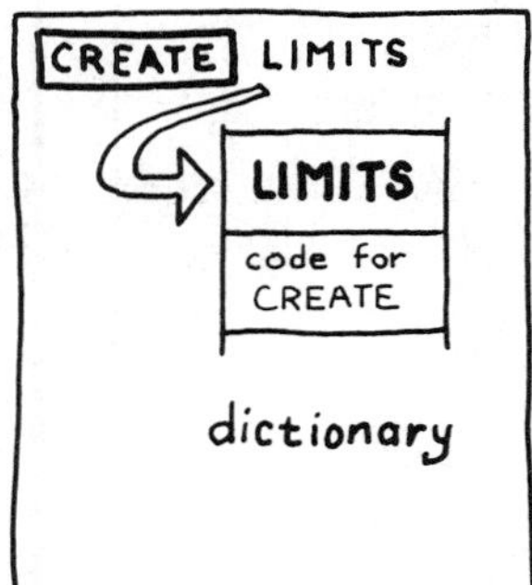

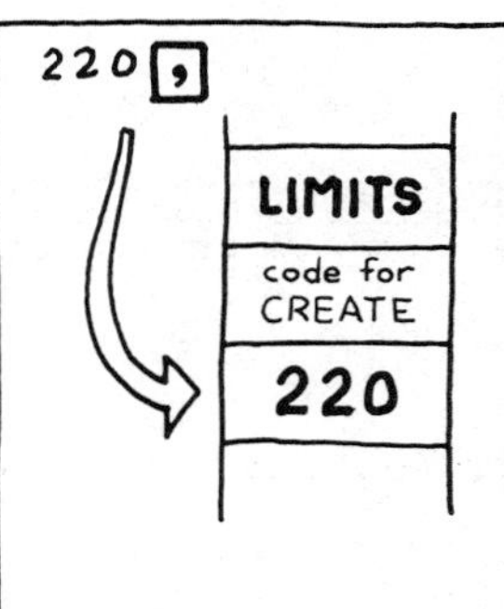

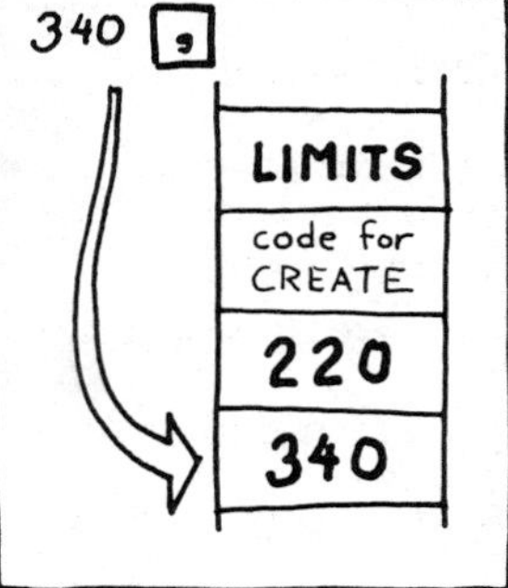

---

† **For Newcomers**

Ingrained habits, learned from English writing, lead some newcomers to forget to type the final , in the line. Remember that , does not separate the numbers, it compiles them.

You can access the elements in a CREATE array just as you would the elements in a VARIABLE array. For example:

```
LIMITS 2+ @ 340 ok
```

You can even store new values into the array, just as you would into a VARIABLE array, as long as you don't do this in an application that you someday hope to target compile.†

To initialize a byte-array that has been defined with CREATE, you can use the word C, (c-comma).‡ For instance, we could store each of the values used in our egg-sorting definition CATEGORY as follows:

```
CREATE SIZES   18 C,  21 C,  24 C,  27 C,  30 C,  255 C,
```

This would allow us to redefine CATEGORY using a DO loop rather than a series of nested IF...THEN statements, as follows‡

```
: CATEGORY   6 0 DO  DUP  SIZES I + C@
     < IF  DROP  I  LEAVE  THEN  LOOP ;
```

Note that we have added a maximum (255) to the array to simplify our definition regarding category 5.

Including the initialization of the SIZES array, this version takes only three lines of source text as opposed to six and takes less space in the dictionary, too.

---

†For People Who Intend to Use polyFORTH's Target Compiler

In a target-compiled application, VARIABLE arrays will reside in RAM; tables defined by CREATE and initialized by , or C, will reside, fixed, in PROM.

‡FORTH-79 Standard

C, is included in the optional Reference Word Set.

‡For People Who Don't Like Guessing How It Works

The idea here is this: since there are five possible categories, we can use the category numbers as our loop index. Each time around, we compare the number on the stack against the element in SIZES, offset by the current loop index. As soon as the weight on the stack is greater than one of the elements in the array, we leave the loop and use I to tell us how many times we had looped before we "left." Since this number is our offset into the array, it will also be our category number.

Here is a list of the FORTH words we've covered in this chapter:

CONSTANT xxx	(n --) xxx: (-- n)	Creates a constant named xxx with the value n; the word xxx returns n when executed.
VARIABLE xxx	(--) xxx: (-- adr)	Creates a variable named xxx; the word xxx returns its address when executed.
CREATE xxx	(--) xxx: (-- adr)	Creates a dictionary entry (head and code pointer only) named xxx; the word xxx returns its address when executed.
!	(n adr --)	Stores a 16-bit number into the address.
@	(adr -- n)	Replaces the address with its contents.
?	(adr --)	Prints the contents of the address, followed by one space.
+!	(n adr --)	Adds a 16-bit number to the contents of the address.
ALLOT	(n --)	Adds n bytes to the parameter field of the most recently defined word.
,	(n --)	Compiles n into the next available cell in the dictionary.
C!	(b adr --)	Stores an 8-bit value into the address.
C@	(adr -- b)	Fetches an 8-bit value from the address.
FILL	(adr n b --)	Fills n bytes of memory, beginning at the address, with value b.
BASE	(n --)	A variable which contains the value of the number base being used by the system.

Double-length Operators (Optional in FORTH-79 Standard)

2VARIABLE xxx	(--)	Creates a double-length variable named xxx;
	xxx: (-- adr)	the word xxx returns its address when executed.
2CONSTANT xxx	(d --)	Creates a double-length constant named xxx with the value d;
	xxx: (-- d)	the word xxx returns the value d when executed.
2!	(d adr --)	Stores a double-length number into the address.
2@	(adr -- d)	Returns the double-length contents of the address.

Words Included in the FORTH-79 Standard Reference Word Set

C,	(b --)	Compiles b into the next available byte in the dictionary.
DUMP	(adr u --)	Displays u bytes of memory, starting at the address.
ERASE	(adr n --)	Stores zeroes into n bytes of memory, beginning at adr.

Additional Words Available in Some Systems

0	(-- 0)	Returns the constant zero.
1	(-- 1)	Returns the constant one.
0.	(-- 0 0)	Returns the double-length constant zero.

KEY

n, n1 ...	16-bit signed numbers	b	8-bit byte
d, d1, ...	32-bit signed numbers	f	Boolean flag
u, u1, ...	16-bit unsigned numbers	c	ASCII character value
ud, ud1, ...	32-bit unsigned numbers	adr	address

Review of Terms

Array	a series of memory locations with a single name. Values can be stored and fetched into the individual locations by giving the name of the array and adding an offset to its address.
Constant	a value which has a name. The value is stored in memory and usually never changes.
Factoring	as it applies to programming in FORTH, simplifying a large job by extracting those elements which might be reused and defining those elements as operations.
Fetch	to retrieve a value from a given memory location.
Initialize	to give a variable (or array) its initial value(s) before the rest of the program begins.
Offset	a number which can be added to the address of the beginning of an array to produce the address of the desired location within the array.
Store	to place a value in a given memory location.
Variable	a location in memory which has a name and in which values are frequently stored and fetched.

Problems -- Chapter 8

1. a) Write two words called BAKE-PIE and EAT-PIE. The first word increases the number of available PIES by one. The second decreases the number by one and thanks you for the pie. But if there are no pies, it types "What pie?" (Make sure you start out with no pies.)

```
EAT-PIE WHAT PIE?
BAKE-PIE ok
EAT-PIE THANK YOU! ok
```

   b) Write a word called FREEZE-PIES which takes all the available pies and adds them to the number of pies in the freezer. Remember that frozen pies cannot be eaten.

```
BAKE-PIE BAKE-PIE FREEZE-PIES ok
PIES ? 0 ok
FROZEN-PIES ? 2 ok
```

2. Define a word called .BASE which prints the current value of the variable BASE in decimal. Test it by first changing BASE to some value other than ten. (This one's trickier than it may seem.)

```
DECIMAL .BASE 10 ok
HEX .BASE 16 ok
```

3. Define a number-formatting word called M. which prints a double-length number with a decimal point. The position of the decimal point within the number is movable and depends on the value of a variable that you will define as PLACES. For example, if you store a "1" into PLACES, you will get

```
200,000 M. 20000.0 ok
```

that is, with the decimal point one place from the right. A zero in PLACES should produce no decimal point at all.

4. In order to keep track of the inventory of colored pencils in your office, create an array, each cell of which contains the count of a different colored pencil. Define a set of words so that, for example, the phrase

   ```
   RED PENCILS
   ```

   returns the address of the cell that contains the count of red pencils, etc. Then set these variables to indicate the following counts:

   ```
   23 red pencils
   15 blue pencils
   12 green pencils
    0 orange pencils
   ```

5. A histogram is a graphic representation of a series of values. Each value is shown by the height or length of a bar. In this exercise you will create an array of values and print a histogram which displays a line of "*"s for each value. First create an array with about ten cells. Initialize each element of the array with a value in the range of zero to seventy. Then define a word PLOT which will print a line for each value. On each line print the number of the cell followed by a number of "*"s equal to the contents of that cell.

   For example, if the array has four cells and contains the values 1, 2, 3, and 4, then PLOT would produce:

   ```
   1 *
   2 **
   3 ***
   4 ****
   ```

6. Create an application that displays a tic-tac-toe board, so that two human players can make their moves by entering them from the keyboard. For example, the phrase

   ```
   4 X!
   ```

   puts an "X" in box 4 (counting starts with 1) and produces this display:

   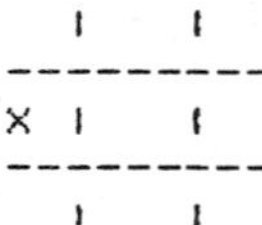

   Then the phrase

   ```
   3 O!
   ```

   puts an "O" in box 3 and prints the display:

   ```
      |   | O
   ---------
    X |   |
   ---------
      |   |
   ```

   Use a byte array to remember the contents of the board, with the value 1 to signify an "X," a -1 to signify a "O," and a 0 to signify an empty box.

   (NOTE: until we explain more about vocabularies, avoid naming anything "X," since this may conflict with the editor's [X].)

9 UNDER THE HOOD

Let's stop for a chapter to lift FORTH's hood and see what goes on inside.

Some of the information contained herein we've given earlier, but, at the risk of redundancy, we're now going to view the FORTH "machine" as a whole, to see how it all fits together.

Inside INTERPRET

Back in the first chapter we learned that the text interpreter, whose name is INTERPRET, picks words out of the input stream and tries to find their definitions in the dictionary. If it finds a word, INTERPRET has it executed.

We can perform these separate operations ourselves by using words that perform the component functions of INTERPRET. For instance, the word ' (an apostrophe, but pronounced *tick*) finds a definition in the dictionary and returns its *address*. If we have defined GREET as we did in Chap. 1, we can now say

```
' GREET U. 25520 ok
```

and discover the address of GREET (whatever it happens to be).

We may also directly use EXECUTE. EXECUTE will execute a definition, given its address on the stack. Thus we can say

    ' GREET EXECUTE HELLO I SPEAK FORTH ok

and accomplish the same thing as if we had merely said GREET, only in a more roundabout way.

If tick cannot find a word in the dictionary, it executes ABORT" and prints a question mark.

FORTH's text interpreter uses a word related to tick that returns a zero flag if the word is found. The name and usage of the word varies,†‡ but the conditional structure of the INTERPRET phrase always looks like this:

```
(find the word)    IF    (convert to a number)
                   ELSE  (execute the word)
                   THEN
```

that is, if the string is not a defined word in the dictionary, INTERPRET tries to convert it as a number. If it is a defined word, INTERPRET executes it.

The word ' has several uses. For instance, you can use the phrase

    ' GREET .

to find out whether GREET has been defined, without actually having to execute it (it will either print the address or respond "?"). In systems that only save the first three characters of a name, you can also use the above phrase to determine whether a name that you want to give to a new definition will conflict with a predefined name.

---

†FORTH-79 Standard

The word FIND attempts to find the next word in the input stream in the dictionary and then returns its address or, if not found, a zero.

‡For polyFORTH Users

The word -' attempts to find the next word in the input stream in the dictionary. If the search is successful, -' leaves the parameter field address and false; if unsuccessful, leaves HERE and true.

You can also use the address to DUMP the contents of the definition, like this:

```
' GREET 12 DUMP
```

Or you can change the value of a constant by first finding its address, then storing the new value into it, like this:

```
110 ' LIMIT !
```

Or you can use tick to implement something called "vectored execution." Which brings us to the next section ...

Vectored Execution

While it *sounds* hairy, the idea of vectored execution is really quite simple. Instead of executing a definition *directly*, as we did with the phrase

```
' GREET EXECUTE
```

we can execute it *indirectly* by keeping its address in a variable, then executing the contents of the variable, like this:

```
' GREET POINTER !
POINTER @ EXECUTE
```

The advantage is that we can change the pointer later, so that a single word can be made to perform different things at different times.

Here is an example that you can try yourself:

```
1 : HELLO    ." HELLO " ;
2 : GOODBYE    ." GOODBYE " ;
3 VARIABLE 'ALOHA
4 : ALOHA    'ALOHA @ EXECUTE ;
5
6 ' HELLO  'ALOHA !
```

In the first two lines, we've simply created words which print the strings "HELLO" and "GOODBYE." In line 3, we've defined a variable called 'ALOHA. This will be our pointer. In line 4, we've defined the word ALOHA to execute the definition whose address is in 'ALOHA. In line 6, we store the address of HELLO into 'ALOHA.

Now if we execute ALOHA, we will get

```
ALOHA HELLO ok
```

Alternatively, if we execute the phrase

```
' GOODBYE 'ALOHA !
```

to store the address of GOODBYE into 'ALOHA, we will get

```
ALOHA GOODBYE ok
```

Thus the same word, ALOHA, can do two different things.

Notice that we named our pointer 'ALOHA (which we would pronounce tick-aloha). Since tick provides an address, we use it as a prefix to suggest "the address of" ALOHA. It is a FORTH naming convention to use this prefix for vectored execution pointers.

Tick always goes to the next word in the input stream.† What if we put tick inside a definition? When we execute the definition, tick will find the next word in the input stream, not the next word in the definition. Thus we could define

```
: SAY   '  'ALOHA ! ;
```

then enter

```
SAY HELLO ok
ALOHA HELLO ok
```

or

```
SAY GOODBYE ok
ALOHA GOODBYE ok
```

to store the address of either HELLO or GOODBYE into 'ALOHA.

But what if we want tick to use the next word in the definition?‡ We must use the word ['] (bracket-tick-bracket) instead of tick. For example:

```
: COMING   ['] HELLO  'ALOHA ! ;
: GOING   ['] GOODBYE 'ALOHA ! ;
```

---

†FORTH-79 Standard

The behavior of tick as described by the Standard differs somewhat from that explained here. See Appendix 3.

‡For Some Small-system, Non-polyFORTH, Users

If your keyboard doesn't have a "[" or "]" key, the documentation that came with your FORTH system should indicate substitutes.

Now we can say

```
COMING ok
ALOHA HELLO ok
GOING ok
ALOHA GOODBYE ok
```

Here's an example of vectored execution that can be found on certain FORTH systems. When FORTH is first loaded, the word NUMBER can only convert single-length numbers. But after double-length routines are loaded, NUMBER can convert double-length or single-length numbers. It would not be enough to simply redefine NUMBER, because then you would also have to redefine INTERPRET and any other word which uses NUMBER. Instead, the definition of NUMBER is something like

```
: NUMBER   'NUMBER @ EXECUTE ;
```

where 'NUMBER is the variable used as a pointer. When FORTH is first loaded, this variable contains the address of the single-length version. But when the double-length routines are loaded, a new definition called (NUMBER), with double-length capability, is added to the dictionary. On the line below the definition in the load block is the phrase

```
' (NUMBER) 'NUMBER !
```

When NUMBER is executed in the future, whether by INTERPRET or whomever, the contents of 'NUMBER are fetched and this definition is executed, giving NUMBER new-found double-length capability.

Here are the commands we've covered so far:†

' xxx	(-- adr)	Attempts to find the address of xxx (the word that follows in the input stream) in the dictionary.
[']	compile time: (--) run time: (-- adr)	Used only in a colon definition, compiles the address of the next word in the definition as a literal.

†FORTH-79 Standard

See Appendix 3.

The Structure of a Dictionary Entry

All definitions, whether they have been defined by :, by VARIABLE, by CREATE, or by any other "defining word," share these basic parts:

name field
link field
code pointer field
parameter field

Using the variable DATE as an example, here's how these components are arranged within each dictionary entry in systems that have a three-character-maximum name field. In this diagram, each horizontal line represents one cell in the dictionary:

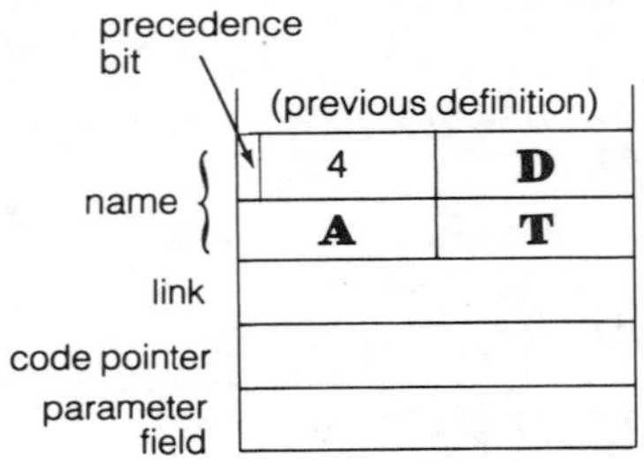

Systems that allow thirty-one-character-maximum name fields usually follow the same pattern, but the name field may take anywhere from two to thirty-two bytes, depending on the name. The order of the four components may also vary.†

---

† FORTH-79 Standard

The FORTH-79 Standard allows thirty-one-character-maximum name fields, but does not specify the order of the field within the dictionary entry. The order is considered implementation-dependent.

In this book, we're only concerned with the functions of the four components, not with their order inside a dictionary entry. We'll use the three-character version as our example because it's the simplest.

Name

In our example, the first byte contains the number of characters in the full name of the defined word (there are four letters in DATE). The next three bytes contain the ASCII representations of the first three letters in the name of the defined word. In a three-character system, this is all the information that tick or bracket-tick-bracket have to go on in matching up the name of a definition with a word in the input stream.

(Notice in the diagram that the sign bit of the "count" byte is called the "precedence bit." This bit is used during compilation to indicate whether the word is supposed to be executed during compilation, or to simply be compiled into the new definition. More on this matter in Chap. 11.)

Link

The "link" cell contains the address of the previous definition in the dictionary list. The link cell is used in searching the dictionary. To simplify things a bit, imagine that it works this way:

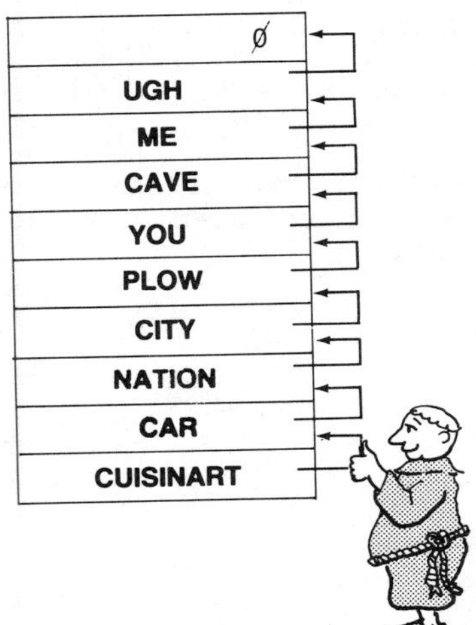

Each time the compiler adds a new word to the dictionary, he sets the link field to point to the address of the previous definition. Here he is setting the link field of CUISINART to point to the definition of CAR.

At search time, tick (or bracket-tick-bracket, etc.) starts with the most recent word and follows the "chain" backwards, using the address in each link cell to locate the next definition back.

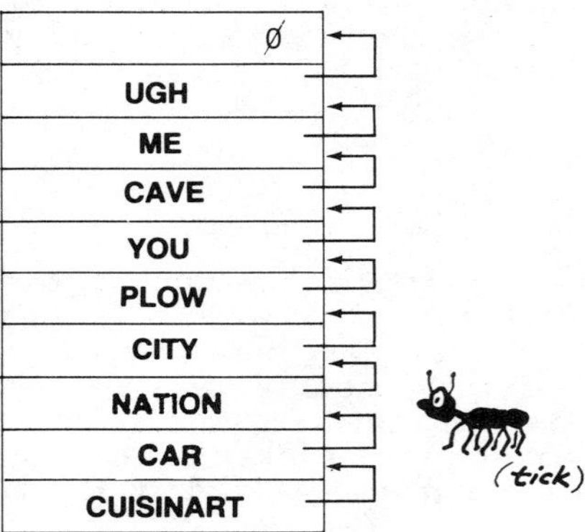

The link field of the first definition in the dictionary contains a zero, which tells tick to give up; the word is not in the dictionary.

Code pointer

Next is the "code pointer." The address contained in this pointer is what distinguishes a variable from a constant or a colon definition. It is the address of the instruction that is executed first when the particular type of word is executed. For example, in the case of a variable, the pointer points to code that pushes the address of the variable onto the stack. In the case of a constant, the pointer points to code that pushes the contents of the constant onto the stack. In the case of a colon definition, the pointer points to code that executes the rest of the words in the colon definition.

The code that is pointed to is called the "run-time code" because it's used when a word of that type is executed (not when a word of that type is defined or compiled).

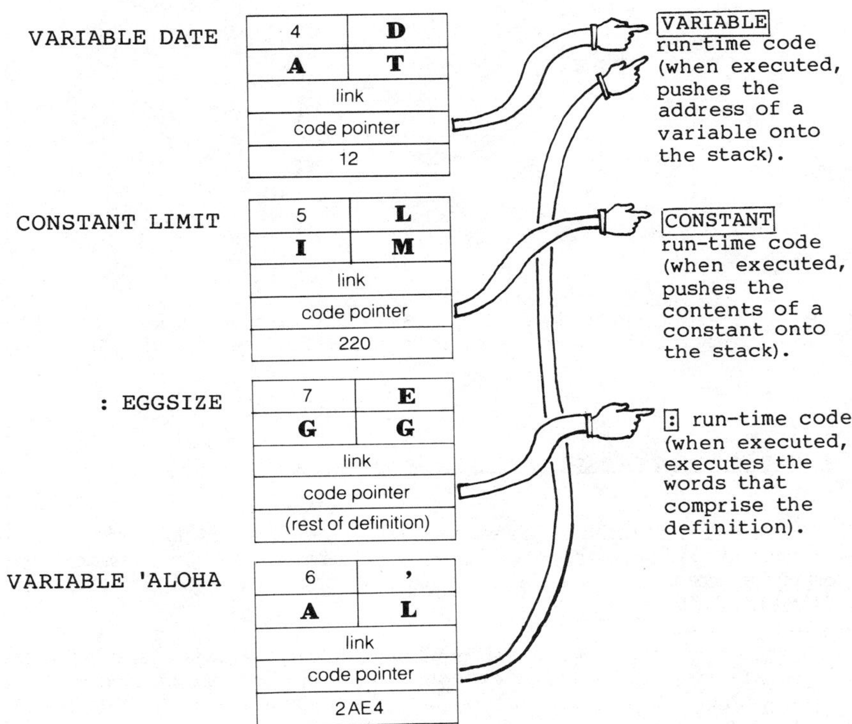

All variables have the same code pointer; all constants have the same code pointer of their own, and so on.

Parameter field

Following the code pointer is the parameter field. In variables and constants, the parameter field is only one cell. In a 2CONSTANT or 2VARIABLE, the parameter field is two cells. In an array, the parameter field can be as long as you want it. In a colon definition, the length of the parameter field depends on the length of the definition, as we'll explain in the next section.

The address that is supplied by tick and expected by EXECUTE is the address of the beginning of the parameter field, called the parameter-field address (pfa).

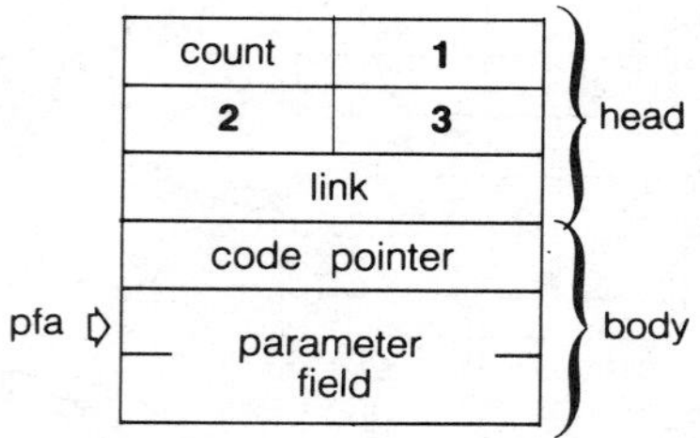

By the way, the name and link fields are often called the "head" of the entry; the code pointer and parameter fields are called the "body."

The Basic Structure of a Colon Definition

While the format of the head and code pointer is the same for all types of definitions, the format of the parameter field varies from type to type. Let's look at the parameter field of a colon definition.

The parameter field of a colon definition contains the addresses of the previously defined words which comprise the definition.† Here is the dictionary entry for the definition of PHOTOGRAPH, which we defined as:

```
: PHOTOGRAPH   SHUTTER  OPEN  TIME EXPOSE  SHUTTER CLOSE ;
```

When PHOTOGRAPH is executed, the definitions that are located at the successive addresses are executed in turn. The mechanism which reads the list of addresses and executes the definitions at each address is called the "address interpreter."

---

†For Experts

The addresses that comprise the body of a colon definition are usually code-field addresses (cfa), not parameter-field addresses.

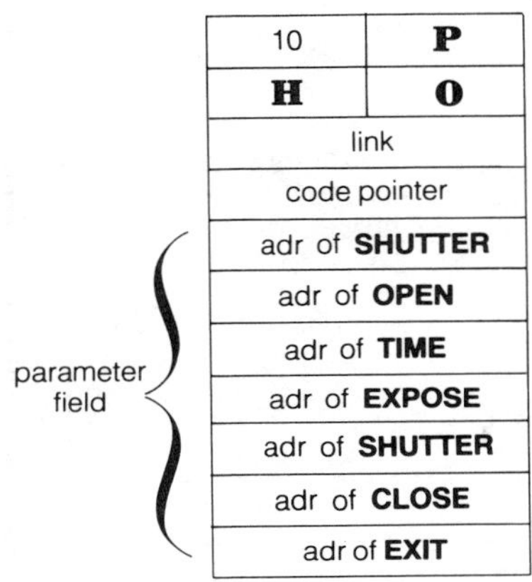

The word [;] at the end of the definition compiles the address of a word called [EXIT]. As you can see in the figure, the address of [EXIT] resides in the last cell of the dictionary entry. The address interpreter will execute [EXIT] when it gets to this address, just as it executes the other words in the definition. [EXIT] terminates execution of the address interpreter, as we will see in the next section.

Nested Levels of Execution

The function of [EXIT] is to return the flow of execution to the next higher-level definition that refers to the current definition. Let's see how this works in simplified terms.

Suppose that DINNER consists of three courses:

```
: DINNER   SOUP ENTREE DESSERT ;
```

and that tonight's ENTREE consists simply of

```
: ENTREE   CHICKEN RICE ;
```

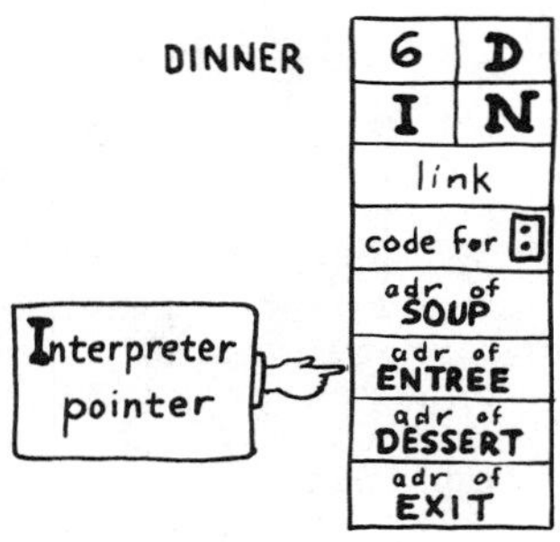

We are executing DINNER and we have just finished the SOUP. The pointer that is used by the address interpreter is called the "interpreter pointer" ([I]). Since the next course after SOUP is the ENTREE, our interpreter pointer is pointing to the cell that contains the address of ENTREE.

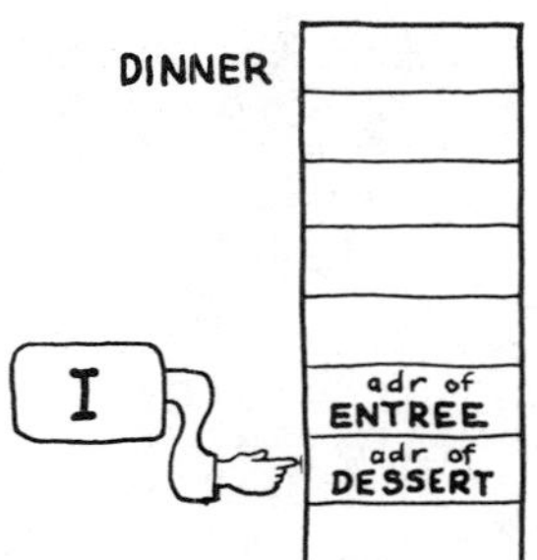

Before we go off and execute ENTREE, we first increment the interpreter pointer so that when we come back it will be pointing to DESSERT.

Now we begin to execute ENTREE. The first thing we execute is ENTREE's "code," i.e., the code that is pointed to by the "code field," common to all colon definitions.

This code does two things:

First, it saves the contents of the interpreter pointer on the return stack ...

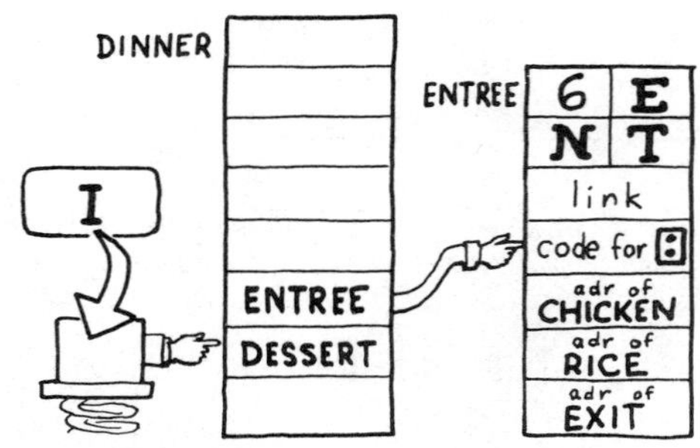

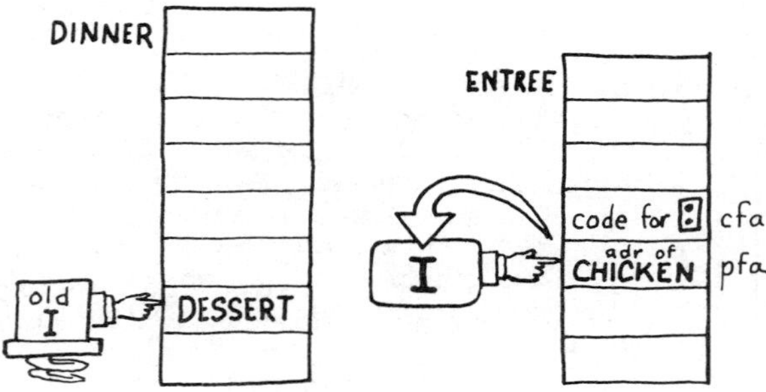

... then it puts the address of its own parameter field address (pfa) into the interpreter pointer. Now the interpreter pointer is pointing to CHICKEN. So the address interpreter gets ready to serve up the chicken.

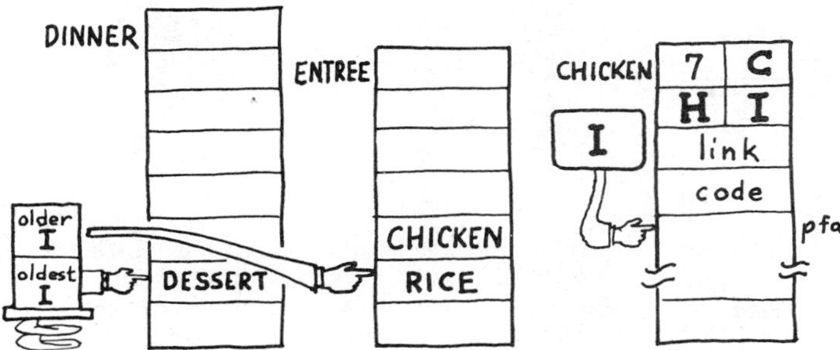

But first, as we did with ENTREE, we increment the pointer so that when we return it will be pointing to RICE. Then CHICKEN's code saves this pointer on the return stack and puts CHICKEN's own pfa into the interpreter pointer.

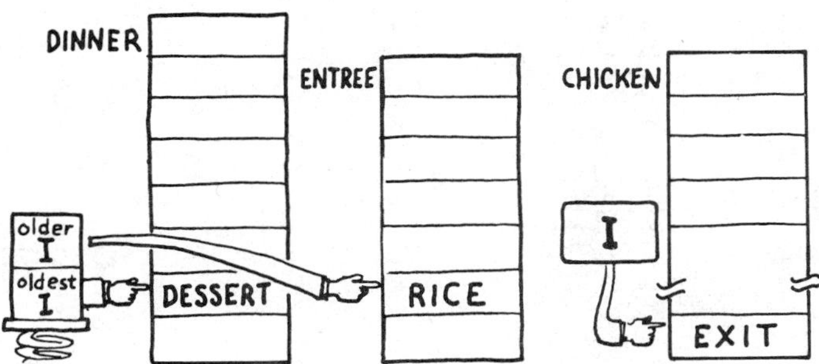

Finally we have our chicken, as the above process contiunes all down the line to the lowest-level definition involved in the making of the succulent poultry. Sooner or later we come to the EXIT in CHICKEN.

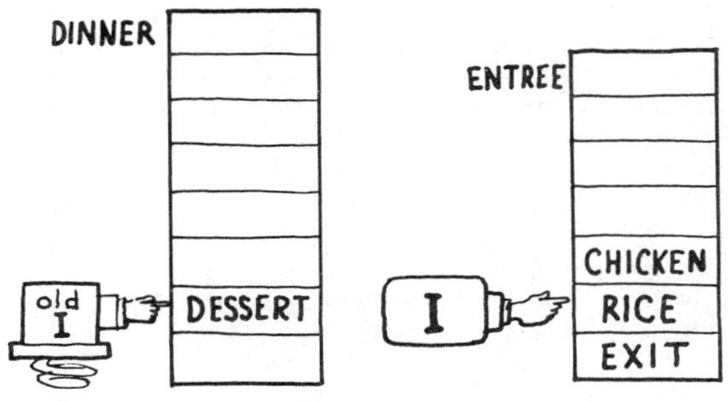

EXIT takes the number off the top of the return stack and puts it in the interpreter pointer. Now the address interpreter continues with the execution of RICE.

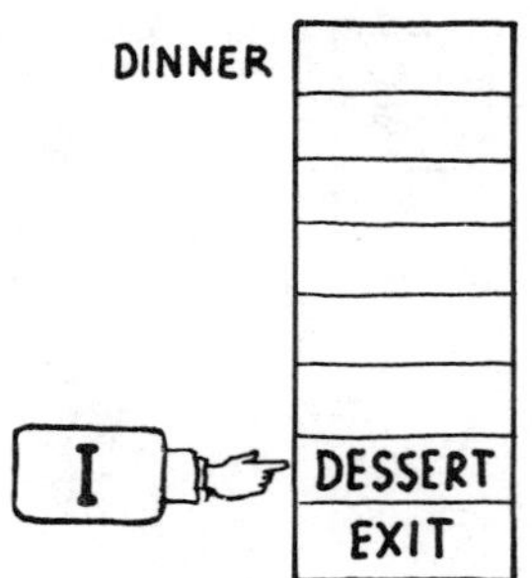

Eventually, of course, the EXIT in ENTREE will put the value on the return stack into the interpreter pointer. At last we're ready for DESSERT.

One Step Beyond

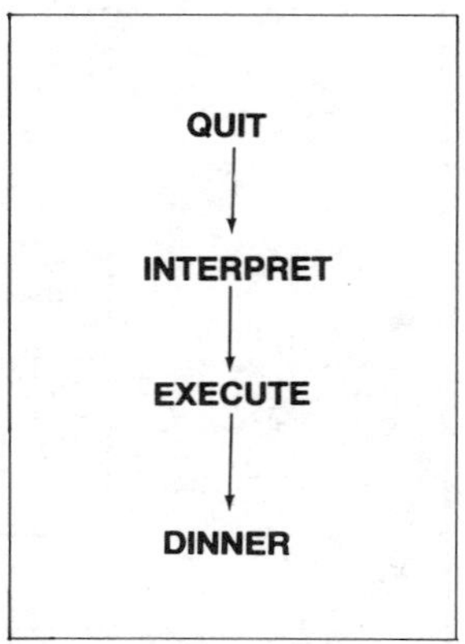

Perhaps you're wondering: what happens when we finally execute the EXIT in DINNER? Whose return address is on the stack? What do we return to?

Well, remember that DINNER has just been executed by EXECUTE, which is a component of INTERPRET. INTERPRET is a loop which checks the entire input stream. Assuming that we entered RETURN after DINNER, then there is nothing more to interpret. So when we exit INTERPRET, where does that leave us? In the outermost definition for each terminal, called QUIT.

QUIT, in simplified form, looks like this:

```
: QUIT   BEGIN  (clear return stack)  (accept input)
          INTERPRET ." ok" CR  0 UNTIL ;
```

(The parenthetical comments represent words and phrases not yet covered.) We can see that after the word INTERPRET comes a dot-quote message, "ok," and a CR, which of course are what we see after interpretation has been completed.

Next is the phrase

```
0 UNTIL
```

which unconditionally returns us to the beginning of the loop, where we clear the return stack and once again wait for input.

If we execute QUIT at any level of execution, we will

immediately cease execution of our application and re-enter QUIT's loop. The return stack will be cleared (regardless of how many levels of return addresses we had there, since we could never use any of them now), and the system will wait for input. You can see why QUIT can be used to keep the message "ok" from appearing at our terminal.

The definition of ABORT" uses QUIT.

Abandoning The Nest

It's possible to skip one level of execution simply by removing one return address from the return stack. For example, consider the three levels of execution associated with DINNER, shown here:

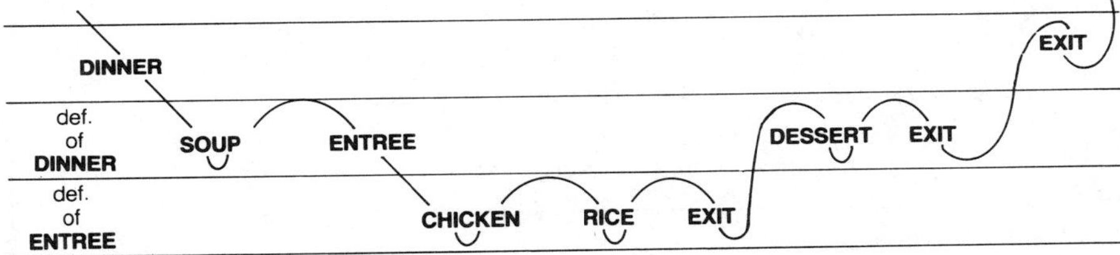

Now suppose that the definition ENTREE is changed to:

```
: ENTREE   CHICKEN RICE  R> DROP ;
```

The phrase "R> DROP" will drop from the return stack the return address of DESSERT, which was put on just prior to the execution of ENTREE. If we reload these definitions and execute DINNER, the EXIT on the third level will take us directly back to the first level. We'll get SOUP, CHICKEN, and RICE but we'll skip DESSERT, as you can see here:

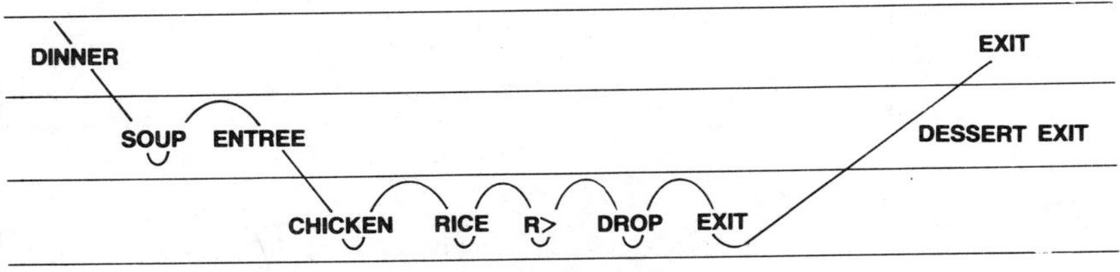

We're not necessarily suggesting that you use "R> DROP" in an application, just illustrating a point.

We've mentioned that the word EXIT removes a return address from atop the return stack and puts it into the interpreter pointer. The address interpreter, which gets its bearings from the interpreter pointer, begins looking at the next level up. It's possible to include EXIT in the middle of a definition. For example, if we were to redefine ENTREE as follows:

```
: ENTREE  CHICKEN  EXIT  RICE ;
```

then when we subsequently execute DINNER, we will exit right after CHICKEN and return to the next course after the ENTREE, i.e., DESSERT.

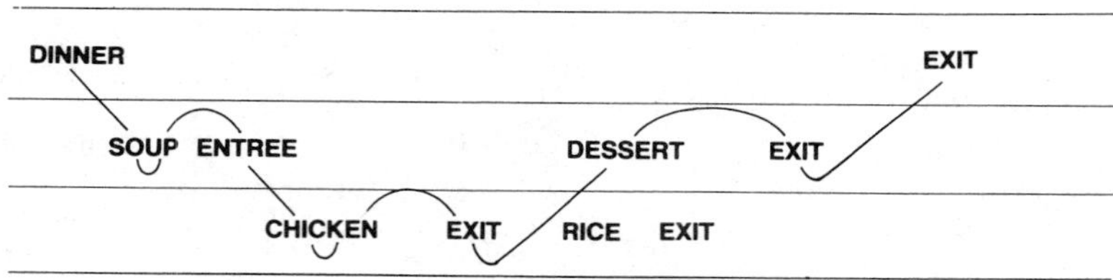

This time we get DESSERT but no RICE.

EXIT is commonly used in a disk block to keep the remainder of the block from being loaded. For example, if you edit EXIT into the end of line 5 of a block and load it, any definitions in line 6 and beyond will not get compiled.

EXIT	(--)	When compiled within a colon definition, terminates execution of that definition at that point. When executed from a load block, terminates interpretation of the block at that point.
QUIT	(--)	Clears both stacks and returns control to the terminal. No message is given.

FORTH Geography

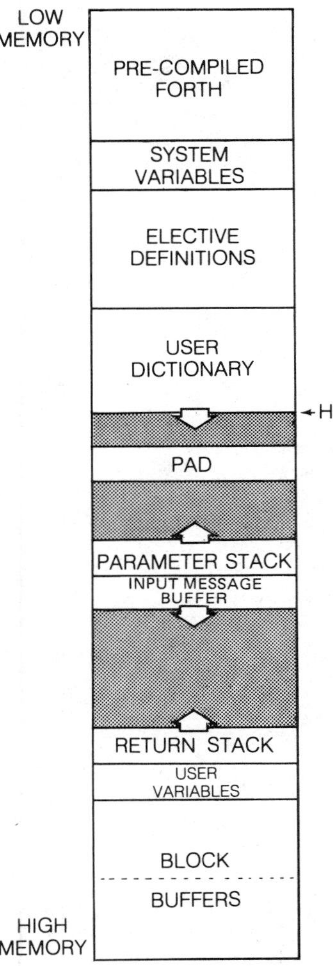

This is a "memory map"† of a typical single-user FORTH system. Multiprogrammed systems such as polyFORTH are more complicated, as we will explain later on. For now let's take the simple case and explore each region of the map, one at a time.

Precompiled Portion

In low memory resides the only precompiled portion of the system (already compiled into dictionary form). On some systems this code is kept on disk (often blocks 1 - 8) and automatically loaded into low RAM when you start up or "boot" the computer. On other systems the precompiled portion resides permanently in PROM, where it is active as soon as you power up the computer.

The precompiled portion usually includes most of the single-length math operators and number-formatting words, single-length stack manipulation operators, editor commands, branching and structure-control words, the assembler, all the defining words we've covered so

---

†For Beginners

A "memory map" depicts how computer memory is divided up for various purposes in a particular system. Here, low-numbered addresses begin at the top ("low memory") and increase as the map goes down. Memory space is measured in groups of 1,024 bytes. This quantity is called a "K" (from "kilo-," meaning a thousand, which is close enough).

far, and, of course, the text and address interpreters.†

System Variables

The next section of memory contains "system variables" which are created by the precompiled portion and used by the entire system. They are not generally used by the user. 'NUMBER, which we discussed earlier, is a system variable.

Elective Definitions

The portion of the FORTH system that is not precompiled is kept on disk in source-text form. You can elect to load or not to load any number of these definitions to better control use of your computer's memory space. The load block for all "electives" is called the "electives block," usually block 9. To compile the electives after you "boot," simply enter

```
9 LOAD
```

(or whichever block is the electives block for your system).

For example, in polyFORTH electives include double- and mixed-length operators, extended editor commands, date and time commands, and the ability to add new multiprogrammed tasks including additional terminals. You can mask any of these electives out of the electives block simply by inserting parentheses.

If your electives block contains this line:

```
( 32-BIT ARITHMETIC)  30 LOAD   31 LOAD   32 LOAD
```

you can avoid loading the double-length routines by changing the line to

```
( 32-BIT ARITHMETIC  30 LOAD   31 LOAD   32 LOAD)
```

If you want to change the electives block after you have already loaded it, you must reload the system (by rebooting) before you can reload the electives. (The word RELOAD, available on some systems, will reload the system and not the electives.)

---

†For Experts

To give you an idea of how compact FORTH can be, all of polyFORTH's precompiled portion resides in less than 8K bytes.

User Dictionary

The dictionary will grow into higher memory as you add your own definitions within the portion of memory called the "user dictionary." The next available cell in the dictionary at any time is pointed to by a variable called H. During the process of compilation, the pointer H is adjusted cell-by-cell (or byte-by-byte) as the entry is being added to the dictionary. Thus H is the compiler's bookmark; it points to the place in the dictionary where the compiler can next compile.

H is also used by the word ALLOT, which advances H by the number of bytes given. For example, the phrase

```
10 ALLOT
```

adds ten to H so that the compiler will leave room in the dictionary for a ten-byte (or five-cell) array.

A related word is HERE, which is simply defined

```
: HERE   H @ ;
```

to put the value of H on the stack. The word , (comma), which stores a single-length value into the next available cell in the dictionary, is simply defined

```
: ,   HERE !  2 ALLOT ;
```

that is, it stores a value into HERE and advances the dictionary pointer two bytes to leave room for it.

You can use HERE to determine how much memory any part of your application requires, simply by comparing the HERE from before with the HERE after compiling. For example:

```
HERE  220 LOAD  HERE SWAP - . 196 ok
```

indicates that the definitions loaded by block 220 filled 196 bytes of memory space in the dictionary.

The Pad

At a certain distance from HERE in your dictionary, you will find a small region of memory called the "pad." Like a scratch pad, it is usually used to hold ASCII character strings that are being manipulated prior to being sent out to a terminal. For example, the number-formatting words use the pad to hold the ASCII numerals during the conversion process, prior to TYPE.

The size of the pad is indefinite. In most systems there are hundreds or even thousands of bytes between the beginning of the pad and the top of the parameter stack.

Since the pad's beginning address is defined relative to the last dictionary entry, it moves every time you add a new definition or execute FORGET or EMPTY. This arrangement proves safe, however, because the pad is never used when any of these events are occurring. The word PAD returns the current address of the beginning of the pad. It is defined simply:

```
: PAD   HERE  34 + ;
```

that is, it returns an address that is a fixed number of bytes beyond HERE. (The actual number may vary.)

Parameter Stack

Far above† the pad in memory is the area reserved for the parameter stack. Although we like to imagine that values actually move up and down somewhere as we "pop them off" and "push them on," in reality nothing moves. The only thing that changes is a pointer to the "top" of the stack.

As you can see below, when we "put a number on the stack," what really happens is that the pointer is "decremented" (so that it points to the next location toward low memory), then our number is stored where the pointer is pointing. When we "remove a number from the stack," the number is fetched from the location where the pointer is pointing, then the pointer is incremented. Any numbers above the stack pointer on our map are meaningless.

---

†For Beginners

"Above" refers to the higher memory addresses, which are "lower" on our map.

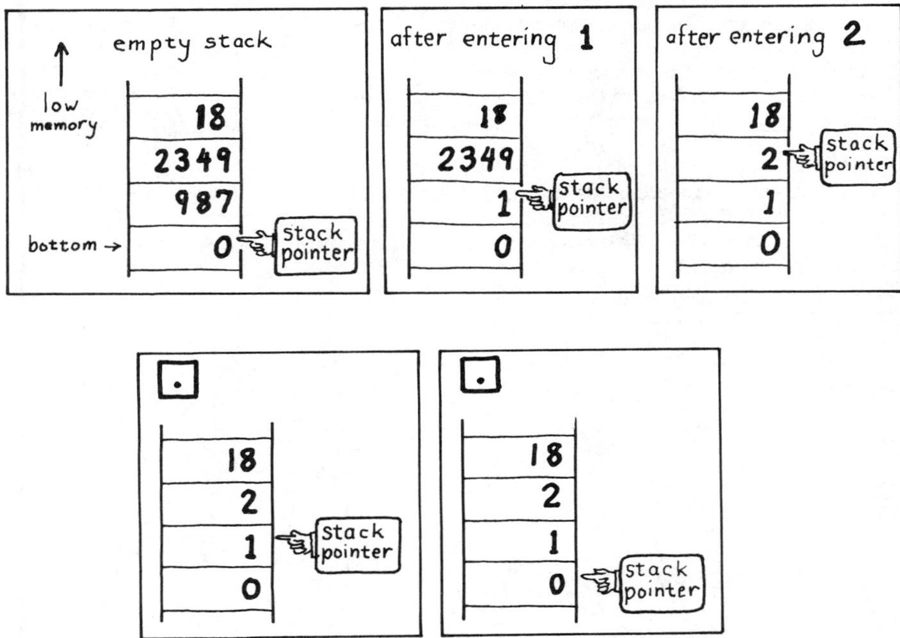

As new values are added to the stack, it "grows toward low memory."

The stack pointer is fetched by the word 'S (pronounced tick-S). Since 'S provides the address of the top stack location, the phrase

```
'S @
```

fetches the contents of the top of the stack. This operation, of course, is identical to that of DUP. If we had five values on the stack, we could copy the fifth one down with the phrase

```
'S 8 + @
```

(but this is generally not considered good programming practice).

The bottom of the stack is pointed to by a variable called S0 (S-zero). S0 always contains the address of the next cell below the "empty stack" cell.

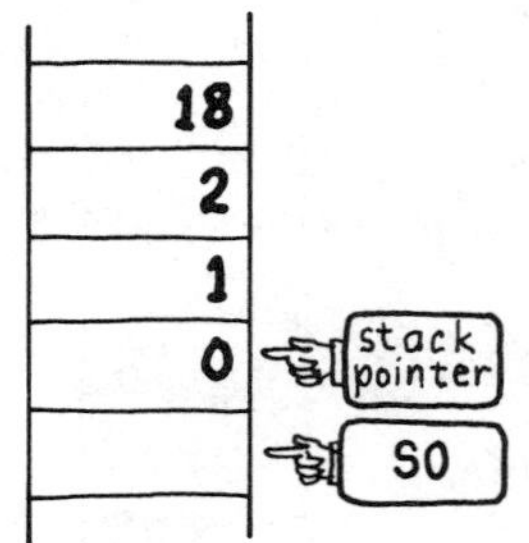

For examples of good uses of 'S and S0, review the definitions of DEPTH and of .S that we gave in the Handy Hint at the end of Chap. 3.

Notice that with double-length numbers, the high-order cell is stored at the lower memory address whether on the stack or in the dictionary. The operators 2! and 2@ keep the order of cells consistent, as you can see here.

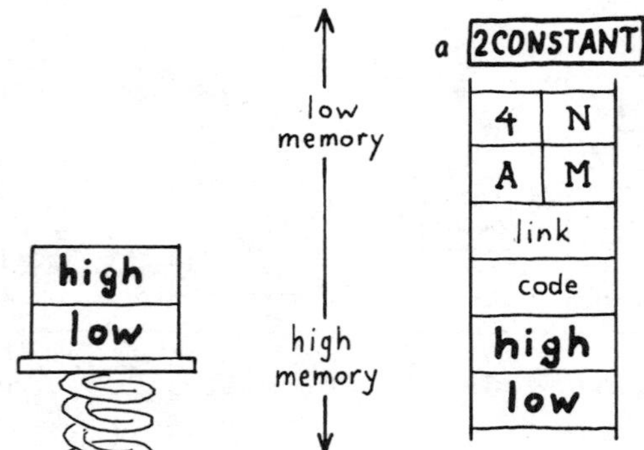

Input Message Buffer

S0 also contains the starting address for the "input message buffer," which grows toward high memory (the same direction as the pad). When you enter text from the terminal, it gets stored into this buffer where the text interpreter will scan it.

Return Stack

Above the buffer resides the return stack, which operates identically to the parameter stack. There are no high-level FORTH words analogous to 'S or S0 that refer to the return stack.

User Variables

The next section of memory contains "user variables." These variables include BASE, S0, and many others that we'll cover in an upcoming section.

Block Buffers

At the high end of memory reside the block buffers. Each buffer provides 1,024 bytes for the contents of a disk block. Whenever you access a block (by listing or loading it, for example) the system copies the block from the disk into the buffer, where it can be modified by the editor or interpreted by LOAD. We'll discuss the block buffers in Chap. 10.

This completes our journey across the memory map of a typical single-user FORTH system. Here are the words we've just covered that relate to memory regions in the FORTH system.†

H	(-- adr)	Returns the address of the dictionary pointer.
HERE	(-- adr)	Returns the next available dictionary location.
PAD	(-- adr)	Returns the beginning address of a scratch area used to hold character strings for intermediate processing.
'S	(-- adr)	Returns the address of the top of the stack before 'S is executed.
S0	(--adr)	Contains the address of the bottom of the parameter stack.

†FORTH-79 Standard

H, 'S, and S0 are not required by the Standard.

The Geography of a Multi-tasked FORTH system

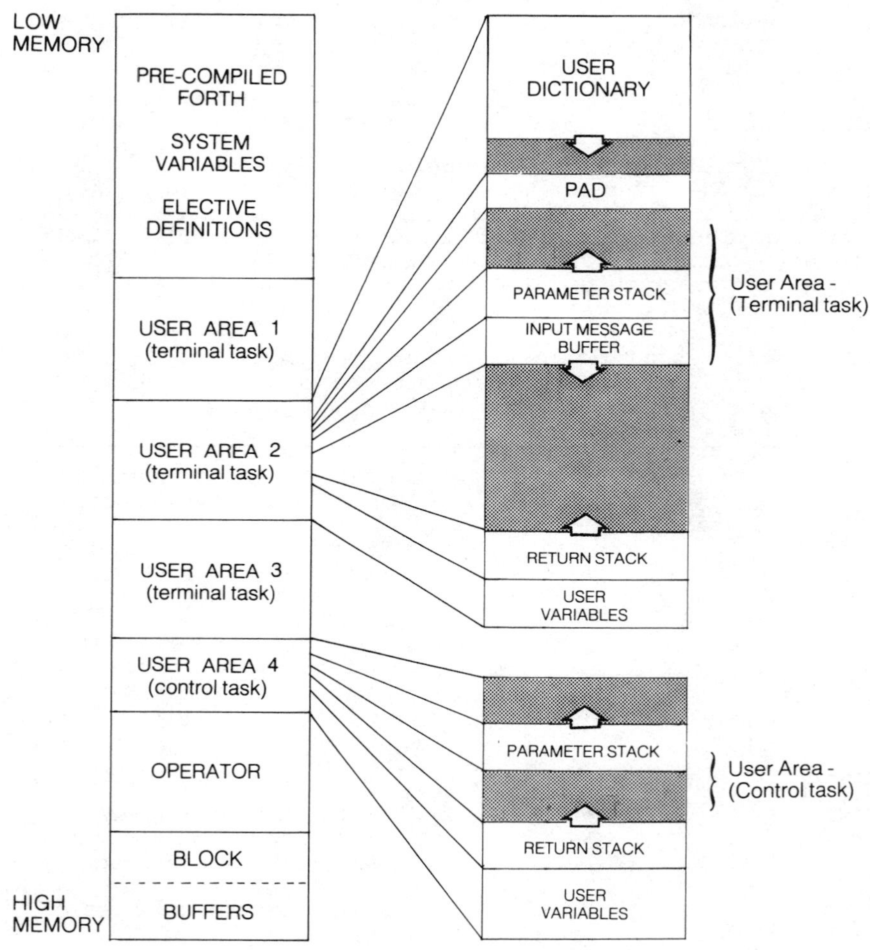

Some FORTH systems (such as polyFORTH) can be multitasked,† so that any number of additional tasks can be added. A task may be

---

†For Beginners

The term "multitasked" describes a system in which numerous tasks operate concurrently on the same computer without interference from one another.

either a "terminal task," which puts the full interactive power of FORTH into the hands of a human at a terminal, or a "control task," which controls a hardware device that has no terminal.

Either type of task requires its own "user area." The size and contents of a user area depends on the type of task, but typical configurations for the two types of tasks are shown in the figure.

Each terminal task has its own private dictionary, pad, parameter stack, input message buffer, return stack, and user variables. This means that any words that you define at your terminal are normally not available to other terminals. Similarly, each task has its own copies of the user variables, such as BASE.

Each control task has a pair of stacks and a small set of user variables. Since a control task uses no terminal, it doesn't need a dictionary of its own; nor does it need a pad or a message buffer.

Following the initial boot there is only one task, called OPERATOR. Loading the electives block will allocate space for the various terminal and control-task partitions. Thus it is possible to reconfigure the subtasks within a system by altering the electives block and reloading it. But it's beyond the scope of this book to explain how.

User Variables

The following list shows most of the user variables. Some we won't ever mention again. Don't try to memorize this table. Just remember where you can find it.

S0	Pointer to the bottom of the parameter stack and, for terminal tasks, the start of the input message buffer.	s-zero
SCR	For the editor, a pointer to the current block number (set by LIST and used by L).	s-c-r
R#	Current character position in the editor.	r-number
BASE	Number conversion base.	
H	Dictionary pointer. Pointer to the next available byte.	
CONTEXT	Contains up to four indexes for vocabularies to be searched.	
CURRENT	Contains the index of the vocabulary to which new definitions will be linked.	
>IN	Pointer to the current position in the input stream.	to-in
BLK	If non-zero, a pointer to the block being interpreted by LOAD. A zero indicates interpretation from the terminal (via the input message buffer).	b-l-k
OFFSET	Block offset to disk drives. The content of OFFSET is added to the stack number by BLOCK.	

User variables are not like ordinary variables. With an ordinary variable (one defined by the word VARIABLE), the value is kept in the parameter field of the dictionary entry.

Each user variable, on the other hand, is kept in an array called the "user table." The dictionary entry for each user variable is located elsewhere; it contains an offset into the user table. When you execute the name of a user variable, such as H, this offset is added to the beginning address of the user table. This gives you the address of H in the array, allowing you to use @ or ! in the normal way.

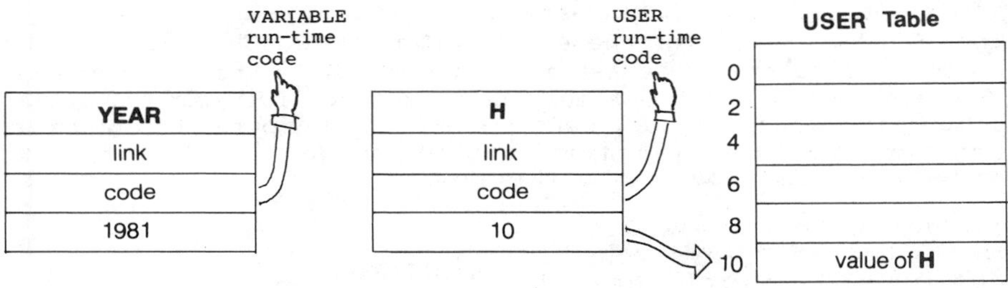

The main advantage of user variables is that any number of tasks can use the same definition of a variable and each get its own value. Each task that executes

```
BASE @
```

gets the value for BASE from its own user table. This saves a lot of room in the system while still allowing each task to execute independently.

User variables are defined by the word USER. The sequence of user variables in the table and their offset values vary from one system to another.

To summarize, there are three kinds of variables: System variables contain values used by the entire FORTH system. User variables contain values that are unique for each task, even though the definitions can be used by all tasks in the system. Regular variables can be accessible either system-wide or within a single task only, depending upon whether they are defined within OPERATOR or within a private task.

Vocabularies

Earlier we mentioned that the reason the [I] in the editor doesn't conflict with the [I] used in a [DO] loop is that they belong to separate "vocabularies." In a simple FORTH system there are three standard vocabularies: FORTH, the editor, and the assembler.

All the words that we've covered so far belong to the FORTH vocabulary, except for the editor commands which belong to the editor vocabulary. The assembler vocabulary contains commands that are used to write assembly-language code for your particular computer. Since assembly code varies from computer to computer, and since assembly-language programming is a whole different subject, we won't cover it in this book.†

All definitions are added to the same dictionary in the order in which they are compiled, regardless of which vocabulary they belong to. So vocabularies are not subdivisions of the dictionary; rather they are independently linked lists that weave through it.

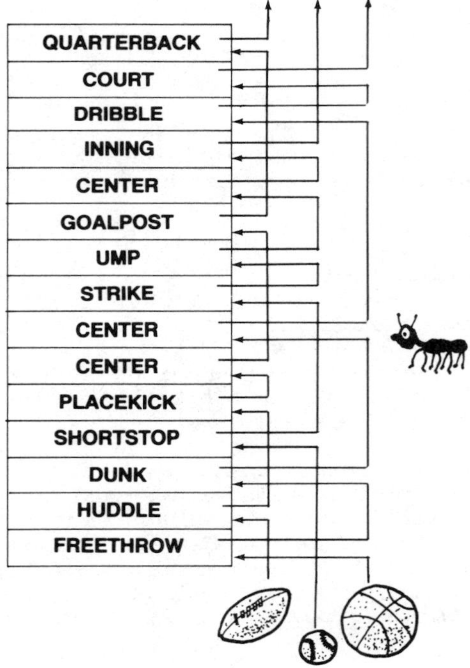

For example, in the figure shown here, there are three vocabularies: football, baseball, and basketball. All three are co-resident in the same dictionary, but when tick follows the basketball chain, for instance, it only finds words in the basketball vocabulary. Even though each vocabulary has a word called CENTER, tick will find whichever version is appropriate for the context.

---

†For the Curious

See Appendix 2.

There is another advantage besides exclusivity, and that is speed of searches. If we are talking about basketball, why waste time hunting through the football and baseball words?

You can change the context in which the dictionary is searched by executing any of the three commands FORTH, EDITOR, or ASSEMBLER. For example, if you enter

```
FORTH
```

you know for sure that the search context is the FORTH vocabulary.

Ordinarily, however, the FORTH system automatically changes the context for you. Here's a typical scenario:

The system starts out with FORTH being the context. Let's say you start entering an application into a block. Certain editor commands switch the context to the editor vocabulary. You will stay in the editor vocabulary until you load the block and begin compiling definitions. The word : will automatically reset the context to what it was before--FORTH.

Different versions of FORTH have different ways of implementing vocabularies. Still, we can make a few general statements that will cover most systems.

The vocabulary to be searched is specified by a user variable called CONTEXT. As we said, the commands FORTH, EDITOR, and ASSEMBLER change the search context.

There is another kind of vocabulary "context": the vocabulary to which new definitions will be linked. The link vocabulary is specified by another variable called CURRENT. Because CURRENT normally specifies the FORTH vocabulary, new definitions are normally linked to the FORTH vocabulary.

But how does the system compile words into the editor and assembler vocabularies? By using the word DEFINITIONS, as in

```
EDITOR DEFINITIONS
```

We know that the word EDITOR sets CONTEXT to "EDITOR." The word DEFINITIONS copies whatever is in CONTEXT into CURRENT. The definition of DEFINITIONS is simply

```
: DEFINITIONS   CONTEXT @  CURRENT ! ;
```

Having entered

```
EDITOR DEFINITIONS
```

any words that you compile henceforth will belong to the editor vocabulary until you enter

    FORTH DEFINITIONS

to reset CURRENT to "FORTH."†

We've presented this introduction to vocabularies mainly to satisfy your curiosity, not to encourage you to add new vocabularies of your own. The problem of defining different subsets of application words with conflicting names is better handled by the use of overlays, which we discussed in Chap. 3.

---

†**For Curious polyFORTH Users**

polyFORTH allows several vocabularies to be chained in sequence. CONTEXT specifies the search order.

The polyFORTH dictionary is comprised of eight "linked lists" which do not correspond with the vocabularies. At compile time a hashing function, based on (usually) the first letter of the word being defined, computes a "hashing index." This index is combined with the "current" vocabulary to produce an index into one of the eight lists.

Thus a single list may contain words from many vocabularies, but any words with identical names belonging to separate vocabularies will be linked to separate lists. The distribution of entries in each chain is balanced, and an entire vocabulary can be searched by searching only one-eighth of the dictionary.

A Handy Hint

How to LOCATE a Source Definition

Some FORTH systems, such as polyFORTH, feature a very useful word called LOCATE. If you enter

```
LOCATE EGGSIZE
```

FORTH will list the block that contains the definition of EGGSIZE. The only requirements are that the word must be resident (currently in the dictionary) and that the word must have been loaded from a block. You therefore can locate system electives and words in your application, but you can't locate words in the precompiled portion.

' xxx	(-- adr)	Attempts to find the address of xxx (the word that follows in the input stream) in the dictionary.
INTERPRET	(--)	Interprets the input stream, indexed by >IN , until exhausted.
EXECUTE	(adr --)	Executes the dictionary entry whose parameter field address is on the stack.
EXIT	(--)	When compiled within a colon definition, terminates execution of that definition at that point. When executed from a load block, terminates interpretation of the block at that point.
QUIT	(--)	Clears both stacks and returns control to the terminal. No message is given.
HERE	(-- adr)	Returns the next available dictionary location.
PAD	(-- adr)	Returns the beginning address of a scratch area used to hold character strings for intermediate processing.
FORTH	(--)	Makes FORTH the CONTEXT vocabulary.
EDITOR	(--)	Makes the editor vocabulary the CONTEXT vocabulary.
ASSEMBLER	(--)	Makes the assembler vocabulary the CONTEXT vocabulary.
DEFINITIONS	(--)	Sets CURRENT to the CONTEXT vocabulary so that subsequent definitions will be linked to this vocabulary.

<u>Common User Variables</u>
(Some not required by the FORTH-79 Standard.)

S0	Pointer to the bottom of the parameter stack and, for terminal tasks, the start of the input message buffer.
SCR	For the editor, a pointer to the current block number (set by LIST and used by L).
R#	Current character position in the editor.
BASE	Number conversion base.
H	Dictionary pointer. Pointer to the next available byte.
CONTEXT	Contains up to four indexes for vocabularies to be searched.
CURRENT	Contains the index of the vocabulary to which new definitions will be linked.
>IN	Pointer to the current position in the input stream.
BLK	If non-zero, a pointer to the block being interpreted by LOAD. A zero indicates interpretation from the terminal (via the input message buffer).
OFFSET	Block offset to disk drives. The content of OFFSET is added to the stack number by BLOCK.

<u>Additional Words Available in Some Systems</u>

[']	compile time: (--) run time: (-- adr)	Used only in a colon definition, compiles the address of the next word in the definition as a literal.
'S	(-- adr)	Returns the address of the top of the stack before 'S is executed.

Review of Terms

Address interpreter — the second of FORTH's two interpreters, the one which executes the list of addresses found in the dictionary entry of a colon definition. The address interpreter also handles the nesting of execution levels for words within words.

Body — the code and parameter fields of a FORTH dictionary entry.

Boot — simply, to load the precompiled portion of FORTH into the computer so that you can talk to the computer in FORTH. This happens automatically when you turn the computer on or press "Reset."

Cfa — code field address; the address of a dictionary entry's code pointer field.

Control task — on a multitasked system, a task which cannot converse with a terminal. Control tasks usually run hardware devices.

Code pointer field — the cell in a dictionary entry which contains the address of the run-time code for that particular type of definition. For example, in a dictionary entry created by `:`, the field points to the address interpreter.

Defining word — a FORTH word which creates a dictionary entry. Examples include `:`, `CONSTANT`, `VARIABLE`, etc.

Electives — the set of FORTH definitions that come with a system but not in the precompiled portion. The "electives block" loads the blocks that contain the elective definitions; the block can be modified as the user desires.

Head — the name and link fields of a FORTH dictionary entry.

Input message buffer — the region of memory within a terminal task that is used to store text as it arrives from a terminal. Incoming source text is interpreted here.

Link field — the cell in a dictionary entry which contains the address of the previous definition, used in searching the dictionary. (On systems which use multiple chains, the link field contains the address of the previous definition in the same chain.)

Name field — the area of a dictionary entry which contains the name (or abbreviation thereof) of the defined word, along with the number of characters in the name.

Pad — the region of memory within a terminal task that is used as a scratch area to hold character strings for intermediate processing.

Parameter field — the area of a dictionary entry which contains the "contents" of the definition: for a CONSTANT, the value of the constant; for a VARIABLE, the value of the variable; for a colon definition, the list of addresses of words that are to be executed in turn when the definition is executed. Depending on its use, the length of a parameter field varies.

Pfa — parameter field address; the address of the first cell in a dictionary entry's parameter field (or, if the parameter field consists of only one cell, its address).

Precompiled portion — the part of the FORTH system which is resident in object form immediately after the power-up or boot operation. The precompiled portion usually includes the text interpreter and the address interpreter; defining, branching, and structure-control words; single-length math and stack operators; single-length number conversion and formatting commands; the editor; and the assembler.

Run-time code — a routine, compiled in memory, which specifies what happens when a member of a given class of words is executed. The run-time code for a colon definition is the address interpreter; the run-time code for a variable pushes the contents of the variable's pfa onto the stack.

System variable — one of a set of variables provided by FORTH which are referred to system-wide (by any task). Contrast with "user variable."

Task	in FORTH, a partition in memory that contains at minimum a parameter and a return stack and a set of user variables.
Terminal task	on a multitasked system, a task which can converse with a human being using a terminal; i.e., one which has a text interpreter, dictionary, etc.
User variable	one of a set of variables provided by FORTH, whose values are unique for each task. Contrast with "system variable."
Vectored execution	the method of specifying code to be executed by providing not the address of the code itself but the address of a location which contains the address of the code. This location is often called the "vector." As circumstances change within the system, the vector can be reset to point to some other piece of code.
Vocabulary	an independently linked subset of the FORTH dictionary.

Problems -- Chapter 9

1. First review Chap. 2, Prob. 6. Without changing any of those definitions, now write a word called COUNTS which will allow the judge to optionally enter the number of counts for any crime. For instance, the entry

    ```
    CONVICTED-OF  BOOKMAKING  3 COUNTS TAX-EVASION
    WILL-SERVE RETURN 17 YEARS ok
    ```

    will compute the sentence for one count of bookmaking and three counts of tax evasion.

2. What is the beginning address of your private dictionary?

3. In your system, how far is the pad from the top of your private dictionary?

4. Assuming that DATE has been defined by VARIABLE, what is the difference between these two phrases:

    ```
    DATE .
    ```

    and

    ```
    ' DATE .
    ```

    What is the difference between these two phrases:

    ```
    BASE .
    ```

    and

    ```
    ' BASE .
    ```

5. In this exercise you will create a "vectored execution array," that is, an array which contains addresses of FORTH words. You will also create an operation word which will execute one word stored in the array when the operation word is executed.

    Define a one-dimensional array of two-byte elements which will return the nth element's address when given a preceding subscript n. Define several words which output something at your terminal and take no inputs. Store the addresses of these output words in various elements of the array. Store the address of a do-nothing word in any remaining elements of the array. Define a word which will take a valid array index and execute the word whose address is stored in the referenced element.

For example,

```
1 DO-SOMETHING HELLO, I SPEAK FORTH. ok
2 DO-SOMETHING 1 2 3 4 5 6 7 8 9 10 ok
3 DO-SOMETHING
**********
**********
**********
**********
**********
4 DO-SOMETHING ok
5 DO-SOMETHING ok
```

10 I/O AND YOU

In this chapter we'll explain how FORTH handles I/O† of character strings to and from the block buffers and the terminal.

Specifically, we'll discuss disk-access commands, output commands, string-manipulation commands, input commands, and number-input conversion.

Block Buffer Basics

The FORTH system is designed so that you don't usually need to think about the mechanics of the block buffers. But sooner or later you _will_, so here's how it works.

As we mentioned earlier, each buffer is large enough to hold the contents of one block (1024 bytes) in RAM so that it can be edited, loaded, or generally accessed in any way. While we can imagine that we're communicating directly to the disk, in reality, the system brings the data from the disk into the buffer where we can read it. We can also write data to the buffer, and the system will send it along to the disk.

---

†For Beginners

I/O is an abbreviation for "input-output," which refers to data, text, or signals that are sent or received by the computer. I/O devices include terminals, printers, disk drives, push buttons, etc.

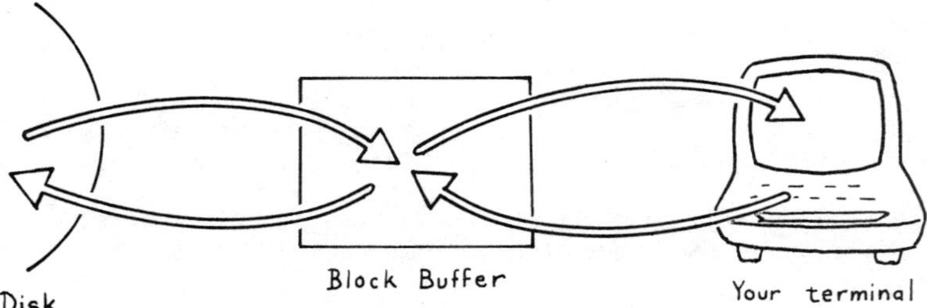

This arrangement is called "virtual memory" because the mass storage memory is made to act like computer memory.

Many FORTH systems use as few as two block buffers, even when the system is multiprogrammed. Let's see how this is possible.

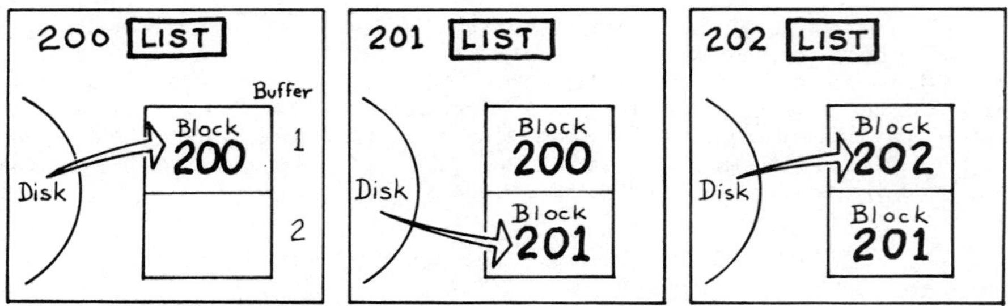

Suppose there are two buffers in your system. Now imagine the following scenario:

First you list block 200. The system reads the disk and transfers the block to buffer 1, from which LIST displays it.

Now you list block 201. The system copies block 201 from the disk into the other buffer.

Now you list block 202. The system copies block 202 from the disk into the less-recently used buffer, namely buffer 1.

What happened to the former contents of buffer 1? They were simply overwritten (erased) by the new contents. This is no loss because block 200 is still on the disk. But what if you had edited block 200? Would your changes be lost? No. Here's what would happen when you listed block 202:

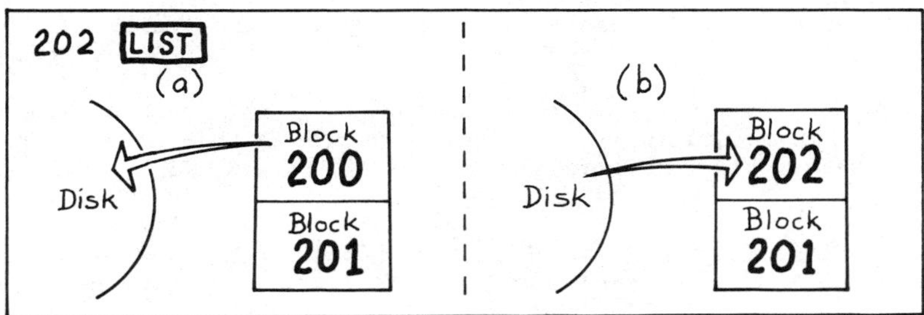

First the modified contents of block 200 would be sent to the disk to update the former contents of 200 there, then the contents of 202 would be brought into the buffer.

The magic word is UPDATE, which sets a flag that indicates that the contents of the most recently accessed buffer should be sent back to disk, rather than erased, the next time that the buffer is needed. All editor commands that change the contents of a block, whether adding or deleting, include UPDATE in their definitions.

Every time you or the system try to access a block, the system first checks whether the block is already in a buffer. If it is, fine. If not, then the system finds the earliest buffer to have been accessed. If the contents of this buffer have been UPDATEd, the system copies the contents back onto disk, then finally copies the newly-accessed block into the buffer.

This arrangement lets you modify the contents of the block any number of times without activating the disk drive each time. Since conversing with the disk takes longer than conversing with RAM, this can save a lot of time.

On the other hand, when there are several users on a single system, this arrangement allows all of them to get by with as few as two buffers (2K of memory), even though each may be accessing a different block.

Some FORTH systems give their owners the option to have as many block buffers as they like, depending on the memory size and the frequency of disk transfers in their own setups.

The word FLUSH† forces all updated buffers to be written to disk

---

†FORTH-79 Standard

The Standard's name for FLUSH is SAVE-BUFFERS.

immediately. Now that you know about the buffers, you can see why we need FLUSH: merely updating a buffer doesn't get it written to disk.

You should also know that when you FLUSH, the system "forgets" that it has your block in a buffer and clears the buffer's update flag. If you list or load the block again, FORTH will have to read it from the disk again.

The effective opposite of FLUSH is EMPTY-BUFFERS, which also makes the system "forget" any block it has and clears any update flags. EMPTY-BUFFERS is useful if you've accidently got "garbage"† in a buffer (e.g., you've deleted some important lines and forgotten what you had originally, or generally messed up) and you *don't* want it to get forced onto the disk. When you list your block again, after entering EMPTY-BUFFERS, the system won't know it ever had your block in memory and will bring it in off the disk anew.‡

Each buffer has an associated cell in memory called the "buffer status cell." It contains the number of the block (e.g., 180).‡ The system uses it to tell whether a requested block is already in memory. When you COPY a block, all you are really doing is changing the number of the block in the buffer status cell and updating the buffer. When it's time for the buffer to be written to disk, it will be written to the new block.

The basic word that brings a block in from the disk, after first finding an available buffer and storing its contents on disk if necessary, is BLOCK. For instance, if you say

```
205 BLOCK
```

the system will copy block 205 from disk into one of the buffers. BLOCK also leaves on the stack the address of the beginning of the buffer that it used. We'll learn how to use this address in a few sections.

---

†For Beginners

"Garbage" is computer jargon for data which is wrong, meaningless, or irrelevant for the use to which it is being put.

‡For Those Using a Multiprogrammed System

Careful! EMPTY-BUFFERS empties *everyone's* buffers.

‡For the Curious

The sign bit of the buffer status cell serves as the "update flag." If the number in the buffer status cell tests as negative by 0<, then the buffer has been "updated."

If your application requires writing a lot of data to the disk without reading what's on the disk already (e.g., to initialize a disk, write raw data, transfer tape to disk, etc.), then you'll want to use BUFFER.

BUFFER is used by BLOCK to assign a block number to the next available buffer. BUFFER doesn't read the contents of the disk into the buffer. Also, BUFFER doesn't check to see whether the block number has already been assigned to a buffer, so you have to make sure that no two buffers get assigned to the same number.

UPDATE	(--)	Marks the most recently referenced block as modified. The block will later be automatically transferred to mass storage if its buffer is needed to store a different block or if FLUSH is executed.
EMPTY-BUFFERS	(--)	Marks all block buffers as empty without necessarily affecting their actual contents. Updated blocks are not written to mass storage.
BLOCK	(u -- adr)	Leaves the address of the first byte in block u. If the block is not already in memory, it is transferred from mass storage into whichever memory buffer has been least recently accessed. If the block occupying that buffer has been updated (i.e., modified), it is rewritten onto mass storage before block u is read into the buffer.
BUFFER	(u -- adr)	Obtains the next block buffer, assigning it to block u. The block is not read from mass storage.

Output Operators

The word EMIT takes a single ASCII representation on the stack, using the low-order byte only, and prints the character at your terminal. For example, in decimal:

```
65 EMIT Aok
66 EMIT Bok
```

The word TYPE prints an entire string of characters at your terminal, given the starting address of the string in memory and the count, in this form:

```
(adr u --  )
```

We've already seen TYPE in our number-formatting definitions without worrying about the address and count, because they are automatically supplied by #>.

Let's give TYPE an address that we know contains a character string. Remember that the starting address of the input message buffer is kept by the user variable S0? Suppose we enter the following command:

```
S0 @ 12 TYPE
```

This will type twelve characters from the input message buffer, which contains the command we just entered:

```
S0 @ 12 TYPE RETURN S0 @ 12 TYPEok
```

Let's digress for a moment to look at the operation of .". At compile time, when the compiler encounters a dot-quote, it compiles the ensuing string right into the dictionary, letter-by-letter, up to the delimiting double-quote. To keep track of things, it also compiles the count of characters into the dictionary entry. Given the definition

```
: TEST  ." SAMPLE " ;
```

and looking at bytes in the dictionary horizontally rather than vertically, here is what the compiler has compiled:

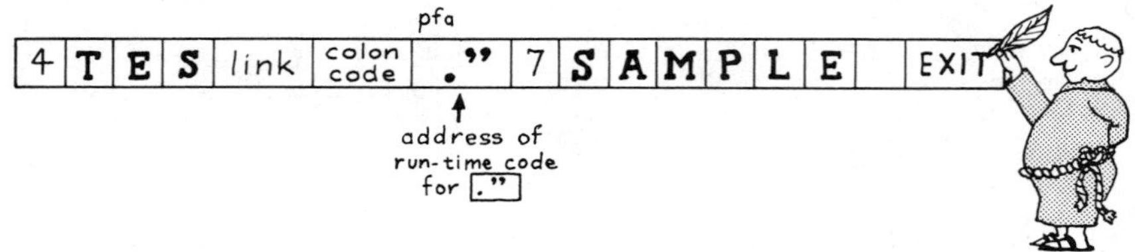

If we wanted to, we could type the word "SAMPLE" ourselves (without executing TEST) with the phrase

```
' TEST 3 + 7 TYPE
```

where

```
' TEST
```

gives us the pfa of TEST,

```
3 +
```

offsets us past the address and the count, to the beginning of the string (the letter "S"), and

```
7 TYPE
```

types the string "SAMPLE."

That little exercise may not seem too useful. But let's go a step further.

Remember how we defined LABEL in our egg-sizing application, using nested IF...THEN statements? We can rework our definition using TYPE. First let's make all the labels the same length and "string them together" within a single definition as a string array. (We can abbreviate the longest label to "XTRA LRG" so that we can make each label eight characters long, including trailing spaces.)

```
: "LABEL"
     ." REJECT  SMALL   MEDIUM  LARGE   XTRA LRGERROR   " ;
```

Once we enter

```
' "LABEL" 3 +
```

to get the address of the start of the string, we can type any particular label by offsetting into the array. For example, if we want label 2, we simply add sixteen (2 x 8) to the starting address and type the eight characters of the name:

```
16 + 8 TYPE
```

Now let's redefine LABEL so that it takes a category-number from zero through five and uses it to index into the string array, like this:

```
: LABEL   8 *  ['] "LABEL" 3 +  +  8 TYPE SPACE ;
```

Recall that the word ['] is just like ' except that it may only be used inside a definition to compile the address of the next word in the definition (in this case, "LABEL").† Later, when we execute LABEL, bracket-tick-bracket will push the pfa of "LABEL" onto the stack. The number three is added, then the string offset is added to compute the address of the particular label name that we want.

This kind of string array is sometimes called a "superstring." As a naming convention, the name of the superstring usually has quotes around it.

Our new version of LABEL will run a little faster because it does not have to perform a series of comparison tests before it hits upon the number that matches the argument. Instead it uses the argument to compute the address of the appropriate string to be typed.

Notice, though, that if the argument to LABEL exceeds the range zero through five, you'll be typing garbage. If LABEL is only going to be used within EGGSIZE in the application, there's no problem. But if an "end user," meaning a person, is going to use it, you'd better "clip" the index, like this:

```
: LABEL   0 MAX  5 MIN  LABEL ;
```

TYPE	(adr u --)	Transmits u characters, beginning at address, to the current output device.

---

†FORTH-79 Standard

See Appendix 3.

Outputting Strings from Disk

We mentioned before that the word BLOCK copies a given block into an available buffer and leaves the address of the buffer on the stack. Using this address as a starting-point, we can index into one of the buffer's 1,024 bytes and type any string we care to. For example, to print line 0 of block 214, we could say

```
CR 214 BLOCK  64 TYPE RETURN
( THIS IS BLOCK 214)                                    ok
```

To print line eight, we could add 512 (8 x 64) to the address, like this:

```
CR 214 BLOCK  512 +  64 TYPE
```

Before we give a more interesting example, it's time to introduce two words that are closely associated with TYPE.

-TRAILING	(adr u1 -- adr u2)	Eliminates trailing blanks from the string that starts at the address by reducing the count from u1 (original byte count) to u2 (shortened byte count).
>TYPE†	(adr u --)	Same as TYPE except that the output string is moved to the pad prior to output. Used in multiprogrammed systems to output strings from disk blocks.

-TRAILING can be used immediately before the TYPE command to adjust the count so that trailing blanks will not be printed. For instance, inserting it into our first example above would give us

```
CR 214 BLOCK  64 -TRAILING TYPE RETURN
( THIS IS BLOCK 214) ok
```

---

†FORTH-79 Standard

>TYPE is not required.

The word >TYPE is only used on multiprogrammed systems to print strings from disk buffers. Instead of typing the string directly from the address given, it first moves the entire string into the pad, then types it from there. Because all users share the same buffers, the system cannot guarantee that by the time TYPE has finished typing, the buffer will still contain the same block. It <u>can</u> guarantee, however, that the buffer will contain the same block during the move to the pad.[†] Since each task has its own pad, >TYPE can safely type from there.

The following example uses TYPE, but you may substitute >TYPE if need be.

```
231 LIST

( BUZZPHRASE GENERATOR -- VER. 1)      EMPTY

181 LOAD  ( RANDOM NUMBERS)

: BUZZ  232 BLOCK +  10 CHOOSE  64 * +  20 -TRAILING TYPE ;
: 1ADJ   0 BUZZ ;
: 2ADJ  20 BUZZ ;
: NOUN  40 BUZZ ;
: PHRASE   1ADJ SPACE 2ADJ SPACE NOUN ;
: PARAGRAPH
     CR  ." BY USING "  PHRASE  ."  COORDINATED WITH "
     CR  PHRASE  ."  IT IS POSSIBLE FOR EVEN THE MOST "
     CR  PHRASE  ."  TO FUNCTION AS "
     CR  PHRASE  ."  WITHIN THE CONSTRAINTS OF "
     CR  PHRASE  ." . " ;
PARAGRAPH
```

(continued)

[†]**For Experts**

In a multiprogrammed system, a task only releases control of the CPU to the next task during I/O or upon explicit command, a command which is deliberately left out of the definition of the word which moves strings.

```
232 LIST

    0 INTEGRATED          MANAGEMENT          CRITERIA
    1 TOTAL               ORGANIZATION        FLEXIBILITY
    2 SYSTEMATIZED        MONITORED           CAPABILITY
    3 PARALLEL            RECIPROCAL          MOBILITY
    4 FUNCTIONAL          DIGITAL             PROGRAMMING
    5 RESPONSIVE          LOGISTICAL          CONCEPTS
    6 OPTIMAL             TRANSITIONAL        TIME PHASING
    7 SYNCHRONIZED        INCREMENTAL         PROJECTIONS
    8 COMPATIBLE          THIRD GENERATION    HARDWARE
    9 QUALIFIED           POLICY              THROUGH-PUT
   10 PARTIAL             DECISION            ENGINEERING
   11
   12
   13
   14
   15
```

Upon loading the application block (in this case block 231), we get something like the following output, although some of the words will be different every time we execute PARAGRAPH.

```
BY USING INTEGRATED POLICY THROUGH-PUT COORDINATED WITH
COMPATIBLE ORGANIZATION CAPABILITY IT IS POSSIBLE FOR EVEN THE MOST
OPTIMAL THIRD GENERATION PROGRAMMING TO FUNCTION AS
SYSTEMATIZED MONITORED CRITERIA WITHIN THE CONSTRAINTS OF
RESPONSIVE POLICY HARDWARE.
```

As you can see, the definition of PARAGRAPH consists of a series of ." strings interspersed with the word PHRASE. If we execute PHRASE alone, we get

PHRASE SYSTEMATIZED MANAGEMENT MOBILITY ok

that is, one word chosen randomly from column 1 in block 232, one word from column 2, and one from column 3.

Looking at the definition of PHRASE, we see that it consists of three application words, 1ADJ, 2ADJ, and NOUN, each of which in turn consists of an offset and the application word BUZZ. The offset indicates which column we want to choose a particular word from; that is, the number of bytes in from the left margin of block 232 that the column begins. The definition of BUZZ breaks down as follows:

232 BLOCK

moves block 232 into an available buffer and returns the address of the buffer's beginning byte.

The word

```
+
```

adds the offset (0, 20, or 40) to offset us into the appropriate column in the block.

```
10 CHOOSE
```

returns a random number† between 0 and 10 to determine which line to take our word from.

```
64 * +
```

multiplies the random number by 64 (the length of one line) and adds this number to the buffer address, to offset into the appropriate line. The address on the stack is the address of the word we are going to type.

```
20 -TRAILING TYPE
```

adjusts the maximum count of 20 downwards so that the count excludes any trailing blanks after the character string and types the string.

---

†The random number generator is given in the following Handy Hint.

A Handy Hint

A Random Number Generator

This simple random number generator can be useful for games, although for more sophisticated applications such as simulations, better versions are available.

```
181 LIST

( RANDOM NUMBER GENERATOR -- HIGH LEVEL)
VARIABLE RND   HERE RND !
: RANDOM   RND @ 31421 *  6927 +  DUP RND ! ;
: CHOOSE   ( u1 --- u2 )
         RANDOM U* SWAP DROP ;

( where CHOOSE returns a random integer within the range
  0 = or < u2 < u1. )
```

Here's how to use it:

To choose a random number between zero and ten (but exclusive of ten) simply enter

```
10 CHOOSE
```

and CHOOSE will leave the random number on the stack.

Internal String Operators

The commands for moving character strings or data arrays are very simple. Each requires three arguments: a source address, a destination address, and a count.

Word	Stack effect	Description	Pronunciation
MOVE†	(adrl adr2 u --)	Copies a region of memory u bytes long, cell-by-cell beginning at adrl, to memory beginning at adr2. The move begins with the contents of adrl and proceeds toward high memory.	move
CMOVE	(adrl adr2 u --)	Copies a region of memory u bytes long, byte-by-byte beginning at adrl, to memory beginning at adr2. The move begins with the contents of adrl and proceeds toward high memory.	c-move
<CMOVE	(adrl adr2 u --)	Copies a region of memory u bytes long, beginning at adrl, to memory beginning at adr2, but starts at the end of the string and proceeds toward low memory.	back-c-move

---

†FORTH-79 Standard

The Standard's MOVE expects a cell count. <CMOVE is not required.

Notice that these commands follow certain conventions we've seen before:

1. When the arguments include a source and a destination (as they do with COPY), the source precedes the destination.

2. When the arguments include an address and a count (as they do with TYPE), the address precedes the count.

And so with these three words the arguments are

    (source destination count --)

To move the entire contents of a buffer into the pad, for example, we would write

```
210 BLOCK  PAD  1024 CMOVE
```

although on cell-address machines the move might be made faster if it were cell-by-cell, like this:

```
210 BLOCK  PAD  1024 MOVE
```

The word <CMOVE lets you move a string to a region that is higher in memory but that overlaps the source region.†

---

†For beginners

Let's say that you want to move a string one byte to the "right" in memory (e.g., when you use the editor command I to insert a character).

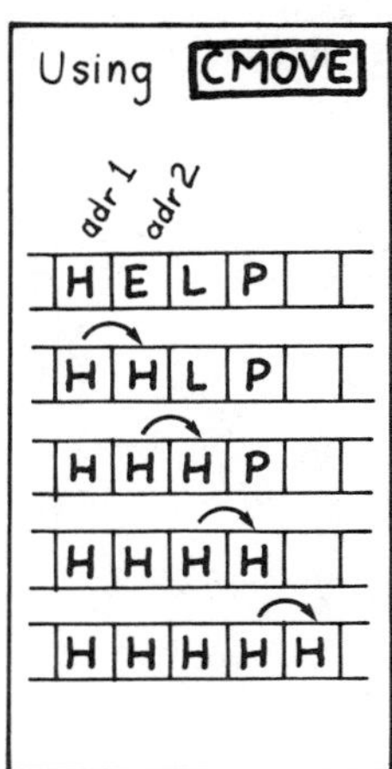

If you were to use CMOVE, the first letter of the string would get copied to the second byte, but that would "clobber" the second letter of the string. The final result would be a string composed of a single character.

Using <CMOVE in this situation keeps the string from clobbering itself during the move.

To blank an array, we can use the word FILL, which we introduced earlier. For example, to store blanks into 1024 bytes of the pad, we say

```
PAD  1024 32 FILL
```

Thirty-two is the ASCII representation of blank.†

Single-character Input

The word KEY awaits the entry of a single key from your terminal keyboard and leaves the character's ASCII equivalent on the stack in the low-order byte.

To execute it directly, you must follow it with a return, like this:

```
KEY RETURN
```

The cursor will advance a space, but the terminal will not print "ok"; it is waiting for your input. Press the letter "A," for example, and the screen will "echo" the letter "A," followed by the "ok." The ASCII value is now on the stack, so enter .:

```
KEY Aok
. RETURN 65 ok
```

This saves you from having to look in the table to determine a character's ASCII code.

You can also include KEY inside a definition. Execution of the definition will stop, when KEY is encountered, until an input character is received. For example, the following definition will list a given number of blocks in series, starting with the current block, and wait for you to press any key before it lists the next one:

```
: BLOCKS  ( count -- )
     SCR @ +  SCR @ DO  I LIST  KEY DROP  LOOP ;
```

---

†For polyFORTH Users

You may use the word BLANK instead, as in

```
PAD  1024 BLANK
```

A Handy Hint

Two Convenient Additions to the Editor

You might want to make the following two additions to your editor vocabulary. The use of these words is a matter of preference; they may or may not already be included with your system.

```
EDITOR DEFINITIONS
: K   #I PAD 132 MOVE  PAD #F 66 MOVE ;
: WIPE   SCR @ BLOCK DUP  1024 32 FILL  0 SWAP !  UPDATE ;
FORTH DEFINITIONS
```

The word K will swap the contents of the find buffer with that of the insert buffer. Here's an example of its use:

```
^YOU HAVE THE RIGHT TO SILENT REMAIN.                    ok
DbbSILENT RETURN
K
F AIN RETURN

YOU HAVE THE RIGHT TO REMAIN^.                           ok
I

YOU HAVE THE RIGHT TO REMAIN SILENT.                     ok
```

Use of D put "SILENT" in the find buffer, and K put it into the insert buffer so that you could insert it where it belongs.

Or if you've just inserted a string in the wrong place, you can put the string into the find buffer with K and then erase it from the line with a simple E.

The word WIPE blanks the current block and stores two nulls in the first two character positions. (On most systems, nulls in the block act just like the word EXIT, to immediately terminate interpretation of the block, should it be loaded.)

In this case we DROP the value left by KEY because we do not care what it is.

Or we might add a feature that allows us either to leave the loop at any time by pressing return or to continue by pressing any other key, such as space. In this case we will perform a conditional test on the value returned by KEY.

```
: BLOCKS   ( count -- )
    SCR @ +  SCR @ DO  I LIST
        KEY 0= ( CR) IF  LEAVE THEN  LOOP ;
```

Note that in most FORTH systems, the carriage-return key is received as a null (zero).

KEY	(-- c)	Returns the ASCII value of the next available character from the current input device.

String Input Commands, from the Bottom up

There are several words involved with string input. We'll start with the lowest-level of these and proceed to some higher-level words. Here are the words we'll cover in this section:

EXPECT	(adr u --)	Awaits u characters (or a carriage return) from the terminal keyboard and stores them, starting at the address.
WORD	(c -- adr)	Reads one word from the input stream, using the character (usually blank) as a delimiter. Moves the string to the address (HERE) with the count in the first byte, leaving the address on the stack.
TEXT	(c --)	Reads a string from the input stream, using the character as a delimiter, then sets the pad to blanks and moves the string to the pad.

The word EXPECT stops execution of the task and waits for input from your keyboard. It expects a given number of keystrokes or a carriage return, whichever comes first. The incoming text is stored beginning at the address given as an argument.

For example, the phrase

```
S0 @  80 EXPECT †
```

will await up to eighty characters and store them in the input message buffer.

This phrase is the one used in the definition of QUIT to get the input for INTERPRET.

In most systems, when you press return or when the limit is reached, EXPECT stores a null (zero) into the string to mark the end, then allows execution to continue.‡

---

† **FORTH-79 Standard**

This phrase is equivalent to the Standard word QUERY.

‡ **For Experts**

You can use EXPECT to accept data from a serial line, such as a measuring device. Since you supply the address and count, such data can be read directly into an array. In a single-user environment, you may read data into a buffer for storage on disk. In a multi-user environment, however, you must use S0 and later move the data into the buffer, since another task may use "your" buffer.

Let's move on to the next higher-level string-input operator. We've just explained that QUIT contains the phrase

```
... S0 @  80 EXPECT  INTERPRET ...
```

But how does the text interpreter scan the input message buffer and pick out each individual word there? With the phrase

```
32 WORD
```

The decimal number 32 is the ASCII representation for "space." WORD scans the input stream looking for the given delimiter, in this case space, and moves the sub-string into a different buffer of its own, with the count in the first byte of the buffer. Finally, it leaves the address of its buffer on the stack, so that INTERPRET (or anyone else) knows where to find it. WORD's buffer usually begins at H, the dictionary pointer, so the address given is HERE.

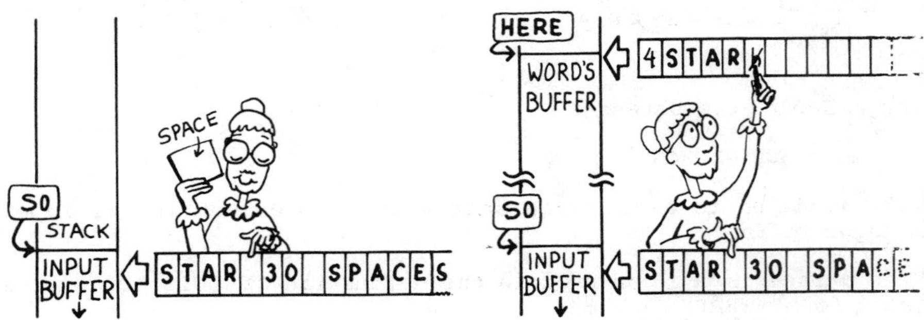

WORD looks for the given delimiter in the input message buffer,

and moves the the sub-string to WORD's buffer, with the count in the first byte.

When you are executing words directly from a terminal, WORD will scan the input buffer, starting at S0. As it goes along, it advances the input buffer pointer, called >IN, so that each time you execute WORD, you scan the next word in the input stream.

>IN is a "relative pointer"; that is, it does not contain the actual address but rather an offset that is to be added to the actual address, which in this case is S0. For example, after WORD has scanned the string "STAR," the value of >IN is five.

WORD ignores initial occurrences of the delimiter (until any other character is encountered). You could type

```
ƀƀƀƀƀSTAR
```

(that is, STAR preceded by several spaces) and get exactly the same string in WORD's buffer as shown above.

When WORD moves the sub-string, it includes a blank at the end but does not include it in the count.

We'll get back to WORD later on in this chapter. For now, though, let's look at a word that uses WORD and that is more useful for handling string input.

TEXT,† like WORD, takes a delimiter and scans the input stream until it finds the string delimited by it. It then moves the string to the pad. What is especially nice about TEXT is that before it moves the string, it blanks the pad for at least sixty-four spaces. This makes it very convenient for use with TYPE. Here's a simple example:

```
CREATE MY-NAME  40 ALLOT
: I'M   32 TEXT  PAD MY-NAME 40 CMOVE ;
```

In the first line we define an array called MY-NAME. In the second line we define a word called I'M which will allow us to enter

```
I'M EDWARD ok
```

---

†**For Those Who Don't Seem to Have TEXT**

TEXT is not required by the FORTH-79 Standard. Its definition, however, is

```
: TEXT   PAD 72 32 FILL  WORD  COUNT PAD SWAP <CMOVE ;
```

If you have a polyFORTH system, the electives block normally does not load the block (usually 34) that contains TEXT. In this case you must add "34 LOAD" to your electives block and reload it.

The definition of I'M breaks down as follows: the phrase

```
32 TEXT
```

scans the remainder of the input stream looking for a space or for the end of the line, whichever comes first. (The delimiter that we give as an argument to TEXT is actually used by WORD, which is included in the definition of TEXT.) TEXT then moves the phrase to a nice clean "pad."

The phrase

```
PAD MY-NAME 40 CMOVE
```

moves forty bytes from the pad into the array called MY-NAME, where it will safely stay for as long as we need it.

We could now define GREET as follows:

```
: GREET  ." HELLO, " MY-NAME 40 -TRAILING TYPE
         ." , I SPEAK FORTH. " ;
```

so that by executing GREET, we get

```
GREET HELLO, EDWARD, I SPEAK FORTH. ok
```

Unfortunately, our definition of I'M is looking for a space as its delimiter. This means that a person named Mary Kay will not get her full name into MY-NAME.

To get the complete input stream, we don't want to "see" any delimiter at all, except the end of the line. Instead of "32 TEXT," we should use the phrase

```
1 TEXT
```

ASCII 1 is a control character that can't be sent from the keyboard and therefore won't ever appear in the input buffer. Thus "1 TEXT" is a convention used to read the entire input buffer, up to the carriage return. By redefining I'M in this way, Mary Kay can get her name into MY-NAME, space and all.

By using other delimiters, such as commas, we can "expect" a series of strings and store each of them into a different array for different purposes. Consider this example, in which the word VITALS uses commas as delimiters to separate three input fields:

```
233 LIST

 ( FORM LOVE LETTER)            EMPTY
 VARIABLE NAME  12 ALLOT     VARIABLE EYES  10 ALLOT
 VARIABLE ME  12 ALLOT
 : VITALS   44 TEXT ( ,)  PAD NAME 14 MOVE
            44 TEXT       PAD EYES 12 MOVE
             1 TEXT       PAD  ME  14 MOVE  ;

 : LETTER       PAGE
        ." DEAR " NAME 14 -TRAILING TYPE ." ,"
    CR ." I GO TO HEAVEN WHENEVER I SEE YOUR DEEP "
                       EYES 12 -TRAILING TYPE ."  EYES.  CAN "
    CR ." YOU GO TO THE MOVIES FRIDAY? "
                              CR 30 SPACES  ." LOVE,"
                              CR 30 SPACES  ME 14 -TRAILING TYPE
    CR ." P.S.  WEAR SOMETHING "  EYES 12 -TRAILING TYPE
      ."  TO SHOW OFF THOSE EYES! " ;
```

which allows you to enter

```
VITALS ALICE,BLUE,FRED ok
```

then enter

```
LETTER
```

It works every time.

So far all of our input has been "FORTH style"; that is, numbers precede commands (so that a command will find its number on the stack) and strings follow commands (so that a command will find its string in the input stream). This style makes use of one of FORTH's unique features: it awaits your commands; it does not prompt you.

But if you want to, you may put EXPECT inside a definition so that it will request input from you under control of the definition. For example, we could combine the two words I'M and GREET into a single word which "prompts" users to enter their names. For example,

```
GREET
WHAT'S YOUR NAME?
```

at which point execution stops so the user can enter a name:

```
GREET
WHAT'S YOUR NAME? TRAVIS MC GEE
HELLO, TRAVIS MC GEE, I SPEAK FORTH. ok
```

We could do this as follows:

```
: GREET   CR ." WHAT'S YOUR NAME?"  S0 @  40 EXPECT
               0 >IN !  1 TEXT   CR  ." HELLO, "
    PAD 40 -TRAILING TYPE   ." , I SPEAK FORTH. " ;
```

We've explained all the phrases in the above definition except this one:

```
0 >IN !
```

Remember that TEXT, because it uses WORD, always uses >IN as its reference point. But when the user enters the word GREET to execute this definition, the string "GREET" will be stored in the input message buffer and >IN will be pointing beyond "GREET". EXPECT does *not* use >IN as its reference, so it will store the user's name beginning at S0, on top of GREET. If you were to execute TEXT *now*, it would miss the first five letters of the user's name. It's necessary to reset >IN to zero so that TEXT will look where EXPECT has put the name.

Number Input Conversions

When you type a number at your terminal, FORTH automatically converts this character string into a binary value and pushes it onto the stack. FORTH also provides two commands which let you convert a character string that begins at any memory location into a binary value.†

Word	Stack	Description
>BINARY or CONVERT	(d1 adr1 -- d2 adr2)	Converts the text beginning at adr1+1 to a binary value with regard to BASE. The new value is accumulated into d1, being left as d2; adr2 is the address of the first non-convertible character.
NUMBER	(adr -- n or d)	Converts the text beginning at adr+1, with regard to BASE, to a binary value that is single-length if no valid punctuation occurs and double-length if valid punctuation does occur. The string may contain a preceding negative sign; adr may contain a count, which will be ignored.

NUMBER exists on most systems and is usually the simpler to use. Here's an example that uses NUMBER:

```
: PLUS   32 WORD  NUMBER + ." = " . ;
```

PLUS allows us to prove to any skeptic that FORTH could use infix notation if it wanted to. We can enter

---

†**FORTH-79 Standard**

The Standard specifies the name CONVERT instead of >BINARY. In FORTH systems which use three-character uniqueness, however, this choice conflicts with the name CONTEXT; hence the name >BINARY is used instead. NUMBER is not required by the Standard.

2 PLUS 13 RETURN = 15 ok

When PLUS is executed, the "2" will be on the stack in binary form, while the "3" will still be in the input stream as a string. The phrase

32 WORD

reads the string; NUMBER converts it to binary and puts the value on the stack; + adds the two values; and . prints the sum.

NUMBER expects on the stack the address of the string that is to be converted, with the count in the first byte and one trailing blank, so it's most appropriate for use after WORD. NUMBER does not actually use the count, however; it only adds one byte to the address before beginning the conversion. Thus you can use NUMBER on a string that does not contain the count in the first byte, simply by subtracting one byte from the starting address of the string.

>BINARY is a more primitive definition, being used in the definition of NUMBER. You can use >BINARY to create your own specialized number input conversion routines. Since >BINARY returns the address of the first non-convertible character, you can make decisions based on whether the character is a hyphen, dot, or whatever. You can also make decisions based on the location of the non-convertible character within the number. For instance, you can write a routine that lets you enter a number with a decimal point in it and then scales it accordingly.

To give a good example of the use of >BINARY, Figure 10-1 shows a definition of NUMBER. This version reads any of the characters

: , - . /

as valid punctuation characters which cause the value to be returned on the stack as a double-length integer. If none of these characters appear in the string, the value is returned as single-length.† This definition uses the word WITHIN as we defined it in the problems for Chap. 4.

Here we use the variable PUNCT to contain a flag that indicates whether punctuation was encountered. We suggest that you use an available user variable instead.

---

†**For polyFORTH Users**

Your version of NUMBER behaves similarly and in addition leaves in the user variable PTR the number of characters that were converted since the last punctuation was encountered.

FIGURE 10-1. A DEFINITION OF NUMBER

VARIABLE PUNCT	Creates a flag that will contain true if the number contains valid punctuation.
: NUMBER (adr -- n or d)	
0 PUNCT !	Initializes flag: no punctuation has occurred.
DUP 1+ C@	Gets the first digit.
45 (-) =	Is it a minus sign?
DUP >R	Saves the flag on the return stack.
+	If the first character is "-", adds 1 (the flag itself) to the address, setting it to point to the first digit.
0 0 ROT	Provides a double-length zero as an accumulator.
BEGIN >BINARY	Begins conversion; converts until an invalid digit.
DUP C@	Fetches the invalid digit.
32 - WHILE	While it is not a blank, checks if it is valid punctuation; that is,
DUP C@ DUP 58 =	a colon, or
SWAP 44 48 WITHIN +	a comma, hyphen, period, or slash.
DUP PUNCT !	Sets PUNCT to indicate whether valid punctuation has occurred.
NOT ABORT" ? "	Otherwise issues an error message.
REPEAT	Exits here if a blank is detected; otherwise repeats conversion.
DROP	Discards the address on the stack.
R> IF DNEGATE THEN	If the flag on the return stack is true, negates d.
PUNCT @ NOT IF DROP THEN ;	If there was no punctuation, returns a single-length value by dropping the high-order cell.

A Closer Look at WORD

So far we have only talked about using WORD to scan the input message buffer (which holds the characters that are EXPECTed from the terminal). But if we recall that the phrase

```
32 WORD
```

is used by the text interpreter, we realize that WORD actually scans the input stream, which is either the input message buffer or a block buffer that is being LOADed.

To achieve this flexibility, WORD uses another pointer in addition to >IN, called BLK (pronounced b-l-k). BLK acts both as a flag and as a pointer. If BLK contains zero, then WORD scans the input message buffer (that is, S0 offset by >IN). But if BLK contains a non-zero number, then WORD is referring to a block buffer and the number in BLK is the number of the block. Here are two examples:

contents of BLK	address currently used by WORD:
0	S0 @ >IN @ + (>IN bytes into the message buffer)
200	200 BLOCK >IN @ + (>IN bytes into the block buffer)

Every time a word is interpreted during a LOAD operation, WORD makes sure that the appropriate block is still in a buffer.

A useful word to use in conjunction with WORD is COUNT. Recall that WORD leaves the length of the word in the first byte of WORD's buffer and also leaves the address of this byte on the stack.

The word COUNT puts the count on the stack and increments the address, like this:

leaving the stack with a string address and a count as appropriate arguments for TYPE, CMOVE, etc.

COUNT is used in the definition of TEXT which we gave in a footnote earlier.

COUNT	(adr -- adr+1 u)	Converts a character string, whose length is contained in its first byte, into the form appropriate for TYPE, by leaving the address of the first character and the length on the stack.

We will further illustrate the use of WORD in one of the examples in Chap. 12.

String Comparisons

Here is a FORTH word that you can use to compare character strings:

-TEXT	(adr1 u adr2 -- f)	Compares two strings that start at adr1 and adr2, each of length u. Returns false if they match; true if no match (positive if binary string 1 > 2, negative if 1 < 2).

not-text

-TEXT can be used to test either whether two character strings are equal or whether one is alphabetically greater or lesser than the other.†‡ Chap. 12 includes an example of using -TEXT to determine whether strings match exactly.

Since for speed -TEXT compares cell-by-cell, you must take care on cell-address machines to give -TEXT even cell addresses only. For example, if you want to compare a string that is being entered as input with a string that is in an array, bring the input string to the pad (using TEXT rather than WORD) because PAD is an even address. Similarly, if you want to test a string that is in a block buffer, you must either guarantee that the string's address is even or, if you cannot know for sure, move the string to an even address (using CMOVE) before making the test.

By the way, the hyphen in -TEXT is as close as ASCII comes to "¬", the logical symbol meaning "not." This is why we conventionally use this prefix for words which return a "negative true" flag. (Negative true means that a zero represents true and a non-zero represents false.) We pronounce such words not-text, etc.

---

†**For Users of Intel, DEC, and Zilog Processors**

To make the "alphabetical" test, you must first reverse the order of bytes.

‡**FORTH-79 Standard**

-TEXT is not included in the Standard. If your system does not have -TEXT, you can load the high-level definition below. Of course, -TEXT is written in assembler code on all polyFORTH systems, for speed.

```
: -TEXT   2DUP + SWAP DO  DROP  2+
    DUP 2- @  I @ -  DUP  IF DUP ABS /  LEAVE THEN
        2 +LOOP  SWAP   DROP ;
```

Here's a list of the FORTH words covered in this chapter.

Word	Stack	Description
UPDATE	(--)	Marks the most recently referenced block as modified. The block will later be automatically transferred to mass storage if its buffer is needed to store a different block or if FLUSH is executed.
EMPTY-BUFFERS	(--)	Marks all block buffers as empty without necessarily affecting their actual contents. Updated blocks are not written to mass storage.
BLOCK	(u -- adr)	Leaves the address of the first byte in block u. If the block is not already in memory, it is transferred from mass storage into whichever memory buffer has been least recently accessed. If the block occupying that buffer has been updated (i.e., modified), it is rewritten onto mass storage before block u is read into the buffer.
BUFFER	(u -- adr)	Obtains the next block buffer, assigning it to block u. The block is not read from mass storage.
TYPE	(adr u --)	Transmits u characters, beginning at address, to the current output device.
-TRAILING	(adr u1 -- adr u2)	Eliminates trailing blanks from the string that starts at the address by reducing the count from u1 (original byte count) to u2 (shortened byte count).

MOVE	(adr1 adr2 u --)	Copies a region of memory u bytes long, cell-by-cell beginning at adr1, to memory beginning at adr2. The move begins with the contents of adr1 and proceeds toward high memory.
CMOVE	(adr1 adr2 u --)	Copies a region of memory u bytes long, byte-by-byte beginning at adr1, to memory beginning at adr2. The move begins with the contents of adr1 and proceeds toward high memory.
KEY	(-- c)	Returns the ASCII value of the next available character from the current input device.
EXPECT	(adr u --)	Awaits u characters (or a carriage return) from the terminal keyboard and stores them, starting at the address.
WORD	(c -- adr)	Reads one word from the input stream, using the character (usually blank) as a delimiter. Moves the string to the address (HERE) with the count in the first byte, leaving the address on the stack.
TEXT	(c --)	Reads a string from the input stream, using the character as a delimiter, then sets the pad to blanks and moves the string to the pad.
>BINARY or CONVERT	(d1 adr1 -- d2 adr2)	Converts the text beginning at adr1+1 to a binary value with regard to BASE. The new value is accumulated into d1, being left as d2; adr2 is the address of the first non-convertible character.

NUMBER	(adr -- n or d)	Converts the text beginning at adr+1, with regard to BASE, to a binary value that is single-length if no valid punctuation occurs, and double-length if valid punctuation does occur. The string may contain a preceding negative sign; adr may contain a count, which will be ignored.
COUNT	(adr -- adr+1 u)	Converts a character string, whose length is contained in its first byte, into the form appropriate for TYPE, by leaving the address of the first character and the length on the stack.

Additional Words Available in Some Systems

>TYPE	(adr u --)	Same as TYPE except that the output string is moved to the pad prior to output. Used in multiprogrammed systems to output strings from disk blocks.
<CMOVE	(adr1 adr2 u --)	Copies a region of memory u bytes long, beginning at adr1, to memory beginning at adr2, but starts at the end of the string and proceeds toward low memory.
-TEXT	(adr1 u adr2 -- f)	Compares two strings that start at adr1 and adr2, each of length u. Returns false if they match; true if no match (positive if binary string 1 > 2, negative if 1 < 2).
BLANK	(adr n --)	Stores ASCII blanks into n bytes of memory, beginning at adr.

Review of Terms

Buffer status cell — in the FORTH operating system, a cell in resident memory associated with each block buffer (usually directly preceding it in memory) which contains the number of the block currently stored in the buffer and a flag (the sign bit) which indicates whether the buffer has been updated.

Relative pointer — a variable which specifies a location in relation to the beginning of an array or string --not the absolute address.

Superstring — in FORTH, a character array which contains a number of strings. Any one string may be accessed by indexing into the array.

Virtual memory — the treatment of mass storage (such as the disk) as though it were resident memory; also the mechanisms of the operating system which make this treatment possible.

Problems -- Chapter 10

1. Enter some famous quotations into an available block, say 228. Now define a word called CHANGE which takes two ASCII values and changes all occurrences within block 228 of the first character into the second character. For example,

   ```
   65 69 CHANGE
   ```

   will change all the "A"s into "E"s.

2. Define a word called FORTUNE which will print a prediction at your terminal, such as "You will receive good news in the mail." The prediction should be chosen at random from a list of sixteen or fewer predictions. Each prediction is sixty-four characters, or less, long.

3. According to Oriental legend, Buddha endows all persons born in each year with special, helpful characteristics represented by one of twelve animals. A different animal reigns over each year, and every twelve years the cycle repeats itself. For instance, persons born in 1900 are said to be born in the "Year of the Rat." The art of fortune-telling based on these influences of the natal year is called "Juneeshee."

   Here is the order of the cycle:

   Rat Ox Tiger Rabbit Dragon Snake
   Horse Ram Monkey Cock Dog Boar

   Write a word called .ANIMAL that types the name of the animal corresponding to its position in the cycle as listed here; e.g.,

   ```
   0 .ANIMAL RAT ok
   ```

   Now write a word called (JUNEESHEE) which takes as an argument a year of birth and prints the name of the associated animal. (1900 is the year of the Rat, 1901 is the Ox, etc.)

   Finally, write a word called JUNEESHEE which prompts the user for his/her year of birth and prints the name of the person's Juneeshee animal. Define it so the user won't have to press "return" after entering the year.

4. Rewrite the definition of LETTER that appears in this chapter so that it uses names and personal descriptions that have been edited into a block, rather than entered into character arrays. In this way, you can keep a file on many "prospects" and produce a letter for any one person with the

appropriate descriptions, just by supplying an argument to LETTER, as in

```
1 LETTER
```

Now define LETTERS so that it prints one letter for each person in your file.

5. In this exercise you will create and use a virtual array, that is, an array which resides on the disk but which is referenced like a memory-resident array (with @ and !).

   First select an unused block in your range of assigned blocks. There can be no text on this block; binary data will be stored in it. Put this block number in a variable. Then define an access word which accepts a cell subscript from the stack, then computes the block number corresponding to this subscript, calls BLOCK and returns the memory address of the subscripted cell. This access word should also call UPDATE. Test your work so far.

   Next use the first cell as a count of how many data items are stored in the array. Define a word PUT which will store a value into the next available cell of the array. Define a display routine which will print the stored elements in the array.

   Now use this virtual array facility to define a word ENTER which will accept pairs of numbers and store them in the array.

   Finally, define TABLE to print the data entered above, eight numbers per line.

11 EXTENDING THE COMPILER: DEFINING WORDS AND COMPILING WORDS

In comparison with traditional languages, FORTH's compiler is completely backwards. Traditional compilers are huge programs designed to translate any foreseeable, legal combination of available operators into machine language. In FORTH, however, most of the work of compilation is done by a single definition, only a few lines long. Special structures like conditionals and loops are not compiled by the compiler but by the words being compiled (IF, DO, etc.).

Lest you scoff at FORTH's simple ways, notice that FORTH is unique among languages in the ease with which you can extend the compiler. Defining new, specialized compilers is as easy as defining any other word, as you will soon see.

When you've got an extensible compiler, you've got a very powerful language!

Just a Question of Time

Before we get fully into this chapter, let's review one particular concept that can be a problem to beginning FORTH programmers. It's a question of time.

We have used the term "run time" when referring to things that occur when a word is executed and "compile time" when referring to things that happen when a word is compiled. So far so good. But things get a little confusing when a single word has both a run-time behavior and a compile-time behavior.

In general there are two classes of words which behave in both ways. For purposes of this discussion, we'll call these two classes "defining words" and "compiling words."

A defining word is a word which, when executed, compiles a new definition. A defining word specifies the compile-time and run-time behavior of each member of the "family" of words that it defines. Using the defining word CONSTANT as an example, when we say

```
80 CONSTANT MARGIN
```

we are executing the compile-time behavior of CONSTANT; that is, CONSTANT is compiling a new constant-type dictionary entry called MARGIN and storing the value 80 into its parameter field. But when we say

```
MARGIN
```

we are executing the run-time behavior of CONSTANT; that is, CONSTANT is pushing the value 80 onto the stack. We'll pursue defining words further in the next few sections.

The other type of word which possesses dual behavior is the "compiling word." A compiling word is a word that we use inside a colon definition and that actually does something during compilation of that definition.

One example is the word .", which at compile time compiles a text string into the dictionary entry with the count in the first byte, and at run time types it. Other examples are control-structure words like IF and LOOP, which also have compile-time behaviors distinct from their run-time behaviors. We'll explore compiling words after we've discussed defining words.

How to Define a Defining Word

Here are the standard FORTH defining words we've covered so far:

```
:
VARIABLE
2VARIABLE
CONSTANT
2CONSTANT
CREATE
USER
```

What do they all have in common? Each of them is used to define a set of words with similar compile-time and run-time characteristics.

And how are all these defining words defined? First we'll answer this question metaphorically.

Let's say you're in the ceramic salt-shaker business. If you plan to make enough salt shakers, you'll find it's easiest to make a mold first. A mold will guarantee that all your shakers will be of the same design, while allowing you to make each shaker a different color.

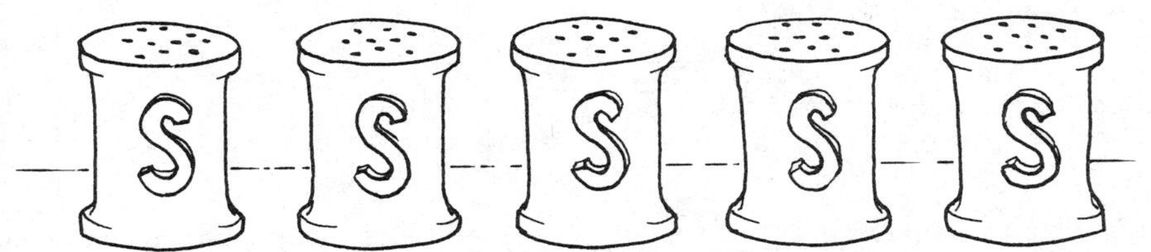

In making the mold, you must consider two things:

1. How the mold will work. (E.g., how will you get the clay into and out of the mold without breaking the mold or letting the seams show?)

2. How the shaker will work. (E.g., how many holes should there be? How much salt should it hold? Etc.)

To bring this analogy back to FORTH, the definition of a defining word must specify two things: the compile-time behavior and the run-time behavior for that type of word.

Hold that thought a moment while we look at the most basic of the defining words in the above list: CREATE. At compile time, CREATE takes a name from the input stream and creates a dictionary heading for it.

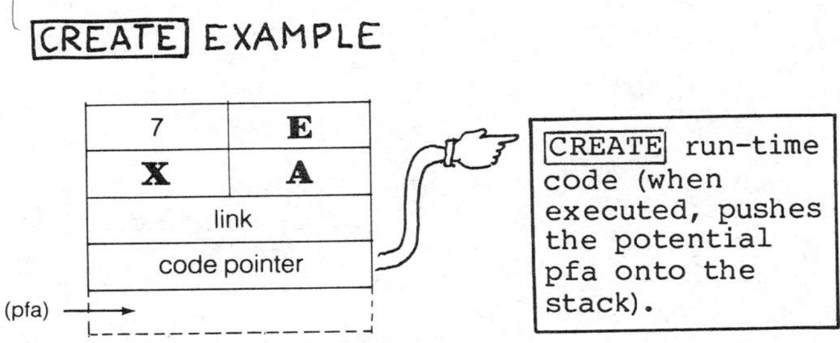

At run time, CREATE pushes the pfa of EXAMPLE onto the stack.

What happens if we use CREATE inside a definition? Consider this example, which is the definition for VARIABLE:

```
: VARIABLE   CREATE  2 ALLOT ;
```

When we execute VARIABLE as in

```
VARIABLE ORANGES
```

we are indirectly using CREATE to create a dictionary head with the name ORANGES and a code pointer that points to CREATE's run-time code. Then we are allotting two bytes for the variable itself.

Since the run-time behavior of a variable is identical to that of a word defined by CREATE, VARIABLE does not need to have run-time code of its own; it can use CREATE's run-time code.

How do we specify a different run-time behavior in a defining word? By using the word DOES>, as shown here:

```
: DEFINING-WORD   CREATE (compile-time operations)
                  DOES> (run-time operations) ;
```

To illustrate, the following could be a valid definition for CONSTANT (although in fact CONSTANT is usually defined in machine code):

```
: CONSTANT   CREATE ,  DOES> @ ;
```

To see how this definition works, imagine we're using it to define a constant named TROMBONES, like this:

```
76 CONSTANT TROMBONES
```

compile-time portion	CREATE	Creates a new dictionary entry (e.g., TROMBONES).
	,	Compiles the value (e.g., 76) for the constant from the stack into the constant's parameter field.
run-time portion	DOES>	Marks the end of the compile-time behavior and the beginning of the run-time behavior. At run time, DOES> will leave the pfa of the word being defined on the stack.
	@	Fetches the contents of the constant, using the pfa that will be on the stack at run time.

The words that precede DOES> specify what the mold will do; the words that follow DOES> specify what the product of the mold will do.

DOES>	run time: (-- adr)	Used in creating a defining word; marks the end of its compile-time portion and the beginning of its run-time portion. The run-time operations are stated in higher-level FORTH. At run time, the pfa of the defined word will be on the stack.

Defining Words You Can Define Yourself

Here are some examples of defining words that you can create yourself.

Recall that in our discussion of "String Input Commands" in Chap. 10, we gave an example that employed character-string arrays called NAME, EYES, and ME. Every time we used one of these names, we followed it with a character count. In the input definition, we wrote

```
... PAD NAME 14 MOVE ...
```

and in the output definition we wrote

```
... NAME 14 -TRAILING TYPE ...
```

and so on.

Let's eliminate the count by creating a defining word called CHARACTERS, whose product definitions will leave the address and count on the stack when executed.

We'll use it like this: if we say

```
20 CHARACTERS ME
```

we will create an array called ME, with twenty bytes available for the character string.

When we execute ME, we'll get the address of the array and the count on the stack. Now we can write:

```
PAD ME MOVE
```

instead of

```
PAD ME 20 MOVE
```

or

```
ME -TRAILING TYPE
```

instead of

```
ME 20 -TRAILING TYPE
```

Here's how we might define CHARACTERS:

: CHARACTERS

compile-time portion	CREATE	Creates a new dictionary entry (e.g., ME).
	DUP , ALLOT	Compiles the count (e.g., twenty) into the first cell of the array for future reference. Then allots an additional twenty bytes beyond the count for the string.
run-time portion	DOES>	Marks the beginning of run-time code, leaving the pfa of the product-word on the stack at run time.
	DUP	Copies the pfa.
	2+	Advances the address to point past the count, to the start of the character string.
	SWAP @	Swaps the string address with the count address and fetches the count. The stack now holds (adr count --).

;

We've just extended our compiler! Our new word CHARACTERS is a defining word that creates a data structure and procedure that we find useful. CHARACTERS not only simplifies our input and output definitions, it also allows us to change the length of any string, should the need arise, in one place only (i.e., where we define it).

Our next example could be useful in an application where a large number of byte arrays are needed. Let's create a defining word called STRING as follows:

```
: STRING   CREATE ALLOT DOES> + ;
```

to be used in the form

```
30 STRING VALVE
```

to create an array thirty bytes in length. To access any byte in this array, we merely say:

```
6 VALVE C@
```

which would give us the current setting of hydraulic valve 6 at an oil-pumping station. At run time, VALVE will add the argument 6 to the pfa left by DOES>, producing the correct byte address.

If our application requires a large number of arrays to be initialized to zero, we might include the initialization in an alternate defining word called 0STRING:

```
: ERASED   HERE OVER  ERASE ALLOT ;
: 0STRING   CREATE ERASED DOES> + ;
```

First we define ERASED to ERASE the given number of bytes, starting at HERE, before ALLOTting the given number of bytes.

Then we simply substitute ERASED for ALLOT in our new version.

By changing the definition of a defining word, you can change the characteristics of all the member words of that family. This ability makes program development much easier. For instance, you can incorporate certain kinds of error checking while you are developing the program, then eliminate them after you are sure that the program runs correctly.

Here is a version of STRING which, at run time, guarantees that the index into the array is valid:

```
: STRING   CREATE DUP , ALLOT
   DOES>  2DUP @ U< NOT  ABORT" RANGE ERROR " + 2+ ;
```

which breaks down as follows:

DUP , ALLOT	Compiles the count and allots the given number of bytes.
DOES> 2DUP @	At run time, given the argument on the stack, produces: (arg pfa arg count --).
U< NOT	Tests that the argument is not less than the maximum, i.e., the stored count. Since U< is an unsigned compare, negative arguments will appear as very high numbers and thus will also fail the test.
ABORT" RANGE ERROR"	Aborts if the comparison check fails.
+ 2+	Otherwise adds the argument to the pfa, plus an additional two to skip over the cell that contains the count.

Here's another way that the use of defining words can help during development. Let's say you suddenly decide that all of the arrays you've defined with STRING are too large to be kept in computer memory and should be kept on disk instead. All you have to do is redefine the run-time portion of STRING. This new STRING will compute which block on the disk a given byte would be contained in, read the block into a buffer using BLOCK, and return the address of the desired byte within the buffer. A string defined in this way could span many consecutive blocks (using the same technique as in Prob. 5, Chap. 10).

You can use defining words to create all kinds of data structures. Sometimes, for instance, it's useful to create multi-dimensional arrays. Here's an example of a defining word which creates two-dimensional byte arrays of given size:

```
: ARRAY  ( #rows #cols --  )
    CREATE  OVER , * ALLOT
    DOES> ( member: row col --  )
    DUP @  ROT *   + +  2+ ;†
```

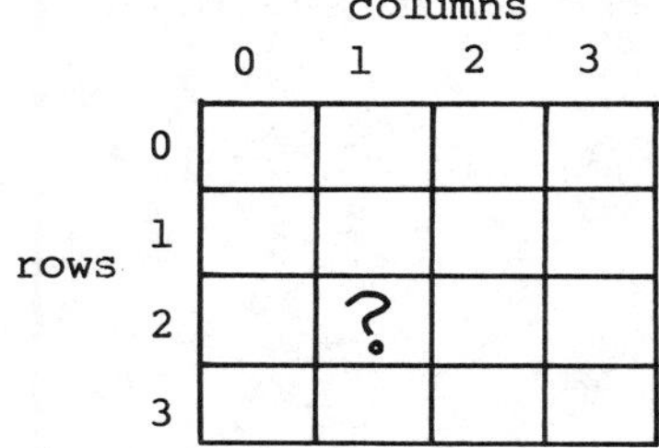

To create an array four bytes by four bytes, we would say

```
4 4 ARRAY BOARD
```

To access, say, the byte in row 2, column 1, we could say

```
2 1 BOARD C@
```

Here's how our ARRAY works in general terms. Since the computer only allows us to have one-dimensional arrays, we must simulate the second dimension. While our imaginary array looks like this: ⟶

column: 0	1	2	3
0	4	8	12
1	5	9	13
2	6	10	14
3	7	11	15

our real array looks like this:

column 0				1				2				3			
0	1	2	3	4	5	6	7	8	9	10	11	12	13	14	15

If you want the address of the byte in row 2, column 1, it can be computed by multiplying your column number (1) by the number of rows in each column (4) and then adding your row number (2), which indicates that you want the sixth byte in the real array.

---

† For Optimizers

This version will run even faster:

```
: ARRAY   OVER  CONSTANT  HERE 2+ ,  * ALLOT
    DOES>  2@  ROT *  + + ;
```

This calculation is what members of ARRAY must do at run time. You'll notice that, to perform this calculation, each member word needs to know how many rows are in each column of its particular array. For this reason, ARRAY must store this value into the beginning of the array at compile time.

For the curious, here are the stack effects of the run-time portion of ARRAY:

Operation	Contents of Stack
	row col pfa
DUP @	row col pfa #rows
ROT	row pfa #rows col
*	row pfa col-index
+ +	address
2+	corrected-address

It is necessary to add two to the computed address because the first cell of the array contains the number of columns.

Our final example is the most visually exciting, if not the most useful.

```
( SHAPES, USING A DEFINING WORD)     EMPTY

: STAR   42 EMIT ;
: .ROW   CR 8 0 DO DUP 128 AND
           IF STAR ELSE SPACE THEN
                        2* LOOP DROP ;

: SHAPE   CREATE  8 0 DO  C,  LOOP
          DOES>  DUP 7 + DO  I C@ .ROW  -1 +LOOP  CR ;

HEX    18 18 3C 5A 99 24 24 24 SHAPE MAN
       81 42 24 18 18 24 42 81 SHAPE EQUIS
       AA AA FE FE 38 38 38 FE SHAPE CASTLE
                                              DECIMAL
```

.ROW prints a pattern of stars and spaces that correspond to the 8-bit number on the stack. For instance:

```
2 BASE ! ok
00111001 .ROW
  ***  * ok
DECIMAL ok
```

Our defining word SHAPE takes eight arguments from the stack and defines a shape which, when executed, prints an 8-by-8 grid that corresponds to the eight arguments. For example:

```
MAN
   **
   **
  ****
 * ** *
*  **  *
  *  *
  *  *
  *  *
ok
```

In summary, defining words can be extremely powerful tools. When you create a new defining word, you extend your compiler. Traditional languages do not provide this flexibility because traditional compilers are inflexible packages that say, "Use my instruction set or forget it!"

The real power of defining words is that they can simplify your problem. Using them well, you can shorten your programming time, reduce the size of your program, and improve readability. FORTH's flexibility in this regard is so radical in comparison to traditional languages that many people don't even believe it. Well, now you've seen it.

The next section introduces still another way to extend the ability of FORTH's compiler.

How to Control the Colon Compiler

Compiling words are words used inside colon definitions to do something at compile time. The most obvious examples of compiling words are control-structure words such as IF, THEN, DO, LOOP, etc. Because FORTH programmers don't often change the way these particular words work, we're not going to study them any further. Instead we'll examine the group of words that control the colon compiler and thus can be used to create any type of compiling word.

Recall that the colon compiler ordinarily looks up each word of a source definition and compiles each word's address into the dictionary entry--that's all. But the colon compiler does not compile the address of a compiling word--it executes it.

How does the colon compiler know the difference? By checking the definition's "precedence bit." If the bit is "off," the address of the word is compiled. If the bit is "on," the word is executed immediately; such words are called "immediate" words.

The word IMMEDIATE makes a word "immediate." It is used in the form

```
: name   definition ;   IMMEDIATE
```

that is, it is executed right after the compilation of the definition.

To give an immediate example, let's define

```
: SAY-HELLO   ." HELLO " ;   IMMEDIATE
```

We can execute SAY-HELLO interactively, just as we could if it were not immediate.

```
SAY-HELLO HELLO ok
```

But if we put SAY-HELLO inside another definition, it will execute at compile time:

```
: GREET   SAY-HELLO   ." I SPEAK FORTH " ; HELLO ok
```

rather than at execution time:

```
GREET I SPEAK FORTH ok
```

Before we go on, let's clarify our terminology. FORTH folks adhere to a convention regarding the terms "run time" and "compile time." In this example, the terms are defined relative to GREET. Thus we would say that SAY-HELLO has a "compile-time behavior" but no "run-time behavior." Clearly, SAY-HELLO does have run-time behavior of its own, but relative to GREET it does not.

To keep our levels straight, let's call GREET in this example the "compilee"; that is, the definition whose compilation we're referring to. SAY-HELLO has no run-time behavior in relation to its compilee.

Here's an example of an immediate word that you're familiar with: the definition of the compiling word BEGIN. It's simpler than you might have thought:

```
: BEGIN   HERE ;   IMMEDIATE
```

BEGIN simply saves the address of HERE at compile time on the stack. Why? Because sooner or later an UNTIL or REPEAT is going to come along, and either has to know what address in the dictionary to return to in the event that it must repeat. This is the address that BEGIN left on the stack.

BEGIN's compile-time behavior is leaving HERE on the stack. But BEGIN compiles nothing into the compilee; there is no run-time behavior for BEGIN.

Unlike BEGIN, most compiling words <u>do</u> have a run-time behavior. To have a run-time behavior, a word has to compile into the compilee the address of the run-time behavior, which must already have been defined as a word.

A good example is DO. Like BEGIN, DO must provide, at compile time, a HERE for LOOP or +LOOP to return to. But unlike BEGIN, DO also has a run-time behavior: it must push the limit and the index onto the return stack.

The run-time behavior of DO is defined by a lower-level word, sometimes called (DO) or 2>R. The definition of DO is this:

```
: DO   COMPILE 2>R  HERE ;   IMMEDIATE
```

The word COMPILE finds the address of the next word in the definition (in this case 2>R) and compiles its address into the compilee definition, so that at run time 2>R will be executed.†

---

†For the Very Curious

Another example is the definition of ;. At compile time, semicolon must do two things:

1. compile the address of EXIT into the dictionary entry being compiled, and

2. leave compilation mode.

Here's the definition of semicolon:

```
: ;   COMPILE EXIT  R> DROP ;   IMMEDIATE
```

The first phrase compiles EXIT, providing the run-time behavior. The second phrase, which is the compile-time behavior, gets us out of the compiler. The top return address at this moment is pointing inside the colon compiler, which is simply a BEGIN...UNTIL loop. When semicolon has finished being executed, execution will return not to the colon compiler, but to INTERPRET.

Don't worry about how we can use a semicolon to end the very definition that defines it. The explanation requires an understanding of polyFORTH's Target Compiler, which is beyond the scope of this book (see Appendix 2).

Another compiler-controlling word is [COMPILE].[†] This word can be used to compile an immediate word as though it were not immediate. Given our previous example, in which SAY-HELLO is an immediate definition, we might define

```
: GREET  [COMPILE] SAY-HELLO  ." I SPEAK FORTH " ; ok
```

to force SAY-HELLO to be compiled rather than executed at compile time. Thus:

```
GREET HELLO I SPEAK FORTH ok
```

Be sure you understand the difference between COMPILE and [COMPILE]. COMPILE compiles the address of any (non-immediate) word into a compilee definition; think of it as deferred compilation. [COMPILE] compiles the address of any immediate word into the definition <u>currently being defined;</u> this is ordinary compilation, but of an immediate word which otherwise would have been executed.

To review, here are three words which are useful in creating new compiling words:

IMMEDIATE	(--)	Marks the most recently defined word as one which, when encountered during compilation, will be executed rather than be compiled.
COMPILE xxx	(--)	Used in the definition of a compiling word. When the compiling word, in turn, is used in a source definition, the code field address of xxx will be compiled into the dictionary entry so that when the new definition is executed, xxx will be executed.
[COMPILE] xxx	(--)	Used in a colon definition, causes the immediate word xxx to be compiled as though it were <u>not</u> immediate; xxx will be executed when the definition is executed.

[†]**For Some Small-system, Non-polyFORTH, Users**

See footnote, page 218.

More Compiler-controlling Words

As you may recall, a number that appears in a colon definition is called a "literal." An example is the "4" in the definition

```
: FOUR-MORE   4 + ;
```

The use of a literal in a colon definition requires two cells. The first contains the address of a routine which, when executed, will push the contents of the second cell (the number itself) onto the stack.†

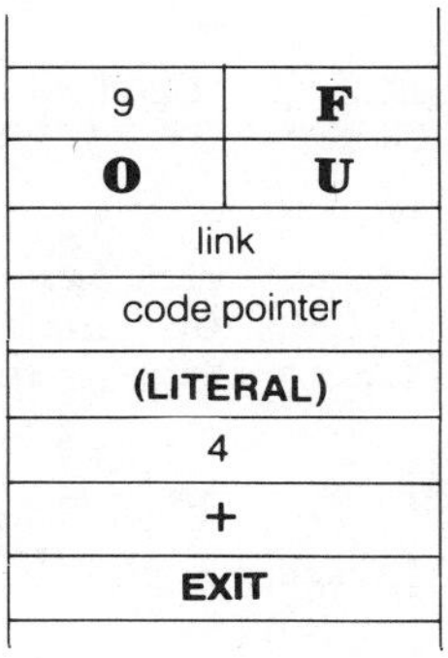

9	F
O	U
link	
code pointer	
(LITERAL)	
4	
+	
EXIT	

The name of this routine may vary; let's call it the "run-time code for a literal," or simply (LITERAL). When the colon compiler encounters a number, it first compiles the run-time code for a literal, then compiles the number itself.

The word you will use most often to compile a literal is LITERAL (no parentheses). LITERAL compiles both the run-time code and the value itself. To illustrate:

```
4  : FOUR-MORE   LITERAL + ;
```

Here the word LITERAL will compile as a literal the "4" that we put on the stack before beginning compilation. We get a dictionary entry that is identical to the one shown above.

For a more useful application of LITERAL, recall that in Chap. 8 we created an array called LIMITS that consisted of five cells, each of which contained the temperature limit for a different burner. To simplify access to this array, we created a word called LIMIT. The two definitions looked like this:

---

† For Memory Conservationists

While a literal requires two cells, a reference to a constant requires only one cell. Since a constant takes only five cells to define, you can see that if you're going to use the same value six times or more, you will save memory by defining the value as a constant. There is hardly any difference between the time required to execute a constant and a literal.

```
VARIABLE LIMITS  8 ALLOT
: LIMIT   2* LIMITS + ;
```

Now let's assume that we will only access the array through the word LIMIT. We can eliminate the head of the array (eight bytes) by using this construction instead:

```
HERE  10 ALLOT
: LIMIT   2* LITERAL + ;
```

In the first line we put the address of the beginning of the array (HERE) on the stack. In the second line, we compile this address as a literal into the definition of LIMIT.

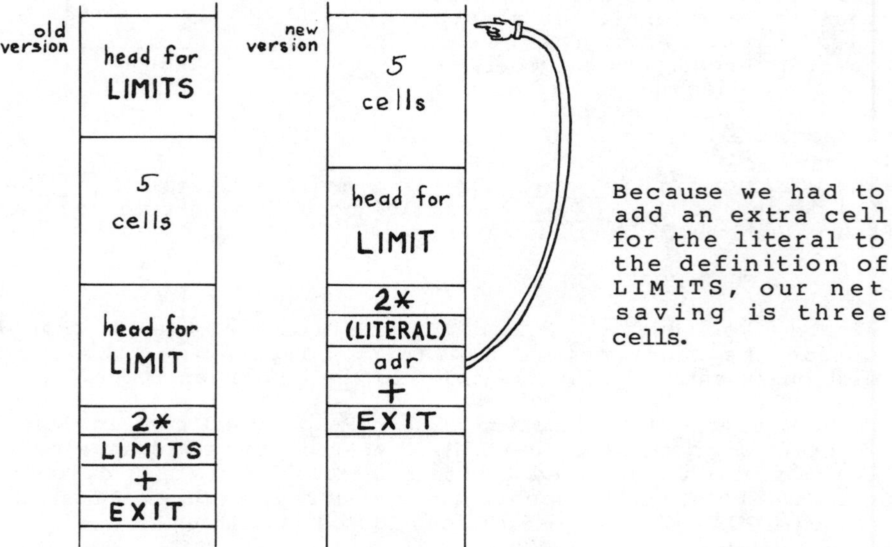

Because we had to add an extra cell for the literal to the definition of LIMITS, our net saving is three cells.

There are two other compiler control words you should know. The words [and] can be used inside a colon definition to stop compilation and start it again, respectively. Whatever words appear between them will be executed "immediately," i.e., at compile time.

Consider this example:

```
: SAY-HELLO   ." HELLO " ;
: GREET   [ SAY-HELLO ] ." I SPEAK FORTH " ; HELLO ok
GREET I SPEAK FORTH ok
```

In this example, SAY-HELLO is not an immediate word, yet when we compile GREET, SAY-HELLO executes "immediately."

For a better example, imagine a colon definition in which we need to type line 3 of block 180. To get the address of line 3, we could use the phrase

```
180 BLOCK 3 64 * +
```

but it's time-consuming to execute

```
3 64 *
```

every time we use this definition. Alternatively, we could write

```
180 BLOCK  192 +
```

but it's unclear to human readers exactly what the 192 means.

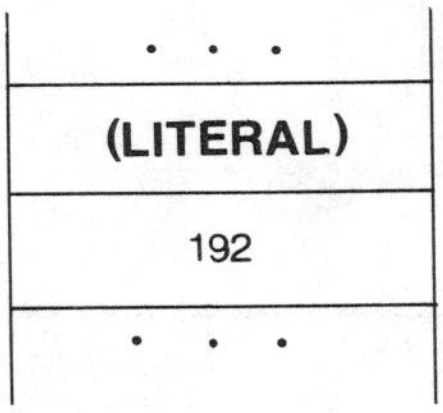

The best solution is to write

```
180 BLOCK [ 3 64 * ] LITERAL +
```

Here the arithmetic is performed only once, at compile time, and the result is compiled as a literal.

. . .
(LITERAL)
192
. . .

Here's a silly example which may give you some ideas for more practical applications. This definition must be loaded from a disk block:

```
: LIST-THIS   [ BLK @ ]  LITERAL  LIST ;
```

When you execute LIST-THIS, you will list whichever block LIST-THIS is defined in. (At compile time, BLK contains the number of the block being loaded. LITERAL compiles this number into the definition as a literal, so that it will serve as the argument for LIST at run time.)

By the way, here's the definition of LITERAL:

```
: LITERAL   COMPILE (LITERAL)  , ;   IMMEDIATE
```

First it compiles the address of the run-time code, then it compiles the value itself (using comma).

To summarize, here are the additional compiler control words we introduced in this section:

LITERAL	compile time: (n --) run time: (-- n)	Used only inside a colon definition. At compile time, compiles a value from the stack into the definition as a literal. At run time, the value will be pushed onto the stack.
[	(--)	Leaves compile mode.
]	(--)	Enters compile mode.

A Handy Hint

Entering Long Definitions from Your Terminal

Let's say you want to enter a definition from your terminal, but the definition won't all fit on one line. The problem is, if you hit "return" in the middle of a colon definition, you will leave compilation mode. (Even if you don't hit "return," EXPECT only accepts eighty characters.)

How can you get FORTH to resume compilation as you enter subsequent lines? By starting them with]. For example:

```
: BOXTEST   6 >  ROT 22 >  ROT 19 >  AND AND RETURN ok
]  IF  ." BIG ENOUGH "  THEN ; RETURN ok
```

(Some FORTH systems stay in compilation mode until a ; is encountered; on such systems the right bracket is unnecessary.)

An Introduction to FORTH Flowcharts

Flowcharts provide a way to visualize the logical structure of a definition, to see where the branches branch and where the loops loop. Old-fashioned flowcharting techniques haven't been adequate for describing FORTH's structured organization. Instead, various FORTH programmers have devised alternate schemes.

The question of which diagramming approach works best for FORTH remains open; programmers use whatever methods work best for them. The subject of flowcharting could occupy a chapter of its own, but we're running out of chapters.

The diagrams that we will use are loosely based on a type of flowchart called the "D-chart," invented by Prof. Edsger W. Dijkstra. Here's how our diagrams work:

Sequential statements are written one below the other, without lines or boxes:

```
statement
next statement
next statement
```

Lines are used to show non-sequential control paths (conditional branches and loops). The FORTH statement

```
condition IF true ELSE false THEN statement
```

would be diagrammed

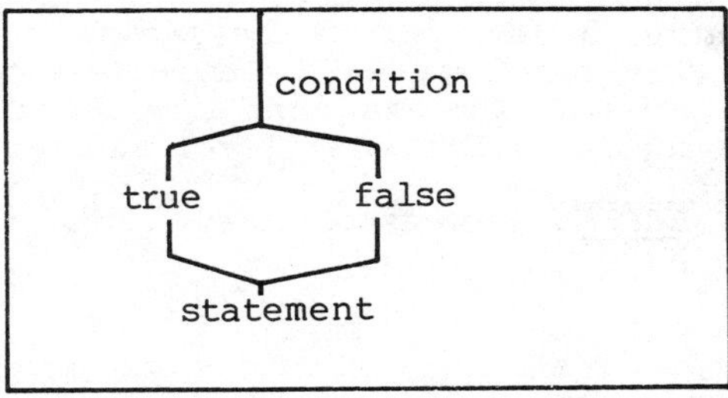

If either phrase is omitted, a vertical line is drawn in its place:

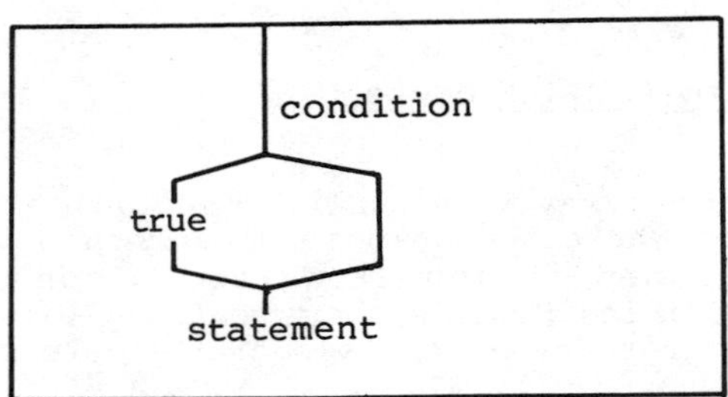

It is immaterial whether "true" is left or right.

A BEGIN...UNTIL structure is diagrammed like this:

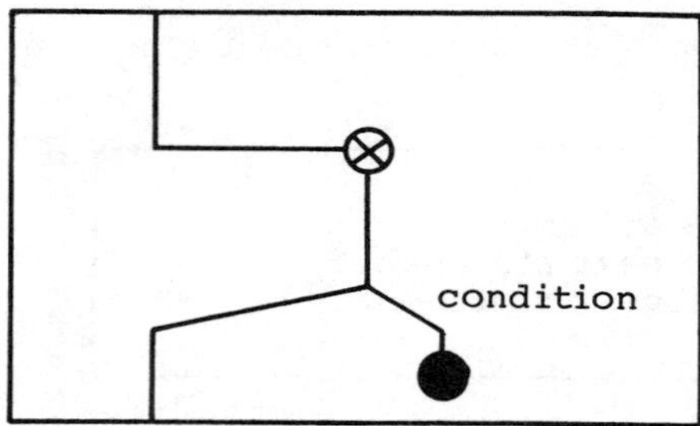

The entire loop structure is shifted to the right from the "normal" flow of execution, connected by a horizontal line at the top. If additional levels of nested loops were to be shown, they would be shifted still further to the right.

The black dot is the symbol for the end of the loop. It indicates that control is returned to the return point, symbolized by the circled X. The condition will cause the loop either to be repeated or to be exited. The diagonal line sloping down to the left indicates the return to the outer level of execution.

A BEGIN...WHILE...REPEAT loop is similar:

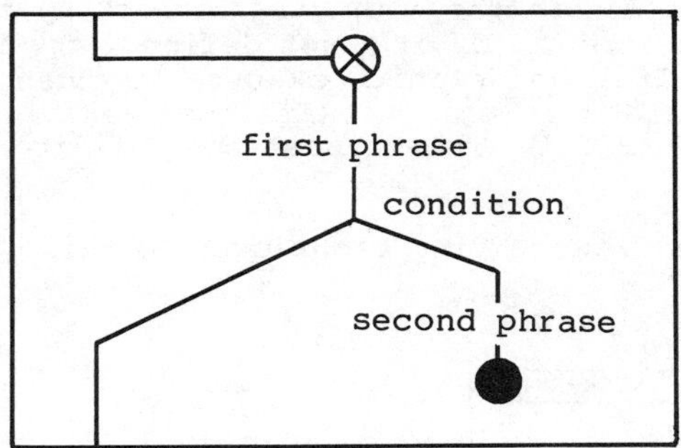

We've given this brief introduction to FORTH flowcharts so that we can visualize the structure of two very important words.

Curtain Calls

This section gives us a chance to say "Goodbye" to the text interpreter and the colon compiler and perhaps to see them in a new light.

Here is the definition of INTERPRET as it is found in many FORTH systems (see page 216 for a discussion of possible variations):

```
: INTERPRET   BEGIN -' IF  NUMBER ELSE  EXECUTE
     ?STACK  ABORT" STACK EMPTY" THEN  0 UNTIL ;
```

We've already covered each of the words contained in this definition; we can describe INTERPRET in English by simply "translating" its definition, like this:

> Begin a loop. Within the loop, try to look up the next word from the input stream. If it's not defined, try to convert it as a number. If it <u>is</u> defined, execute it, then check to see whether the stack <u>is</u> empty. (If it is, exit the loop and print "STACK EMPTY.") Then repeat the infinite loop.

Now let's apply our flowcharting techniques to this definition.

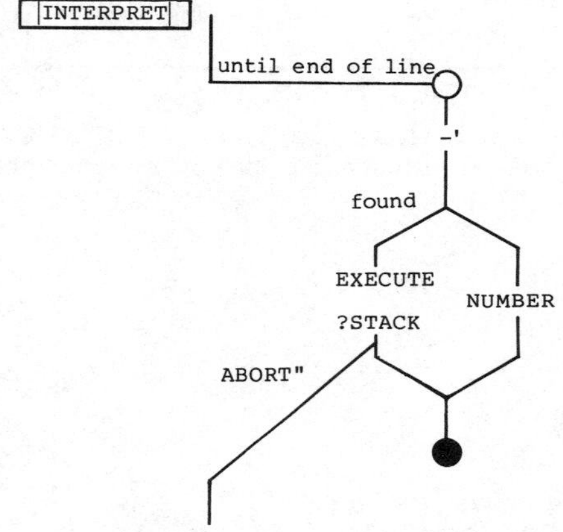

As you can see, the FORTH text interpreter is a simple yet powerful structure. Now let's compare its structure with that of the colon compiler:

---

† **For the Very Curious**

You may have wondered, if INTERPRET is an infinite loop, how do we exit it and get back to QUIT? The answer varies for different implementations of FORTH, but the most common answer is this:

When you enter a line of text from the terminal and press "return," the word EXPECT places a "null" (zero) at the end of the input stream. This null is actually a defined FORTH word; its code field points directly to EXIT. The result: when INTERPRET gets to the end of the line, it finds null in the dictionary and executes it. EXIT immediately transports us up to QUIT. Simple and fast.

```
: ]   BEGIN -' IF (NUMBER)  LITERAL
        ELSE ( check precedence bit)  IF  EXECUTE  ?STACK
           ABORT" STACK EMPTY"
        ELSE 2- ,  THEN THEN  0 UNTIL ;
```

The first thing you probably noticed is that the name of the colon compiler is not [:] but []]. The definition of [:] invokes []] after creating the dictionary head and performing a few other odd jobs.

The next thing you may have noticed is that the compiler is somewhat similar to the interpreter. Let's translate the above definition into English:

> Begin a loop. Within the loop, try to look up the next word from the input stream. If it's not defined, try to convert it as a number † and, if it is a number, compile it as a literal.
>
> If it is defined, then treat it as a word. If the word is immediate, then execute it and check to see if the stack is empty. If it is not immediate, change the pfa to a cfa (code-field address) and compile this address. Then repeat the infinite loop.

Picture it this way:

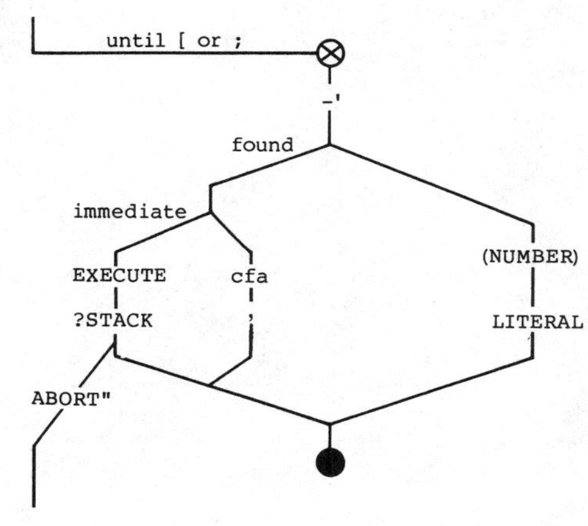

† **For the Curious**

The version of [NUMBER] that the colon compiler uses is the 16-bit version. That's why you can't have a double-length literal in a colon definition (except by making it two single-length literals).

Compare this to the diagram of INTERPRET and you'll see that] could be called an interpreter with the ability to decide whether to execute or to compile any given word. It is the simplicity of this design that lets you add new compiling words so easily.

In summary, we've shown two ways to extend the FORTH compiler:

1. Add new, specialized compilers, by creating new defining words.

2. Extend the existing colon compiler by creating new compiling words.

While traditional compilers try to be universal tools, the FORTH compiler is a collection of separate, simple tools ... with room for more. Which approach seems more useful:

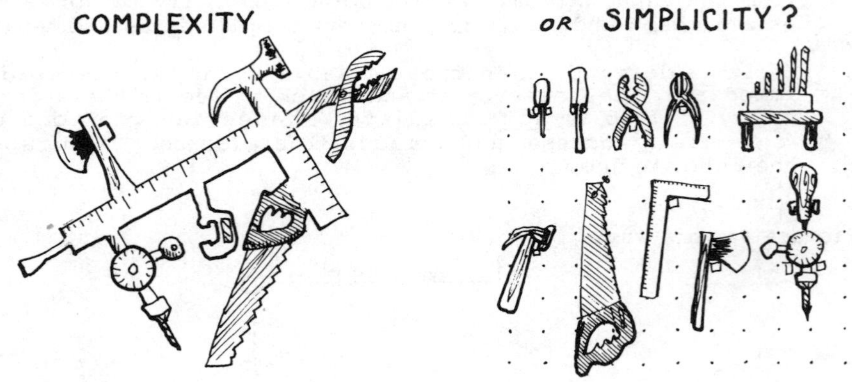

Here's a summary of the words we've covered in this chapter:

Word	Stack	Description
DOES>	run time: (-- adr)	Used in creating a defining word; marks the end of its compile-time portion and the beginning of its run-time portion. The run-time operations are stated in higher-level FORTH. At run time, the pfa of the defined word will be on the stack.
IMMEDIATE	(--)	Marks the most recently defined word as one which, when encountered during compilation, will be executed rather than be compiled.
COMPILE xxx	(--)	Used in the definition of a compiling word. When the compiling word, in turn, is used in a source definition, the code field address of xxx will be compiled into the dictionary entry so that when the new definition is executed, xxx will be executed.
[COMPILE] xxx	(--)	Used in a colon definition, causes the immediate word xxx to be compiled as though it were not immediate; xxx will be executed when the definition is executed.
LITERAL	compile time: (n --) run time: (--n)	Used only inside a colon definition. At compile time, compiles a value from the stack into the definition as a literal. At run time, the value will be pushed onto the stack.
[	(--)	Leaves compile mode.
]	(--)	Enters compile mode.

Review of Terms

Compile-time behavior
1. when referring to <u>defining</u> words: the sequence of instructions which will be carried out when the defining word is executed--these instructions perform the compilation of the member words;
2. when referring to <u>compiling</u> words: the behavior of a compiling word, contained within a colon definition, during compilation of the definition.

Compilee
a definition being compiled. In relation to a compiling word, the compilee is the definition whose compilation the compiling word affects.

Compiling word
a word used inside a colon definition to take some action during the compilation process.

Defining word
a word which, when executed, compiles a new dictionary entry. A defining word specifies the compile-time and run-time behavior of each member of the "family" of words that it defines.

Flowcharts
a graphic representation of the logical structure of a program or, in FORTH, of a definition.

Precedence bit
in FORTH dictionary entries, a bit which indicates whether a word should be executed rather than be compiled when it is encountered during compilation.

Run-time behavior
1. when referring to <u>defining</u> words: the sequence of instructions which will be carried out when any member word is executed;
2. when referring to <u>compiling</u> words: a routine which will be executed when the compilee is executed. Not all compiling words have run-time behavior.

Problems -- Chapter 11

1. Define a defining word named LOADED-BY that will define words which load a block when they are executed. Example:

```
6000 LOADED-BY CORRESPONDENCE
```

would define the word CORRESPONDENCE. When CORRESPONDENCE is executed, block 6000 would get loaded.

2. Define a defining word BASED. which will create number output words for specific bases. For example,

```
16 BASED. H.
```

would define H. to be a word which prints the top of the stack in hex but does not permanently change BASE.

```
DECIMAL
17 DUP H. . RETURN 11 17 ok
```

3. Define a defining word called PLURAL which will take the address of a word such as CR or STAR and create its plural form, such as CRS or STARS. You'll provide PLURAL with the address of the singular word by using tick. For instance, the phrase

```
' CR  PLURAL  CRS
```

will define CRS in the same way as though you had defined it

```
: CRS   ?DUP IF  0 DO CR  LOOP THEN ;
```

4. The French words for DO and LOOP are TOURNE and RETOURNE. Using the words DO and LOOP, define TOURNE and RETOURNE as French "aliases." Now test them by writing yourself a French loop.

5. The FORTH-79 Standard Reference Word Set contains a word called ASCII that can be used to make certain definitions more readable. Instead of using a numeric ASCII code within a definition, such as

```
: STAR   42 EMIT ;
```

you can use

```
: STAR   ASCII *  EMIT ;
```

The word ASCII reads the next character in the input stream, then compiles its ASCII equivalent into the definition as a literal. When the definition STAR is executed, the ASCII value is pushed onto the stack.

Define the word ASCII.

6. Write a word called LOOPS which will cause the remainder of the input stream, up to the carriage return, to be executed the number of times specified by the value on the stack. For example,

```
7 LOOPS  42 EMIT  SPACE RETURN * * * * * * * ok
```

12 THREE EXAMPLES

Programming in FORTH is more of an "art" than programming in any other language. Like painters drawing brushstrokes, FORTH programmers have complete control over where they are going and how they will get there. Charles Moore has written, "A good programmer can do a fantastic job with FORTH; a bad programmer can do a disastrous job." A good FORTH programmer must be conscious of "style."

FORTH style is not easily taught; it's a subject that deserves a book of its own. Some elements of good FORTH style include:

- simplicity,
- the use of many short definitions rather than a few longer ones,
- a correspondence between words and easy-to-understand actions or data structures,
- well-chosen names, and
- well laid-out blocks, clearly commented.

One good way to learn style, aside from trial and error, is to study existing FORTH applications, including FORTH itself. In this book we've included the definitions of many FORTH system words, and we encourage you to continue this study on your own.

This chapter introduces three applications which should serve as examples of good FORTH style.

The first example will show you the typical process of programming in FORTH: starting out with a problem and working step-by-step towards the solution.

The second example involves a more complex application already written: you will see the use of well-factored definitions and the creation of an application-specific "language."

The third example demonstrates the way to translate a mathematical equation into a FORTH definition; you will see how speed and compactness can be increased by using fixed-point arithmetic.

WORD Game

The example in this section is a refinement of the buzzphrase generator which we programmed back in Chap. 10. (You might want to review that version before reading this section.) The previous version did not keep track of its own carriage returns, causing us to force CRs into the definition and creating a very ragged right margin. The job of deciding how many whole words can fit on a line is a reasonable application for a computer and not a trivial one.

The problem is this: to draft a "brief" which consists of four paragraphs, each paragraph consisting of an appropriate introduction and sentence. Each sentence will consist of four randomly-chosen phrases linked together by fillers to create gramatically logical sentences and a period at the end.

The words and phrases have already been edited into blocks 234, 235, and 236 in the listing at the end of this section. Look at these blocks now, without looking at the two blocks that follow them (we're pretending we haven't written the application yet).

Block 234 contains the four introductions. They must be used in sequence. Block 235 contains four sets of fillers. The four sets must be used in sequence, but any of the three versions within a set may be chosen at random. Block 236 contains the three columns of buzzwords from our previous version, with some added words.

You might also look at the sample output that precedes the listing of the application, to get a better idea of the desired result.

"Top-down design" is a widely accepted approach to programming that can help to reduce development time. The idea is that you first study your application as a whole, then break the problem into smaller processes, then break these processes into still smaller units. Only when you know what all the units should do, and how they will connect together, do you begin to write code.

The FORTH language encourages top-down design. But in FORTH you can actually begin to write top-level definitions immediately. Already we can imagine that the "ultimate word" in our application might be called PAPER, and that it will probably be defined something like this:

```
: PAPER   4 0 DO I INTRO  SENTENCE LOOP ;
```

where INTRO uses the loop index as its argument to select the appropriate introduction. SENTENCE could be defined

```
: SENTENCE   4 0 DO I FILLER  PHRASE LOOP ;
```

where FILLER uses the loop index as its argument to select the appropriate set, then chooses at random one of the three versions within the set. The function of PHRASE will be the same as before.

Using FORTH's editor, we can enter these top-level definitions into a block. Of course we can't load the block until we have written our lower-level definitions.

In complicated applications, FORTH programmers often test the logic of their top-level definitions by using "stubs" for the lower-level words. A stub is a temporary definition. It might simply print a message to let us know its been executed. Or it may do nothing at all, except resolve the reference to its name in the high-level definition.

While the top-down approach helps to organize the programming process, it isn't always feasible to code in purely top-down fashion. Usually we have to find out how certain low-level mechanisms will work before we can design the higher-level definitions.

The best compromise is to keep a perspective on the problem as a whole while looking out for low-level problems whose solutions may affect the entire application.

In our example application, we can see that it will no longer be possible to force CRs at predictable points. Instead we've got to invent a mechanism whereby the computer will perform carriage returns automatically.

The only way to solve this problem is to count every character that is typed. Before each word is typed, the application must decide whether there is room to type it on the current line or do a carriage return first.

So let's define the variable LINECOUNT to keep the count and the constant RMARGIN with the value 78, to represent the maximum count per line. Each time we type a word we will add its count to LINECOUNT. Before typing each word we will execute this phrase:

```
(length of next word) LINECOUNT @ +  RMARGIN >  IF CR
```

that is, if the length of the next word added to the current length of the line exceeds our right margin, then we'll do a carriage return.

But we have another problem: how do we isolate words with a known count for each word? You got it, we use WORD.

Let's write out a "first draft" of this low-level part of our application. It will type a single word, making appropriate calculations for carriage returns.

32 WORD	Finds one word delimited by a space.
COUNT DUP	Leaves the count and a copy of the count on the stack, with the address of the first character beneath.
LINECOUNT @ +	Computes how long the current line would be if the word were to be included on it.
RMARGIN >	Decides if it would exceed the margin.
IF CR 0 LINECOUNT !	If so, resets the carriage and the count.
ELSE SPACE THEN	Otherwise, leaves a space between the words.
DUP 1+ LINECOUNT +!	Increases the count by the length of the word to be typed, plus one for the space.
TYPE	Types the word using the count and the address left by COUNT.

Now the problem is getting WORD to look at the strings on disk. WORD gets its bearings from BLK and >IN, so if we say,

```
234 BLK !   0 >IN !
```
[†]

then WORD will begin scanning block 234, starting at the top (byte zero).

[†] **For polyFORTH Users**

The user variables >IN and BLK are adjacent to each other in the user table. This design allows you to fetch and store both together with 2@ and 2!. For example,

```
234 0 >IN 2!
```

This causes another problem: by storing new values into the input stream pointers, we've destroyed the old values. If we now execute a definition that contains the above phrase, the interpreter will not come back to us when it's done; it will continue trying to interpret the rest of block 234. To solve this problem, our definition must save the pointer values somewhere before it changes them, then restore them just before it's done. Let's define a double-length variable called HOMEBASE, so we have a place to save the pointers. Then let's write a word whose job it will be to save the pointers in HOMEBASE. Finally, let's write a word which will restore the pointers.

```
VARIABLE HOMEBASE  2 ALLOT
: <WRITE   BLK @  >IN @  HOMEBASE 2! ;
: WRITE>   HOMEBASE 2@  >IN !  BLK ! ;
```

Now we have to modify our highest-level definition slightly, by editing in <WRITE at the beginning and WRITE> at the end:

```
: PAPER   <WRITE  4 0 DO I INTRO SENTENCE LOOP WRITE> ;
```

The next question is: how do we know when we've gotten to the end of the string?

Since we are typing word by word, we have to check whether >IN has advanced sixty-four places from its starting point every time we have found a new word. But the limit is not always sixty-four places; in the case of the buzzwords, the limit is twenty places.

For this reason, we should probably make the limit be an argument to a word. For example, the phrase

```
64 WORDS
```

should type out the contents of the 64-byte string, word by word, performing carriage returns where necessary.

How should we structure our definition of WORDS? Let's re-examine what it must do:

1. Determine whether there is still a word in the string to be typed.

2. If there is, type the word (with margin checking), then repeat. If there isn't, exit.

The two part nature of this structure suggests that we need a BEGIN...WHILE...REPEAT loop. Let's write our problem this way, if only to understand it better.

```
... BEGIN ANOTHER WHILE .WORD REPEAT ...
```

ANOTHER will do step 1; .WORD will do step 2.

How should ANOTHER determine whether there is still a word to be typed from the string? It must scan for the next word in the block, by using the phrase

```
32 WORD
```

then compare the new value of >IN against the limit for >IN, and finally return a "true" if the value is less than or equal to the limit. This flag will serve as the argument for WHILE.

How do we compute the limit for >IN? Before we can begin the above loop, we have to add the argument (sixty-four or whatever) to the beginning value of >IN and save this limit on the stack for ANOTHER to use each time through the loop. Thus our definition of WORDS might be

```
: WORDS   ( u -- )  >IN @ +  BEGIN ANOTHER WHILE
     .WORD REPEAT  2DROP ;
```

We need the 2DROP because, when we exit the loop, we will have the address of WORD's buffer and the limit for >IN on the stack, neither of which we need any longer.

Now we can define ANOTHER. We've already decided that the first thing it must do is find the next word, by using the phrase

```
32 WORD
```

At this point, there will be two values on the stack:

```
limit adr
```

We can perform the comparison with the phrase

```
OVER  >IN @  < NOT
```

By using OVER we save the limit on the stack for future loops. Remember that the phrase

```
< NOT
```

is the same as "greater than *or* equal to." Our definition of ANOTHER, then, might be

```
32 CONSTANT BL
: ANOTHER   ( limit -- limit adr)
     BL WORD  OVER  >IN @  < NOT ;
```

(The abbreviation BL is a common mnemonic† for "blank." We have used it here to improve program readability.)

How do we define .WORD? Actually, we've defined it already, a few pages back, with the exception that

```
32 WORD
```

should be omitted from the beginning of the definition, since it will have been performed in ANOTHER.

Now we have our word-typing mechanism. But let's see if we're overlooking anything. For example, consider that every time we start a new paragraph, we must remember to reset LINECOUNT to zero. Otherwise our .WORD will think that the current line is full when it isn't. We should ask ourselves this question: is there ever a case in this application where we would want to perform a CR without resetting LINECOUNT? The answer is no, by the very nature of the application. For this reason we can define

```
: CR   CR 0 LINECOUNT ! ;
```

to create a version of CR that is appropriate for this application. We can use this CR in our definition of .WORD.

We should also consider our handling of spaces between words. By using the phrase

```
IF CR ELSE SPACE THEN
```

before typing each word, we guarantee that there will be a space between each pair of words on the same line but no space at the beginning of successive lines. And since we are typing a space before each word rather than after, we can place a period immediately after a word, as we must at the end of a sentence.

But there's still a problem with this logic: at the beginning of a new paragraph, we will always get one space before the first word. Our solution: to redefine SPACE so that it will be sensitive to whether or not we're at the beginning of a line, and will not space if we are:

```
: SPACE   LINECOUNT @  IF SPACE THEN ;
```

If LINECOUNT is "0" then we know we are at the beginning of a line, because of the way we have redefined CR.

---

† For Beginners

As a general term, a "mnemonic" is a symbol or abbreviation chosen as an aid in remembering.

While we are redefining SPACE, it would be logical to include the phrase

```
1 LINECOUNT +!
```

in the redefinition. Again our reasoning is that we should never perform a space without incrementing the count. Now we can eliminate the word 1+ from the definition of .WORD, thereby eliminating a bug in the previous .WORD, namely that LINECOUNT was getting incremented even at the beginning of the line.

Let's assume that we have edited our definitions into a block. (In fact, we've done this already in block 237.) Notice that we had very little typing to do, compared with the amount of thinking we've done. FORTH source tends to be concise.†

Now we can define our in-between-level words--words like INTRO and PHRASE that we have already used in our highest-level words, but which we didn't define because we didn't have the low-level mechanism.

Let's start with INTRO. First we must set our input-stream pointers. The introductions are all in block 234, so the phrase

```
234 BLK !
```

takes care of them. Since each line is sixty-four bytes long, we can calculate the desired offset into the block by multiplying the loop index by sixty-four, then storing the offset into >IN.

Now we're ready to use WORDS to type all the words in the next sixty-four bytes. The finished definition of INTRO looks like this:

```
: INTRO   ( u -- ) 64 * >IN !  234 BLK !  CR  64 WORDS ;
```

Our mechanism has given us a very easy way to select strings. Unfortunately we cannot test this definition by itself, because it does not reset the input-stream pointers to their original values when it's done. But we can get around this by writing ourselves a definition called TEST, as follows:

```
: TEST  CR  '  <WRITE EXECUTE WRITE> SPACE ;
```

Now we can say

---

†For Experts

On the other hand, FORTH is not as compressed as APL, which in our opinion is not nearly as readable as FORTH.

```
0 TEST INTRO

IN THIS PAPER WE WILL DEMONSTRATE THAT ok
```

The "tick" in TEST will find the next word in the input stream, INTRO, which will then be executed "between" <WRITE and WRITE>. Notice that we put the argument to INTRO on the stack first.

The definition for FILLER will be a little more complicated. Since we are dealing with sets, not lines, and since the sets are four lines apart, we must multiply the loop index not by 64, but by (64 * 4). To pick one of the 3 versions within the set, we must choose a random number under three and multiply it by 64, then add this result to the beginning of the set. Recalling our discussion of compile-time arithmetic in Chap. 11., we can define

```
: FILLER   ( u -- ) [ 4 64 * ] LITERAL *
        3 CHOOSE  64 * +  >IN !  235 BLK !  64 WORDS ;
```

Again, we can test this definition by writing

```
3 TEST FILLER
TO FUNCTION AS ok
```

The remaining words in the application are similar to their previous counterparts, stated in terms of the new mechanism.

Here is a sample of the output, followed by our finished listing. (We've added block 239 as an afterthought so that we'd be able to print the same paper more than once.)

```
IN THIS PAPER WE WILL DEMONSTRATE THAT BY APPLYING AVAILABLE
RESOURCES TOWARDS FUNCTIONAL DIGITAL CAPABILITY COORDINATED WITH
COMPATIBLE ORGANIZATIONAL UTILITIES IT IS POSSIBLE FOR EVEN THE
MOST RESPONSIVE DIGITAL OUTFLOW TO AVOID TRANSIENT UNILATERAL
MOBILITY.

ON THE ONE HAND, STUDIES HAVE SHOWN THAT WITH STRUCTURED DEPLOYMENT
OF TOTAL FAIL-SAFE MOBILITY BALANCED BY SYSTEMATIZED UNILATERAL
THROUGH-PUT IT BECOMES NOT UNFEASABLE FOR ALL BUT THE LEAST RANDOM
ORGANIZATIONAL PROJECTIONS TO AVOID RESPONSIVE LOGISTICAL CONCEPTS.

ON THE OTHER HAND, HOWEVER, PRACTICAL EXPERIENCE INDICATES THAT
WITH STRUCTURED DEPLOYMENT OF QUALIFIED TRANSITIONAL MOBILITY
BALANCED BY REPRESENTATIVE LOGISTICAL THROUGH-PUT IT IS NECESSARY
FOR ALL REPRESENTATIVE UNILATERAL ENGINEERING TO FUNCTION AS
OPTIONAL DIGITAL SUPERSTRUCTURES.

IN SUMMARY, THEN, WE PROPOSE THAT WITH STRUCTURED DEPLOYMENT OF
RANDOM MANAGEMENT FLEXIBILITY BALANCED BY STAND-ALONE DIGITAL
CRITERIA IT IS NECESSARY FOR ALL QUALIFIED FAIL-SAFE OUTFLOW TO
AVOID PARTIAL UNDOCUMENTED ENGINEERING.
```

```
234 LIST

IN THIS PAPER WE WILL DEMONSTRATE THAT
ON THE ONE HAND, STUDIES HAVE SHOWN THAT
ON THE OTHER HAND, HOWEVER, PRACTICAL EXPERIENCE INDICATES THAT
IN SUMMARY, THEN, WE PROPOSE THAT
```

```
235 LIST

BY USING
BY APPLYING AVAILABLE RESOURCES TOWARDS
WITH STRUCTURED DEPLOYMENT OF
COORDINATED WITH
TO OFFSET
BALANCED BY
IT IS POSSIBLE FOR EVEN THE MOST
IT BECOMES NOT UNFEASABLE FOR ALL BUT THE LEAST
IT IS NECESSARY FOR ALL
TO FUNCTION AS
TO GENERATE A HIGH LEVEL OF
TO AVOID
```

```
236 LIST

INTEGRATED          MANAGEMENT          CRITERIA
TOTAL               ORGANIZATIONAL      FLEXIBILITY
SYSTEMATIZED        MONITORED           CAPABILITY
PARALLEL            RECIPROCAL          MOBILITY
FUNCTIONAL          DIGITAL             PROGRAMMING
RESPONSIVE          LOGISTICAL          CONCEPTS
OPTIMAL             TRANSITIONAL        TIME PHASING
SYNCHRONIZED        INCREMENTAL         PROJECTIONS
COMPATIBLE          THIRD GENERATION    HARDWARE
QUALIFIED           POLICY              THROUGH-PUT
PARTIAL             DECISION            ENGINEERING
STAND-ALONE         UNDOCUMENTED        OUTFLOW
RANDOM              CONTEXT SENSITIVE   SUPERSTRUCTURES
REPRESENTATIVE      FAIL-SAFE           INTERACTION
OPTIONAL            OMNIRANGE           CONGRUENCE
TRANSIENT           UNILATERAL          UTILITIES
```

```
237 LIST

( BUZZPHRASE GENERATOR II -- MARGIN SETTING)     EMPTY
181 LOAD ( RANDOM NUMBERS)
32 CONSTANT BL                78 CONSTANT RMARGIN
VARIABLE LINECOUNT            VARIABLE HOMEBASE  2 ALLOT
: <WRITE   BLK @  >IN @  HOMEBASE 2! ;
: WRITE>   HOMEBASE 2@  >IN !  BLK ! ;

: CR   CR  0 LINECOUNT ! ;
: SPACE   LINECOUNT @  IF SPACE  1 LINECOUNT +!  THEN ;
: .WORD    ( adr)  COUNT DUP LINECOUNT @ + RMARGIN >
           IF CR ELSE SPACE THEN
           DUP  LINECOUNT +!  TYPE ;
: ANOTHER  ( lim -- lim adr)  BL WORD  OVER >IN @ < NOT ;
: WORDS   ( u)
        >IN @ +  BEGIN ANOTHER WHILE .WORD REPEAT  2DROP ;
238 LOAD    239 LOAD
```

```
238 LIST

( BUZZPHRASE GENERATOR -- HIGH LEVEL WORDS)

: BUZZ   16 CHOOSE 64 * + >IN !  236 BLK !  20 WORDS ;
: 1ADJ   0 BUZZ ;
: 2ADJ   20 BUZZ ;
: NOUN   40 BUZZ ;
: PHRASE   1ADJ 2ADJ NOUN ;
: FILLER   ( u)  [ 4 64 * ] LITERAL *
     3 CHOOSE 64 * + >IN !  235 BLK !    64 WORDS ;
: SENTENCE   4 0 DO I FILLER PHRASE LOOP ." ." CR ;
: INTRO   ( u)   64 * >IN !  234 BLK !  CR 64 WORDS ;

: PAPER   <WRITE  CR CR  4 0 DO I INTRO SENTENCE LOOP WRITE> ;


: TEST   CR '  <WRITE EXECUTE WRITE> SPACE ;
```

```
239 LIST

( RETRIEVAL OF MORE SUCCESSFUL PAPERS)

VARIABLE SEED

: 4POSTERITY   RND @ SEED ! ;
( execute BEFORE producing a paper)

: REDO   SEED @ RND ! ;
( execute AFTER a paper, to reprint it.
  Usage:  REDO PAPER   )
```

File Away!

Our second example consists of a simple filing system.† It is a powerful and useful application, and a good one to learn FORTH style from. We have divided this section into four parts:

1. A "How to" for the end user. This will give you an idea of what the application can do.
2. Notes on the way the application is structured and the way certain definitions work.
3. A glossary of all the definitions in the application.
4. A listing of the application, including the blocks that contain the files themselves.

How to Use the Simple File System

This computer filing system lets you store and retrieve information quickly and easily. At the moment, it is set up to handle people's names, occupations, and phone numbers.‡ Not only does it allow you to enter, change, and remove records, it also allows you to search the file for any piece of information. For example, if you have a phone number, you can find the person's name; or, given a name, you can find the person's job, etc.

For each person there is a "record" which contains four "fields." The names which specify each of these four fields are

SURNAME   GIVEN   JOB   PHONE

("Given," of course, refers to the person's given name, or first name.)

---

† For Serious File-Users

FORTH, Inc. offers a very powerful File Management Option.

‡ For Programmers

You can easily change these categories or extend the number of fields the system will handle.

File Retrieval

You can search the file for the contents of any field by using the word FIND, followed by the field-name and the contents, as in

FIND JOB NEWSCASTER RETURN DAN RATHER ok

If any "job" field contains the string "NEWSCASTER," then the system prints the person's full name. If no such file exists, it prints "NOT IN FILE."

Once you have found a field, the record in which it was found becomes "current." You can get the contents of any field in the current record by using the word GET. For instance, having entered the line above, you can now enter

GET PHONE RETURN 555-9876 ok

The FIND command will only find the first instance of the field that you are looking for. To find out if there is another instance of the field that you last found, use the command ANOTHER. For example, to find another person whose "job" is "NEWSCASTER," enter

ANOTHER RETURN JESSICA SAVITCH ok

and

ANOTHER RETURN FRANK REYNOLDS ok

When there are no more people whose job is "NEWSCASTER" in the file, the ANOTHER command will print "NO OTHER."

To list all names whose field contains the string that was last found, use the command ALL:

```
ALL RETURN
DAN RATHER
JESSICA SAVITCH
FRANK REYNOLDS
ok
```

Since the surname and given name are stored separately, you can use FIND to search the file on the basis of either one. But if you know the person's full name, you can often save time by locating both fields at once, by using the word FULLNAME. FULLNAME expects the full name to be entered with the last name first and the two names separated by a comma, as in

FULLNAME WONDER,STEVIE RETURN STEVIE WONDER ok

(There must not be a space after the comma, because the comma marks the end of the first field and the beginning of the second field.) Like FIND and ANOTHER, FULLNAME repeats the name to indicate that it has been found.

You can actually find any pair of fields by using the word PAIR. You must specify both the field names and their contents, separated by a comma. For example, to find a newscaster whose given name is Dan, enter

PAIR JOB NEWSCASTER,GIVEN DAN RETURN DAN RATHER ok

File Maintenance

To enter a new record, use the command ENTER, followed by the surname, given name, job, and phone, each separated by a comma only. For example,

ENTER NUREYEV,RUDOLF,BALLET DANCER,555-1234 RETURN ok

To change the contents of a single field within the current record, use the command CHANGE followed by the name of the field, then the new string. For example,

CHANGE JOB CHOREOGRAPHER RETURN ok

To completely remove the current record, use the command REMOVE:

REMOVE RETURN ok

After adding, changing, or removing records, and before turning off the computer or changing disks, be sure to use the word

FLUSH ok

Comments

This section is meant as a guide, for the novice FORTH programmer, to the glossary and listing which follow. We'll describe the structure of this application and cover some of the more complicated definitions. As you read this section, study the glossary and listing on your own, and try to understand as much as you can.

Turn to the listing now and look at block 242. This block contains the definitions for all nine end-user commands we've just discussed. Notice how simple these definitions are, compared to their power!

This is a characteristic of a well-designed FORTH application. Notice that the word -FIND, the elemental file-search word, is factored in such a way that it can be used in the definitions of FIND, ANOTHER, and ALL, as well as in the internal word, (PAIR), which is used by PAIR and by FULLNAME.

We'll examine these definitions shortly, but first let's look at the overall structure of this application.

One of the basic characteristics of this application is that each of the four fields has a name which we can enter in order to specify the particular field. For example, the phrase

```
SURNAME PUT
```

will put the character string that follows in the input stream into the "surname" field of the current record. The phrase

```
SURNAME .FIELD
```

will print the contents of the "surname" field of the current record, etc.

There are two pieces of information that are needed to identify each field: the field's starting address relative to the beginning of a record and the length of the field.

In this application, a record is laid out like this:

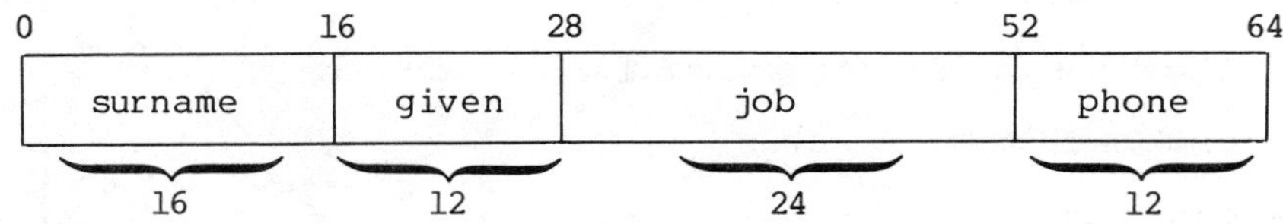

For instance, the "job" field starts twenty-eight bytes in from the beginning of every record and continues for twenty-four bytes.

We chose to make a record exactly sixty-four bytes long so that the fields will line up in columns when we LIST the file. This was for our convenience in programming, but this system could be modified to hold records of any length and any number of fields.[†]

We've taken the two pieces of information for each field and put them into a double-length table associated with each field name. Our definition of JOB, therefore, is

```
CREATE JOB  28 , 24 ,
```

3	J
O	B
link	
code pointer	
28	
24	

Thus when we enter the name of a field, we are putting on the stack the address of the table that describes the "job" field. We can fetch either or both pieces of information relative to this address.

Let's call each of these entries a "field specifying table," or a "spec table" for short.

[†]For Those Who Want to Modify This File System

To change the parameters of the fields, just make sure that the beginning byte ("tab") for each field is consistent with the lengths of the fields that precede it. For example, if the first field is thirty bytes long, as in

```
CREATE 1FIELD  0 , 30 ,
```

then make the tab for the second field thirty, as in

```
CREATE 2FIELD  30 , 12 ,
```

etc. Finally, set the value of R-LENGTH in line 4 to the length of the entire record (the last field's tab plus its length). Using R-LENGTH, the system automatically computes the number of records that can fit into a single block (1024 R-LENGTH /) and defines the constant REC/BLK accordingly.

You may also change the location of the new file (e.g., to create several different files) by changing the value of the constant FILE in line 5. You may also change the maximum number of blocks that your file can contain by replacing the "2" in the same line. This value will be converted into a maximum number of records, by being multiplied by REC/BLK, and kept as the constant MAXRECS.

Part of the design for this application is derived from the requirements of FIND, ANOTHER, and ALL; that is, FIND not only has to find a given string within a given type of field, but also needs to "remember" the string and the type of field so that ANOTHER and ALL can search for the same thing.

We can specify the kind of field with just one value, the address of the spec table for that type of field. This means that we can "remember" the type of field by storing this address into KEEP.

KIND was created for this purpose, to indicate the "kind" of field.

To remember the string, we have defined a buffer called WHAT to which the string can be moved. (WHAT is defined relative to the pad, where memory can be reused, so as not to waste dictionary space.)

The word KEEP serves the dual purpose of storing the given field type into KIND and the given character string into WHAT. If you look at the definition of the end-user word FIND, you will see that the first thing it does is KEEP the information on what is being searched for. Then FIND executes the internal word -FIND, which uses the information in KIND and WHAT to find a matching string.

ANOTHER and ALL also use -FIND, but they don't use KEEP. Instead they look for fields that match the one most recently "kept" by FIND.

So that we can GET any piece of information from the record which we have just "found," we need a pointer to the "current" record. This need is met with the variable #RECORD. The operations of the words TOP and DOWN in block 240 should be fairly obvious to you.

The word RECORD uses #RECORD to compute the absolute address (the computer-memory address, somewhere in a disk buffer) of the beginning of the current record. Since RECORD executes BLOCK, it also guarantees that the record really is in a buffer.

Notice that RECORD allows the file to continue over a range of blocks. /MOD divides the value of #RECORD by the number of records per block (sixteen in this case, since each record is sixty-four bytes long). The quotient indicates which block the record will be in, relative to the first block; the remainder indicates how far into that block this record will be.

While a spec table contains the relative address of the field and its length, we usually need to know the field's absolute address and length for words such as TYPE, MOVE, and -TEXT. Look at the definition of the word FIELD to see how it converts the address of a spec table into an absolute address and length.

Then examine how FIELD is applied in the definition of .FIELD.

The word PUT also employs FIELD. Its phrase

```
PAD SWAP FIELD
```

leaves on the stack the arguments

```
adr-of-PAD  absolute-adr-of-field  count
```

for MOVE to move the string from the pad into the appropriate field of the current record.

There are two things worth noting about the definition of FREE in block 241. The first is the method used to determine whether a record is empty. We've made the assumption that if the first byte of a record is empty, then the whole record is empty, because of the way ENTER works. If the first byte contains a character whose ASCII value is less than thirty-three (thirty-two is blank), then it is not a printing character and the line is empty. (Sometimes an empty block will contain all nulls, other times all blanks; either way, such records will test as "empty.") As soon as an empty record is found, LEAVE ends the loop. #RECORD will contain the number of the free record.

Another thing worth noting about FREE is that it aborts if the file is full, that is, if it runs through all the records without finding one empty. We can use a DO loop to run through all the records, but how can we tell that the loop has run out before it has found an empty record?

The best way is to leave a "1" on the stack, to serve as a flag, before beginning the loop. If an empty record is found, we can change the flag to zero (with the word NOT) before we leave the loop. When we come out of the loop, we'll have a "1" if we never found an empty record, a "0" if we did. This flag will be the argument for ABORT".

We use a similar technique in the definition of -FIND. -FIND must return a flag to the word that executed it: FIND, ANOTHER, ALL, or (PAIR). The flag indicates whether a match was found before the end of the file was reached. Each of these outer words needs to make a different decision based on the state of this flag. This flag is a "1" if a match is not found (hence the name -FIND). The decision to use negative logic was based on the way -FIND is used.

Because the flag needs to be a "1" if a match is not found, the easiest way to design this word is to start with a "1" on the stack and change it to a "0" only if a match is found. But notice: while the loop is running, there are two values on the stack: the flag we just mentioned and the spec table address for the type of field to be searched. Since we need the address every time through the loop and the flag only once, if at all, we have decided to keep the address on top of the stack and the flag underneath. For this reason, we use the phrase

```
SWAP NOT SWAP
```

By the way, we could have avoided the problem of carrying both values on the stack by putting the phrase

```
KIND @ FIELD
```

inside the loop, instead of

```
KIND @
```

at the beginning and

```
DUP FIELD
```

inside. But we didn't, because we always try to keep the number of instructions inside a loop to a minimum. Naturally, it is the loops that take the most time running.

Now that you understand the basic design of this application, you should have no trouble understanding the rest of the listing, using the glossary as a guide.†

---

† For polyFORTH Users

This type of glossary is generated by an application called DOCUMENTOR, which is included in the File Management Option.

```
FORTH, Inc.                                          Page 1   3/06/81
                  SIMPLE FILES GLOSSARY
 WORD             VOCABULARY   BLOCK   STACK EFFECTS


 #RECORD          FORTH          240     ( -- adr)
     A variable that points to the current record.

 (PAIR)           FORTH          241     ( adr)
     Starting from the top, attempts to find a match on the contents
     of WHAT, using KIND to indicate the type of field.  If a match
     is made, then attempts to match a second field, whose type is
     indicated by adr, with the contents of PAD.  If both match,
     prints the name; otherwise repeats until a match is made or
     until the end of the file is reached, in which case prints
     an error message.

 -FIND            FORTH          241     ( -- f)
     Beginning with #RECORD and proceeding down, compares the contents
     of the field indicated by KIND against the contents of WHAT.

 .FIELD           FORTH          240     ( adr)
     From the current record, types the contents of the field that is
     associated with the field-specifying table at adr.

 .NAME            FORTH          240
     From the current record, types the name, first name first.

 ALL              FORTH          242
     Beginning at the top of the file, uses KIND to determine type of
     field and finds all matches on WHAT.  Types the full name(s).

 ANOTHER          FORTH          242
     Beginning with the next record after the current one, and using
     KIND to determine type of field, attempts to find a match on WHAT.
     If successful, types the name; otherwise an error message.

 CHANGE           FORTH          242
     Changes the contents of the given field in the current record.
     usage:  CHANGE  field-name  new-contents

 DOWN             FORTH          240
     Moves the record pointer down one record.

 ENTER            FORTH          242
     Finds the first free record, then moves four strings separated
     by commas into the surname, given, job, and phone fields of
     that record.

 FIELD            FORTH          240     ( adr -- adr length)
     Given the address of a field-specifying table, insures that
     the associated field in the current record is in a disk buffer
     and returns the address of the field in the buffer along with
     its length.

 FILES            FORTH          240     ( -- u)
     The number of the block where the files begin.
```

```
FORTH, Inc.                                          Page 2   3/06/81
                SIMPLE FILES GLOSSARY
 WORD           VOCABULARY  BLOCK  STACK EFFECTS

 FIND           FORTH          242
    Finds the record in which there is a match between the contents
    of the given field and the given string.
       Usage:  FIND field-name  string

 FREE           FORTH          241
    Starting at the top of the file, finds the first record that is
    free, that is, whose first byte contains a blank or zero.
    Aborts if the file is full.

 FULLNAME       FORTH          242
    Finds the record in which there is a match on both the first and
    last names given.   Usage:  FULLNAME lastname,firstname

 GET            FORTH          242
    Prints the contents of the given type of field from the current
    record.

 GIVEN          FORTH          240     ( -- adr)
    Returns the address of the field-specifying table for the
    "given" (first name) field.

 JOB            FORTH          240     ( -- adr)
    Returns the address of the field-specifying table for the
    "job" field.

 KEEP           FORTH          241     ( adr)
    Moves a character string, delimited either by a comma or by a
    carriage return, from the input stream into WHAT, and saves the
    address of the given field-specifying table in KIND, for future
    use by -FIND.

 KIND           FORTH          240     ( -- adr)
    A variable that contains the address of the field-specifying
    table for the type of field that was last searched for by FIND.

 MAXRECS        FORTH          240     ( -- u)
    The maximum number of records to be allowed in the system.

 MISSING        FORTH          241
    Prints the message "NOT IN FILE."

 PAIR           FORTH          242
    Finds the record in which there is a match between both the
    contents of the first given field and the first given string, and
    and also the contents of the second given field and the second
    given string.  Comma is the delimiter.
       Usage:   PAIR  field1 string1,field2 string2

 PHONE          FORTH          240     ( -- adr)
    Returns the address of the field-specifying table for the
    "phone" field.
```

SIMPLE FILES GLOSSARY

WORD	VOCABULARY	BLOCK	STACK EFFECTS

PUT FORTH 241 (adr)
Moves a character string, delimited either by a comma or by a carriage return, from the input stream into the field whose field-specifying table address is given on the stack.

R-LENGTH FORTH 240 (-- u)
The length in bytes of a single record.

READ FORTH 241
Moves a character string, delimited either by a comma or by a carriage return, from the input stream into PAD.

REC/BLK FORTH 240 (-- u)
The number of records that will fit in a single block, given MAXRECS.

RECORD FORTH 240 (-- adr)
Insures that the current record is in a disk buffer, and returns the address of the first byte of that record.

REMOVE FORTH 242
Erases the current record.

SURNAME FORTH 240 (-- adr)
Returns the address of the field-specifying table for the "surname" (last name) field.

TOP FORTH 240
Resets the record pointer to the top of the file.

WHAT FORTH 240 (-- adr)
Returns the address of a buffer that contains the string that is being searched for, or was last searched for, by FIND.

```
240 LIST

( SIMPLE FILES)                                  EMPTY
               ( tab length)                            ( tab length)
CREATE SURNAME   0 ,  16 ,        CREATE GIVEN  16 ,  12 ,
CREATE JOB      28 ,  24 ,        CREATE PHONE  52 ,  12 ,
64 CONSTANT R-LENGTH        1024 R-LENGTH / CONSTANT REC/BLK
243 CONSTANT FILES              2 REC/BLK * CONSTANT MAXRECS
VARIABLE #RECORD                  VARIABLE KIND
: WHAT    ( -- adr)  PAD 80 + ;
: RECORD    ( -- first adr of current record)
   #RECORD @ REC/BLK /MOD  FILES + BLOCK  SWAP R-LENGTH * + ;
: FIELD    ( field --adr length)  2@ RECORD +  SWAP ;
: TOP    0 #RECORD ! ;
: DOWN    1 #RECORD +! ;
: .FIELD    ( field)  FIELD  -TRAILING TYPE  SPACE ;
: .NAME   GIVEN .FIELD   SURNAME .FIELD ;
241 LOAD  242 LOAD
```

```
241 LIST

( SIMPLE FILES, CONT'D)
: READ    44 TEXT ;
: PUT    ( field)  READ  PAD SWAP FIELD MOVE  UPDATE ;
: KEEP    ( field) DUP KIND !
                     2+ @  READ  PAD WHAT ROT MOVE ;
: FREE    1  MAXRECS 0 DO  I #RECORD !  RECORD C@
   ( ASCII) 33 <  IF NOT LEAVE THEN  LOOP ABORT" FILE FULL " ;
: -FIND    ( -- f)   1  KIND @  MAXRECS  #RECORD @ DO
         I #RECORD !  DUP FIELD WHAT -TEXT NOT IF
            SWAP NOT SWAP  LEAVE THEN  LOOP  DROP ;
: MISSING   ." NOT IN FILE " ;
: (PAIR)   ( field)    MAXRECS 0 DO  I #RECORD !
   -FIND IF  MISSING LEAVE ELSE  DUP FIELD PAD -TEXT NOT
                     IF .NAME LEAVE THEN   THEN   LOOP DROP ;
```

```
242 LIST

( SIMPLE FILES -- END USER WORDS)
: ENTER   FREE   SURNAME PUT    GIVEN PUT
                 JOB PUT        PHONE PUT ;
: REMOVE   RECORD R-LENGTH 32 FILL  UPDATE ;
: CHANGE    '  PUT ;
: FIND    '  KEEP  TOP -FIND  IF MISSING ELSE .NAME THEN ;
: GET   '  .FIELD ;
: ANOTHER   DOWN -FIND  IF ." NO OTHER "  ELSE .NAME THEN ;
: ALL    TOP BEGIN  CR -FIND NOT  WHILE  .NAME DOWN  REPEAT ;
: PAIR   '  KEEP   '  READ (PAIR) ;
: FULLNAME   SURNAME KEEP  GIVEN READ (PAIR) ;
```

```
243 LIST

FILLMORE          MILLARD      PRESIDENT                   NO PHONE
LINCOLN           ABRAHAM      PRESIDENT                   NO PHONE
BRONTE            EMILY        WRITER                      NO PHONE
RATHER            DAN          NEWSCASTER                  555-9876
FITZGERALD        ELLA         SINGER                      555-6789
SAVITCH           JESSICA      NEWSCASTER                  555-9653
MC CARTNEY        PAUL         SONGWRITER                  555-1212
WASHINGTON        GEORGE       PRESIDENT                   NO PHONE
REYNOLDS          FRANK        NEWSCASTER                  555-8765
SILLS             BEVERLY      OPERA STAR                  555-9876
FORD              HENRY        CAPITALIST                  NO PHONE
DEWHURST          COLEEN       ACTRESS                     555-9876
WONDER            STEVIE       SONGWRITER                  555-0097
FULLER            BUCKMINSTER WORLD ARCHITECT              555-7604
RAWLES            JOHN         PHILOSOPHER                 555-9721
TRUDEAU           GARRY        CARTOONIST                  555-9832


244 LIST

VAN BUREN         ABIGAIL      COLUMNIST                   555-8743
ABZUG             BELLA        POLITICIAN                  555-4443
THOMPSON          HUNTER S.    GONZO JOURNALIST            555-9854
SINATRA           FRANK        SINGER                      555-9412
JABBAR            KAREEM ABDULBASKETBALL PLAYER            555-4439
MC GEE            TRAVIS       FICTITIOUS DETECTIVE        555-8887
DIDION            JOAN         WRITER                      555-0009
FRAZETTA          FRANK        ARTIST                      555-9991
HENSON            JIM          PUPPETEER                   555-0001


245 LIST
```

No Weighting

Our final example is a math problem which many people would assume could only be solved by using floating point. It will illustrate how to handle a fairly complicated equation with fixed-point arithmetic and demonstrate that for all the advantages of using fixed-point, range and precision need not suffer.

In this example we will compute the weight of a cone-shaped pile of material, knowing the height of the pile, the angle of the slope of the pile, and the density of the material.

To make the example more "concrete," let's weigh several huge piles of sand, gravel, and cement. The slope of each pile, called the "angle of repose," depends on the type of material. For example, sand piles itself more steeply than gravel.

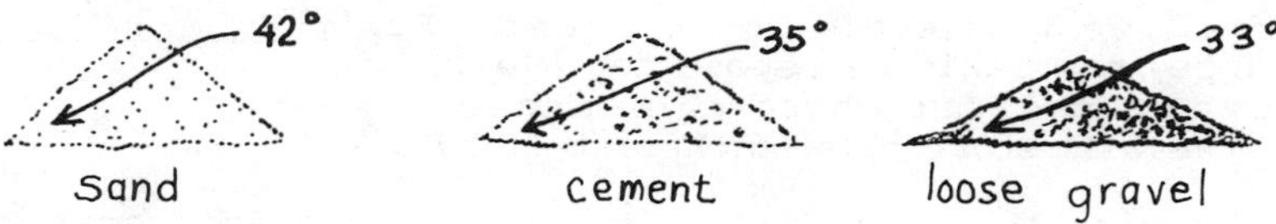

(In reality these values vary widely, depending on many factors; we have chosen approximate angles and densities for purposes of illustration.)

Here is the formula for computing the weight of a conical pile h feet tall with an angle of repose of θ degrees, where D is the density of the material in pounds per cubic foot:†

---

†For Skeptics

The volume of a cone, V, is given by

$$V = \frac{1}{3}\pi b^2 h$$

where b is the radius of the base and h is the height. We can compute the base by knowing the angle or, more specifically, the tangent of the angle. The tangent of an angle is simply the ratio of the segment marked h to the segment marked b in this drawing:

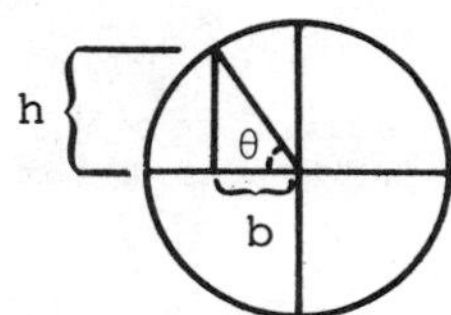

(continued...)

$$W = \frac{\pi h^3 D}{3 \tan^2(\theta)}$$

This will be the formula which we must express in FORTH.

Let's design our application so that we can enter the name of a material first, such as

DRY-SAND

then enter the height of a pile and get the result for dry sand.

Let's assume that for any one type of material the density and angle of repose never vary. We can store both of these values for each type of material into a table. Since we ultimately need each angle's tangent, rather than the number of degrees, we will store the tangent. For instance, the angle of repose for a pile of cement is 35°, for which the tangent is .700. We will store this as the integer 700.

CEMENT
131
700

Bear in mind that our goal is not just to get an answer; we are programming a computer or device to get the answer for us in the fastest, most efficient, and most accurate way possible. As we indicated in Chap. 5, to write equations using fixed-point arithmetic requires an extra amount of thought. But the effort pays off in two ways:

For Skeptics (continued)

If we call this angle "θ" (<u>theta</u>), then

$$\tan \theta = \frac{h}{b}$$

Thus we can compute the radius of the base with

$$b = \frac{h}{\tan \theta}$$

When we substitute this into the expression for V, and then multiply the result by the density D in pounds per cubic foot, we get the formula shown above.

1. vastly improved run-time speed, which can be very important when there are millions of steps involved in a single calculation, or when we must perform thousands of calculations every minute. Also,

2. program size, which would be critical if, for instance, we wanted to put this application in a hand-held device specifically designed as a pile-measuring calculator. FORTH is often used in this type of instrument.

Let's approach our problem by first considering scale. The height of our piles ranges from 5 to 50 feet. By working out our equation for a pile of cement 50 feet high, we find that the weight will be nearly 35,000,000 pounds.

But because our piles will not be shaped as perfect cones and because our values are averages, we cannot expect better than four or five decimal places of accuracy.† If we scale our result to tons, we get about 17,500. This value will comfortably fit within the range of a single-length number. For this reason, let's write this application entirely with single-length arithmetic operators.

Applications which require greater accuracy can be written using double-length arithmetic; to illustrate we've even written a second version of this application using 32-bit math, as you'll see later on. But we intend to show the accuracy that FORTH can achieve even with 16-bit math.

By running another test with a pile 40 feet high, we find that a difference of one-tenth of a foot in height can make a difference of 25 tons in weight. So we decide to scale our input to feet and inches rather than merely to whole feet.

---

† For Math Experts:

In fact, since our height will be expressed in three digits, we can't expect greater than three-digit precision. But for purposes of our example, we'll keep better than four-digit precision.

We'd like the user to be able to enter

```
15 FOOT  2 INCH  PILE
```

where the words FOOT and INCH will convert the feet and inches into tenths of an inch, and PILE will do the calculation. Here's how we might define FOOT and INCH:

```
: FOOT   10 * ;
: INCH   100 12 */ 5 +  10 / + ;
```

The use of INCH is optional.

(By the way, we could as easily have designed input to be in tenths of an inch with a decimal point, like this:

```
15.2
```

In this case, NUMBER would convert the input as a double-length value. Since we are only doing single-length arithmetic, PILE could simply begin with DROP, to eliminate the high-order byte.)

In writing the definition of PILE, we must try to maintain the maximum number of places of precision without overflowing 15 bits. According to the formula, the first thing we must do is cube the argument. But let's remember that we will have an argument which may be as high as 50 feet, which will be 500 as a scaled integer. Even to square 500 produces 250,000, which exceeds the capacity of single-length arithmetic.

We might reason that, sooner or later in this calculation, we're going to have to divide by 2000 to yield an answer in tons. Thus the phrase

```
DUP DUP 2000 */
```

will square the argument and convert it to tons at the same time, taking advantage of */'s double-length intermediate result. Using 500 as our test argument, the above phrase will yield 125.

But our pile may be as small as 5 feet, which when squared is only 25. To divide by 2000 would produce a zero in integer arithmetic, which suggests that we are scaling down too much.

To retain maximum accuracy, we should scale down no more than necessary. 250,000 can be safely accommodated by dividing by 10. Thus we will begin our definition of PILE with the phrase

```
DUP DUP 10 */
```

The integer result at this stage will be scaled to one place to the right of the decimal point (25000 for 2500.0).

Now we must <u>cube</u> the argument. Once again, straight multiplication will produce a double-length result, so we must use */ to scale down. We find that by using 1000 as our divisor, we can stay just within single-length range. Our result at this stage will be scaled to one place to the <u>left</u> of the decimal point (12500 for 125000.) and still accurate to 5 digits.

According to our formula, we must multiply our argument by pi. We know that we can do this in FORTH with the phrase

```
355 113 */
```

We must also divide our argument by 3. We can do both at once with the phrase

```
355 339 */
```

which causes no problems with scaling.

Next we must divide our argument by the tangent squared, which we can do by dividing the argument by the tangent <u>twice</u>. Because our tangent is scaled to 3 decimal places, to divide by the tangent we multiply by 1000 and divide by the table value. Thus we will use the phrase

```
1000 THETA @ */
```

Since we must perform this twice, let's make it a definition, called /TAN (for <u>divide-by-the-tangent</u>) and use the word /TAN twice in our definition of PILE. Our result at this point will still be scaled to one place to the left of the decimal (26711 for 267110, using our maximum test values).

All that remains is to multiply by the density of the material, of which the highest is 131 pounds per cubic foot. To avoid overflowing, let's try scaling down by two decimal places with the phrase

```
DENSITY @ 100 */
```

But by testing, we find that the result at this point for a 50-foot pile of cement will be 34,991, which just exceeds the 15-bit limit. Now is a good time to take the 2000 into account. Instead of

```
DENSITY @ 100 */
```

we can say

```
DENSITY @ 200 */
```

and our answer will now be scaled to whole tons.

You will find this version in the listing of block 246 that

follows. As we mentioned, we have also written this application using double-length arithmetic, in block 248. In this version you enter the height as a double-length number scaled to tenths of a foot, followed by the word FEET, as in 50.0 feet.

By using double-length integer arithmetic, we are able to compute the weight of the pile to the nearest whole pound. The range of double-length integer arithmetic compares with that of most floating-point arithmetic. Below is a comparison of the results obtained using a 10-decimal-digit calculator, single-length FORTH, and double-length FORTH. The test assumes a 50-foot pile of cement, using the table values.

	in pounds	in tons
calculator	34,995,634	17,497.817
FORTH 16-bit	---	17,495
FORTH 32-bit	34,995,634	17,497.817

Here's a sample of our application's output:

```
246 LOAD ok
CEMENT ok
10 FOOT PILE = 138 TONS OF CEMENT ok
10 FOOT 3 INCH PILE = 151 TONS OF CEMENT ok
DRY-SAND ok
10 FOOT PILE = 81 TONS OF DRY SAND ok
248 LOAD CEMENT ok
10.0 FEET = 279939 POUNDS OF CEMENT OR 139.969 TONS ok
```

A note on "

The defining word MATERIAL takes three arguments for each material, one of which is the address of a string. .SUBSTANCE uses this address to type the name of the material.

To put the string in the dictionary and to give an address to MATERIAL, we have defined a word called ". As you can see from its definition, " compiles the string (delimited by a second quotation mark, ASCII 34) into the dictionary, with the count in the first byte, and leaves its address on the stack for MATERIAL. To compile the count and string into the dictionary, we simply have to execute WORD, since WORD's buffer is HERE. We get the string's address as a fillip, since WORD also leaves HERE.

All that remains is to ALLOT the appropriate number of bytes. This number is obtained by fetching the count from the first byte of the string and adding one for the count's byte.

246 LIST

```
( WEIGHT OF CONICAL PILES -- SINGLE-LENGTH)     EMPTY
VARIABLE DENSITY   VARIABLE THETA   VARIABLE STRING
34 CONSTANT QUOTE
: "   QUOTE WORD  DUP C@ 1+ ALLOT ;
: .SUBSTANCE   STRING @  COUNT  TYPE SPACE ;

: MATERIAL   ( STRING DENSITY THETA) CREATE  , , ,
    DOES> DUP @ THETA !  2+ DUP @ DENSITY !  2+ @ STRING ! ;

: FOOT   10 * ;
: INCH   100 12 */  5 + 10 /  + ;

: /TAN   1000 THETA @  */ ;
: PILE   DUP DUP 10 */  1000 */  355 339 */ /TAN /TAN
       DENSITY @  200 */   ." = "  .  ." TONS OF " .SUBSTANCE ;
247 LOAD
```

247 LIST

```
( TABLE OF MATERIALS)
( STRING-ADDRESS   DENSITY  THETA)
" CEMENT"              131       700   MATERIAL CEMENT
" LOOSE GRAVEL"         93       649   MATERIAL LOOSE-GRAVEL
" PACKED GRAVEL"       100       700   MATERIAL PACKED-GRAVEL
" DRY SAND"             90       754   MATERIAL DRY-SAND
" WET SAND"            118       900   MATERIAL WET-SAND
" CLAY"                120       727   MATERIAL CLAY
CEMENT
```

248 LIST

```
( WEIGHT OF CONICAL PILES -- DOUBLE-LENGTH)     EMPTY
VARIABLE DENSITY   VARIABLE THETA   VARIABLE STRING
34 CONSTANT QUOTE
: "   QUOTE WORD  DUP C@ 1+ ALLOT ;
: .SUBSTANCE   STRING @  COUNT  TYPE SPACE ;
: U.3   <#  # # # 46 HOLD #S  #>  TYPE SPACE ;
: MATERIAL   ( STRING DENSITY THETA) CREATE  , , ,
    DOES> DUP @ THETA !  2+ DUP @ DENSITY !  2+ @ STRING ! ;

: CUBE   ( d -- d)  2DUP OVER 10 M*/  DROP  10 M*/ ;
: /TAN   ( d -- d)  1000 THETA @  M*/ ;
: FEET   ( d -- d)   CUBE  355 339 M*/  DENSITY @ 1 M*/
           /TAN  /TAN 5 M+  1 10 M*/
          2DUP  ." = " D. ." POUNDS OF "  .SUBSTANCE
       1 2 M*/    ." OR " U.3  ." TONS " ;
247 LOAD
```

 3/06/81 11:45 Starting FORTH

Review of Terms

Stub — in FORTH, a temporary definition created solely to allow testing of a higher-level definition.

Top-down programming — a programming methodology by which a large application is divided into smaller units, which may be further subdivided as necessary. The design process starts with the overview, or "top," and proceeds down to the lowest level of detail. Coding of the low-level units begins only after the entire structure of the application has been designed.

APPENDIX 1
ANSWERS TO PROBLEMS

Chapter 1

1. ```
   : GIFT   ." BOOKENDS " ;
   : GIVER   ." STEPHANIE " ;
   : THANKS   ." DEAR "  GIVER ." , THANKS FOR THE "
       GIFT ." . " ;
   ```

2. ```
   : TEN-LESS   -10 + ;   or
   : TEN-LESS   10 - ;
   ```

3. When THANKS was compiled, the definition included a reference to the first version of GIFT (the only version of GIFT at that time). Thus THANKS will always execute the same version of GIFT.

Chapter 2

1. ```
   DUP DUP:   (1 2 -- 1 2 2 2)
   2DUP:      (1 2 -- 1 2 1 2)
   ```

2. SWAP 2SWAP SWAP

3. `: 3DUP   DUP 2OVER ROT ;`

4. `: 2-4   OVER + * + ;`

5. `: 2-5   2DUP -  ROT ROT + / ;`

6. ```
   : CONVICTED-OF   0 ;
   : WILL-SERVE   . ." YEARS " ;
   : HOMICIDE   20 + ;
   : ARSON   10 + ;
   : BOOKMAKING   2 + ;
   : TAX-EVASION   5 + ;
   ```

7. ```
   : EGG.CARTONS   12 /MOD .  ." CARTONS AND "
       . ." LEFTOVERS " ;
   ```

Chapter 4

1. ```
   1 0= NOT . 1 ok
   0 0= NOT . 0 ok
   200 0= NOT . 1 ok
   ```

2. Don't ask.

3. (assuming the legal age is 18 or over:)

```
: CARD   17 >  IF ." ALCOHOLIC BEVERAGES PERMITTED "
             ELSE ." UNDER AGE " THEN ;
```

4.
```
: SIGN.TEST    DUP 0=  IF ." ZERO " ELSE
               DUP 0<  IF ." NEGATIVE " ELSE
                          ." POSITIVE " THEN THEN DROP ;
```
(or anything else that works)

5.
```
: STARS   ?DUP  IF STARS THEN ;
```

6.
```
: <ROT   ROT ROT ;
: WITHIN   <ROT OVER > NOT  <ROT >  AND ;
```
Or here's a more efficient version, using tricks introduced in the next chapter:
```
: WITHIN   >R 1- OVER < SWAP R> < AND ;
```

7.
```
: GUESS ( answer guess -- answer      or  -- )
     2DUP =  IF ." CORRECT! " 2DROP ELSE
     2DUP <  IF ." TOO HIGH " ELSE ." TOO LOW "
                                 THEN DROP THEN ;
```

8.
```
: SPELLER      DUP ABS 4 >  IF ."OUT OF RANGE "  ELSE
               DUP 0<  IF ." NEGATIVE "  ABS  THEN
               DUP 0=  IF ." ZERO "  ELSE
               DUP 1 =  IF ." ONE "  ELSE
               DUP 2 =  IF ." TWO "  ELSE
               DUP 3 =  IF ." THREE "  ELSE
                          ." FOUR "
               THEN THEN THEN THEN THEN  DROP ;
```

9. assuming <ROT and WITHIN are still loaded:
```
: 3DUP   DUP 2OVER ROT ;
: TRAP    ( answer low-try hi-try -- answer        or   --
   3DUP OVER =  <ROT = AND  IF ." YOU GOT IT! " DROP ELSE
   3DUP SWAP 1 + SWAP  WITHIN IF ." BETWEEN "
      ELSE ." NOT BETWEEN " THEN THEN 2DROP ;
```

Chapter 5

1. `*/ MINUS`

2. `MAX MAX MAX .`

3.
   a) 0 32 - 10 18 */ . -17 ok
   b) 212 32 - 10 18 */ . 100 ok
   c) -32 32 - 10 18 */ . -35 ok
   d) 16 18 10 */ 32 + . 60 ok
   e) 233 273 - . -40 ok

4.
```
: F>C   32 -  10 18 */ ;
: C>F   18 10 */  32 + ;
: K>C   273 - ;
: C>K   273 + ;
: F>K   F>C  C>K ;
: K>F   K>C  C>F ;
```

```
186 LIST

( ANSWERS, CHAP. 6)                EMPTY
( PROBLEMS 1 - 6)
: STARS   0 DO ." *" LOOP ;
: BOX   0 DO CR DUP STARS LOOP DROP ;
: \STARS   ( #-of-lines)  0 DO   CR   I SPACES  10 STARS LOOP ;
: /STARS   ( #-of-lines)  1 SWAP DO   CR  I SPACES  10 STARS
                 -1 +LOOP ;
: ( USING BEGIN & UNTIL FOR /STARS :)
: A/STARS   ( #-of-lines)  BEGIN CR   DUP SPACES 10 STARS
      1- DUP 0= UNTIL  DROP ;

( DIAMONDS DEFINED IN TWO STAGES:)
: TRIANGLE  DO CR 9 I - SPACES
            I 2* 1+ STARS DUP +LOOP DROP ;
: DIAMONDS   0 DO 1 10 0 TRIANGLE
                 -1 0 9 TRIANGLE LOOP ;
```

```
187 LIST

( ANSWERS, CHAP. 6, CONT'D)        EMPTY

( PROB. 7)
: R%   10 */ 5 +  10 / ;
: DOUBLED   ( AMT INT -- )
      OVER 2* ROT ROT SWAP 21 1 DO
            CR ." YEAR "  I 2 U.R 3 SPACES
                    2DUP R% + DUP ." BAL " .
              DUP 2OVER DROP > IF
        CR CR ." MORE THAN DOUBLED IN " I . ." YEARS " LEAVE
                                 THEN LOOP 2DROP DROP ;

( PROB. 8)
: **   1- ?DUP IF
     OVER ROT ROT  0 DO OVER * LOOP SWAP DROP THEN ;
```

```
188 LIST

( ANSWERS, CHAP. 7)               EMPTY
( PROB. 1)
: N-MAX   0 BEGIN 1+ DUP  0< UNTIL 1- . ;
( Keeps incrementing the number on the stack by one until
  it looks negative, which means the limit has been passed.
  The final 1- sets it back to what it was just before it
  surpassed the limit.)
( PROB. 2 -- Assume that HUMOROUS and SENSITIVE are
   both true.  The "anded" result is "1".  Now assume
   that ART-LOVING and MUSIC-LOVING are also both true.
   If we "+" their flags instead of "OR"ing them, we get "2."
            But 0001 [one]
      ANDed with 0010 [two]
           gives 0000, which is false.)
```

```
189 LIST

( ANSWERS, CHAP. 7 -- CONT'D)     EMPTY
( PROB. 3)
: BEEP   ." BEEP "  7 EMIT ;
: DELAY   20000 0 DO LOOP ;
: 3BELLS   BEEP DELAY BEEP DELAY BEEP ;
( PROB. 4-a)
: F>C    -320 M+  10 18 M*/ ;
: C>F    18 10 M*/  320 M+ ;
: K>C    -2732 M+ ;
: C>K     2732 M+ ;
: F>K    F>C C>K ;
: K>F    K>C C>F ;
( PROB. 4-b)
: .DEG    SWAP OVER DABS
     <#  # 46 HOLD  #S SIGN #>  TYPE SPACE ;
```

```
190 LIST

( ANSWERS, CHAP. 7 -- CONT'D)
( PROB. 5)
: DPOLY   ( x -- dv)
        DUP 7 M*  20 M+  ROT 1 M*/  5 M+ ;
: ?DMAX   0 BEGIN  1+ DUP DPOLY 0 0 D< UNTIL 1- . ;
(   ?DMAX /ret/ 17513 ok   -- this takes a while)
( PROB. 6)
: BINARY  2 BASE ! ;
: 3-BASES
    17 0 DO  CR ." DECIMAL"  DECIMAL   I 4 U.R  8 SPACES
                ." HEX "     HEX       I 3 U.R  8 SPACES
                ." BINARY"   BINARY    I 8 U.R  8 SPACES
                                               LOOP DECIMAL ;
```

```
191 LIST

( ANSWERS, CHAP. 7 -- CONT'D)
( PROB. 7 -- It tells you that double-length routines are
  loaded.  Two dots are interpreted as a double-length zero.)
( PROB. 8)
: .PH#   <#  # # # #  45 HOLD  # # #
              OVER IF 47 HOLD #S THEN  #> TYPE SPACE ;
( OVER supplies IF with the low-order cell of the
  number being converted.  This cell contains zero only
  when conversion has completely "used up" the number.)
```

```
192 LIST

( ANSWERS, CHAP. 8)                    EMPTY
( PROB. 1-a)
VARIABLE PIES   0 PIES !
: BAKE-PIE   1 PIES +! ;
: EAT-PIE   PIES @  IF -1 PIES +!   ." THANK YOU "
                    ELSE  ." WHAT PIE? " THEN ;
( PROB 1-b)
VARIABLE FROZEN-PIES     0 FROZEN-PIES !
: FREEZE-PIES   PIES @  FROZEN-PIES +!  0 PIES ! ;
( PROB. 2)
: .BASE   BASE @  DUP DECIMAL .  BASE ! ;
( PROB. 3)
VARIABLE PLACES   0 PLACES !
: M.   SWAP OVER DABS  <#
     PLACES @ ?DUP  IF  0 DO  #  LOOP  46 HOLD  THEN
                              #S  SIGN  #>  TYPE SPACE ;
```

```
193 LIST

( ANSWERS, CHAP. 8 -- CONT'D)        EMPTY

( Prob. 4)
VARIABLE #PENCILS  6 ALLOT
0 CONSTANT RED                  2 CONSTANT BLUE
4 CONSTANT GREEN                6 CONSTANT ORANGE

: PENCILS   #PENCILS + ;

23 RED PENCILS !
15 BLUE PENCILS !
12 GREEN PENCILS !
 0 ORANGE PENCILS !

( To test, we can enter
        BLUE PENCILS ? 15 ok   )
```

```
194 LIST

( ANSWERS, CHAP. 8, CONT'D)   EMPTY

( PROB. 5)
CREATE 'SAMPLES   20 ALLOT   ( 10 CELLS)
: STARS   ?DUP IF 0 DO 42 EMIT LOOP THEN ;
: SAMPLES   ( index# -- adr )   2* 'SAMPLES + ;
: INIT-SAMPLES   ( -- )
      11 0 DO  I 7 MOD  I SAMPLES !  LOOP ;

: PLOT   ( -- )
     11 0 DO  CR  I 2 U.R  SPACE  I SAMPLES @  STARS LOOP CR ;

INIT-SAMPLES
```

```
194 LOAD
PLOT
 0
 1 *
 2 **
 3 ***
 4 ****
 5 *****
 6 ******
 7
 8 *
 9 **
10 ***
```

```
195 LIST

( ANSWERS, CHAP. 8)        EMPTY
( PROB. 6)
VARIABLE BOARD 7 ALLOT
: CLEAR   BOARD  10 0 FILL ;    CLEAR
: SQR   BOARD + ;
: BAR   ." | " ;
: DASHES   CR  9 0 DO ." -" LOOP CR ;
: .BOX   SQR C@  DUP  0= IF 2 SPACES ELSE
              DUP 1 = IF ." X "   ELSE
                         ." O "   THEN THEN DROP ;
: DISPLAY    CR  9 0 DO
    I IF  I 3 MOD 0= IF DASHES ELSE BAR THEN THEN
       I .BOX  LOOP  CR QUIT ;
: PLAY   1-  0 MAX  8 MIN  SQR C! ;
: X!   1 SWAP  PLAY  DISPLAY ;
: O!  -1 SWAP  PLAY  DISPLAY ;

196 LIST

( ANSWERS, CH. 9)                        EMPTY
( PROB. 1)
: COUNTS   '  ROT ROT 0 DO  OVER EXECUTE  LOOP  SWAP DROP ;

( PROB. 2)
( You can find out by entering
     EMPTY  HERE .            )

( PROB. 3)
( You can find out by entering
     PAD HERE - .             )

( PROB. 4)
( a. No difference.  A VARIABLE returns its own pfa.
  b. A user variable returns the address of a cell in the user
  table.  The dictionary entry, which ' finds, is elsewhere.)

197 LIST

( ANSWERS, CHAP. 9, CONT'D)
( PROB. 5, SOLUTION #1)
VARIABLE 'TO-DO  10 ALLOT   ( 6 CELLS)
: TO-DO   ( index -- adr)  1-  2*  'TO-DO + ;

: GREET   ." HELLO, I SPEAK FORTH. " ;
: SEQUENCE    11 1 DO I . LOOP ;
: TILE   10 5 BOX ;    ( see answers, Ch. 6)
: NOTHING ;

' GREET     1 TO-DO !        ' SEQUENCE  2 TO-DO !
' TILE      3 TO-DO !        ' NOTHING   4 TO-DO !
' NOTHING   5 TO-DO !        ' NOTHING   6 TO-DO !

: DO-SOMETHING   ( index -- )  TO-DO @  EXECUTE ;
```

```
198 LIST

( ANSWERS, CHAP. 9, CONT'D)
( PROB. 5, SOLUTION #2)
VARIABLE 'TO-DO  10 ALLOT  ( 6 CELLS)
: TO-DO   ( index -- adr)  1-  2*  'TO-DO + ;

: GREET   ." HELLO, I SPEAK FORTH. " ;
: SEQUENCE    11 1 DO I . LOOP ;
: TILE   10 5 BOX ;   ( see answers, Ch. 6)
: NOTHING ;

: INIT"TO-DO"   ( -- )  7 1 DO ['] NOTHING  I TO-DO ! LOOP
   ['] GREET  1 TO-DO !     ['] SEQUENCE  2 TO-DO !
   ['] TILE   3 TO-DO !  ;
INIT"TO-DO"

: DO-SOMETHING   ( index -- )  TO-DO @  EXECUTE ;
```

```
199 LIST

 0 ( ANSWERS, CHAP. 10)                EMPTY
 1
 2 ( PROB. 1)
 3 : CHANGE   ( c1 c2 -- )   ( changes c1 to c2)
 4    SWAP   228 BLOCK  1024 OVER + SWAP DO
 5                  2DUP I C@  = IF I C!  ELSE DROP THEN
 6                                 LOOP 2DROP ;
 7
 8 ( PROB. 2)
 9 181 LOAD  ( RANDOM NUMBERS)
10 : FORTUNE   CR 16 CHOOSE  64 *  ( block#) BLOCK +
11                   64 -TRAILING TYPE SPACE ;
12 ( You'll have to invent your own "fortunes".  Edit them
13  into an available block, one per line.  Then edit the
14  block number into line 11 above, where indicated.)
15
```

```
200 LIST

( ANSWERS, CHAP. 10, CONT'D)
( PROB. 3)
: ANIMALS   ." RAT   OX    TIGER RABBITDRAGONSNAKE HORSE RAM   M
ONKEYCOCK  DOG   BOAR  " ;
: .ANIMAL   ( u -- )
      6 *  ['] ANIMALS  3 +   + 6 -TRAILING TYPE ;
( .ANIMAL takes an argument from 0 to 11.)

: (JUNEESHEE)   ( yr -- )
       1900 - 12 MOD
        ." YOU WERE BORN IN THE YEAR OF THE "  .ANIMAL
                               46 EMIT ( dot)   CR ;

: JUNEESHEE    CR
   ." IN WHAT YEAR WERE YOU BORN? "
   S0 @  4 EXPECT  0 >IN !  1 WORD  NUMBER  CR (JUNEESHEE) ;
```

```
201 LIST

( ANSWERS, CHAP. 10, CONT'D)                 EMPTY
( PROB. 4)

: NAME      64 *  202 BLOCK +           24 -TRAILING TYPE ;
: HAIR      64 *  202 BLOCK +  24 +   20 -TRAILING TYPE ;
: EYES      64 *  202 BLOCK +  44 +   20 -TRAILING TYPE ;

: LETTER     CR CR        DUP DUP
   ." DEAR " NAME  ." ,"  CR
CR ." YOU'RE THE ONLY ONE FOR ME.  LET ME RUN MY FINGERS "
CR ." THROUGH YOUR NICE " HAIR ."  HAIR.  LET ME LOOK INTO "
CR ." YOUR DEEP " EYES ."  EYES. "  ;

: LETTERS   4 0 DO I LETTER LOOP ;
```

```
202 LIST

LATICIA                 BLACK               BROWN
ALICE                   BLONDE              BLUE
STACEY                  BROWN               HAZEL
BARBARA                 BROWN               GREEN
```

```
203 LIST

( ANSWERS, CHAP. 10, CONT'D)                  EMPTY
( PROB. 5)
VARIABLE #START   222 #START ! ( file begins at block 222)
: ELEMENT   ( index -- adr)
     2*  1024 /MOD  #START @  +  BLOCK  +  UPDATE ;
( Test virtual array:)
: INIT-ARRAY   500 0 DO  I   I ELEMENT  !  LOOP ;
: .ARRAY   0 DO  CR   I . SPACE  I ELEMENT ?  LOOP ;

( Now make the virtual array into a file:)
: AVAILABLE   ( -- adr)  #START @  BLOCK  UPDATE ;
0 AVAILABLE !
( Redefine ELEMENT to skip over AVAILABLE:)
: ELEMENT   ( index -- adr)
   1+  2*  1024 /MOD  #START @  +  BLOCK  +  UPDATE ;
```

```
204 LIST

( ANSWERS, CHAP. 10, CONT'D)
( PROB. 5, CONT'D)

: PUT   ( value -- )  AVAILABLE @ ELEMENT !  1 AVAILABLE +!  ;

: SHOW   ( -- )   AVAILABLE @  0 DO   CR   I .
           I ELEMENT ?     LOOP ;

: ENTER   ( value1 value2 -- )   SWAP  PUT  PUT  ;

: TABLE   AVAILABLE @   ?DUP IF
   CR  0 DO   I 8 MOD  0=  IF   CR  THEN
          I ELEMENT @   8 U.R   LOOP  CR
          THEN ;



205 LIST

( ANSWERS, CHAP. 11)                    EMPTY
( PROB. 1)
: LOADED-BY   CREATE  ,  DOES>  @ LOAD ;

( PROB. 2)
: BASED.   CREATE  ,   DOES> @  BASE @  SWAP BASE !
    SWAP  .   BASE !  ;

( PROB. 3)
: PLURAL   ( adr -- )    CREATE  ,
    DOES> @  SWAP  ?DUP IF  0 DO  DUP EXECUTE LOOP THEN  DROP ;
' CR PLURAL CRS
5 CRS
: BEEP   7 EMIT  20000 0 DO LOOP ;    ' BEEP  PLURAL BEEPS
4 BEEPS


206 LIST

( ANSWERS, CHAP. 11, CONT'D)

( PROB. 4)
: TURNE   [COMPILE] DO ;   IMMEDIATE
: RETURNE   [COMPILE] LOOP ;   IMMEDIATE
: TRY   10 0 TURNE  I .  RETURNE ;

( PROB. 5)
: ASCII   32 WORD  1+  C@  [COMPILE] LITERAL ;   IMMEDIATE
: STAR   ASCII *  EMIT ;

( PROB. 6)
: LOOPS   >IN @  SWAP  0 DO  DUP >IN !  INTERPRET  LOOP  DROP ;
10 LOOPS   CR  30 SPACES  STAR
```

APPENDIX 2
FURTHER FEATURES OF polyFORTH

polyFORTH is a total software development environment designed especially for the professional programmer. polyFORTH is currently available for the most popular minicomputers and microprocessors.

In this book we've covered all the polyFORTH commands that might be used in a high-level, single-task application. We've left out several categories of words that are also included in polyFORTH. These categories are:

The Assembler

All versions of FORTH, not just polyFORTH, include an assembler vocabulary. Using the assembler, it is possible to code directly in the assembly language of a particular processor.

The assembler is primarily used to code time-critical words in a real-time application. Often an entire application can be coded in high-level FORTH, then after the application has been tested, critical low-level words can be redefined in machine code.

polyFORTH's assembler vocabulary includes interrupt-handling capability.

Printing Utility

polyFORTH provides a multiprogrammed task that sends output to a printer instead of your terminal. Among the printing utility commands are several which list disk blocks in the standard format of three to a page.

Date and Time Support

The current date and, when supported by a system clock, time of day are maintained by the system.

The Multiprogrammer

As many tasks as are needed, either terminal or control tasks, can be easily added. A single command builds a new task, given certain size parameters. Another command activates the task and gives it a specified behavior.

Disking Utility

polyFORTH includes commands for copying entire disks or portions thereof, for error checking, and for formatting when it is needed by the system.

Target Compiler

polyFORTH provides the capability to develop an application that ultimately will run on a different processor, in some cases even a different variety of processor. The compiled code can either be executed directly or be compressed and burned into ROM.

FORTH, Inc., which licenses and sells polyFORTH, was founded in 1973 by the inventor of FORTH, Charles H. Moore, and his associates. FORTH, Inc. also provides full documentation, hot-line support, educational services in all parts of the country, software options, and custom application programming. For further information write or call FORTH, Inc., 2309 Pacific Coast Hwy., Hermosa Beach, CA, 90254, 213/372-8493, TWX 910 344-6408.

APPENDIX 3
FORTH-79 STANDARD

The purpose of FORTH-79 Standard is to allow transportability of standard FORTH programs in source form among standard FORTH systems. A program written according to the Standard will run equivalently on any FORTH system that adheres to the Standard.

The current Standard was developed by the FORTH Standards Team. (The Standards Team is not affiliated with FORTH, Inc., but the company does have three voting members on the team.) This Standard is a descendant of FORTH-78 (proposed by the FORTH International Standards Team) and before that of FORTH-77 (the work of an informal group of European and American FORTH users). Efforts at standardization go back as far as 1973, at Kitt Peak Observatory in Arizona.

Having voted to accept the FORTH-79 Standard, FORTH, Inc. revised its product line to adopt most of the Standard's features and naming conventions. Of course the Standard attempts to cover only a minimal system. Therefore it doesn't address many powerful words and features included in FORTH, Inc.'s polyFORTH, which represents the state-of-the-art in FORTH implementations. In this book we've included many words which we feel are likely to be adopted by future Standards.

A small number of issues raised by the FORTH-79 Standard remain controversial. In a few cases, the functions of words as described in this book don't follow the FORTH-79 Standard, but rather the FORTH, Inc. product line. Most of these discrepancies have been marked with footnotes; however, a few are more general in nature and deserve special discussion.

The most noticeable difference is in the length of the name field for each dictionary entry. The Standard specifies that dictionary entries include up to 31 characters of the name to avoid "collisions." FORTH, Inc. implementations use a count and three characters not only to save memory, but also to support dictionary search routines that are significantly faster than any 31 character implementation seen to date. FORTH, Inc. is presently researching algorithms which may offer users greater flexibility in naming, without unacceptable sacrifice in performance.

The FORTH-79 Standard includes a few words which change their behavior depending on a variable called STATE, which indicates whether the user is in "compile mode." One is `."`. In FORTH,

Inc. implementations, ." is a compiling word, and therefore it may only be used inside a colon definition. In FORTH-79 languages, it has two functions: if the system is in execution mode, it will type the string which follows it at the terminal from which it was just entered.

A more significant controversy related to STATE is the behavior of the word ' (tick). In FORTH, Inc. languages, tick always reads the next word in the input stream when tick is executed. The Standard tick however, has two behaviors: when the system is in execution mode, it behaves in the normal way, but in compile mode it behaves like ['] (bracket-tick-bracket); that is, it compiles the address of the next word in the definition as a literal. To define a word which must "tick" the next word in the input stream when the word is executed, you must use the phrase

```
[COMPILE] '
```

if you're using the Standard tick .

There's one other difference worth mentioning here. The FORTH-79 Standard does not make the assumption that the DO loop index and limit will be kept on the return stack. Presumably a system may have a third stack. For this reason, the Standard includes the word R@ to copy the top value from the return stack onto the parameter stack. In all systems that we know of, however, R@ would be identical to the FORTH I.

For more information or for copies of the FORTH-79 Standard, write to the FORTH Interest Group (FIG), P.O. Box 1105, San Carlos, CA 94070.

APPENDIX 4
SUMMARY OF FORTH WORDS

ARITHMETIC

Single-length

word	page
+	53
-	53
*	53
/	53
/MOD	53
MOD	53
*/	123
*/MOD	123
U*	177
U/MOD	177
1+	123
1-	123
2+	123
2-	123
2*	123
2/	123
ABS	123
NEGATE	123

Double-length

word	page
D+	178
D-	178
DNEGATE	178
DABS	178

Mixed-length

word	page
M+	179
M/	179
M*	179
M*/	179

ASCII CHARACTERS AND EQUIVALENTS

See table on p. 157

CHARACTER INPUT

word	page
KEY	284
EXPECT	284
WORD	284
TEXT	284
COUNT	285

CHARACTER OUTPUT

word	page
CR	27
SPACE	27
SPACES	27
EMIT	27
."	27
PAGE	143
TYPE	283
>TYPE	285
-TRAILING	283

COMPARISONS

Single-length

word	page
=	103
-	103
<	103
U<	177
>	103
0=	103
0<	103
0>	103
MIN	123
MAX	123

Double-length

word	page
D=	179
D0=	179
D<	179
DU<	179